DISPUTE SETTLEMENT UNDER THE NAFTA: MANUAL AND SOURCE BOOK

LEON E. TRAKMAN

WITH THE ASSISTANCE OF
KIRTI JADEJA

Transnational Publishers, Inc.
Irvington-on-Hudson, New York

Library of Congress Cataloging-in-Publication Data

Trakman, Leon E.
Dispute settlement under the NAFTA: manual and source book / Leon E. Trakman; with the assistance of Kirti Jadeja.
p. cm.
Includes index.
ISBN 1–57105–043–4
1. Dispute resolution (Law)—United States. 2. Dispute resolution (Law)—Canada. 3. Dispute resolution (Law)—Mexico. I. Jadeja, Kirti. II. Title.
KDZ525.T73 1996
341.7'543—dc21 96–37022
CIP

Manufactured in the United States of America

CONTENTS

ABOUT THE AUTHORS xiii

ACKNOWLEDGMENTS xv

PREFACE xvii

PART I
DISPUTE RESOLUTION PROCEDURES 1

CHAPTER 1:
GENERAL DISPUTE RESOLUTION MEASURES: CHAPTER 20 5

1.1 SCOPE AND COVERAGE 5
1.11 APPLICABLE TO 5
1.12 PROVISIONS THAT PRECLUDE THE APPLICATION OF CHAPTER 20 6
1.13 ADDITIONAL DISPUTE RESOLUTION PROCEDURES AND THEIR RELATIONSHIP TO CHAPTER 20 6
1.14 ISSUES DEALT WITH 7
1.2 WHO CAN INITIATE A CLAIM 7
1.3 ADMINISTRATIVE STRUCTURE OF THE NAFTA 8
1.31 FREE TRADE COMMISSION 8

1.32 SECRETARIAT 9
1.33 COMMITTEES AND WORKING GROUPS 9
1.34 TRANSPARENCY AND DUE PROCESS REQUIREMENTS 12
1.4 STAGES OF PROCEEDINGS 12
1.41 STEP I: CONSULTATIONS 13
1.42 STEP II: FREE TRADE COMMISSION 14
1.43 STEP III: PANEL PROCEEDINGS 15
1.5 POST-PANEL PROCEEDINGS 18
1.6 CHOICE OF FORUMS: GATT V. NAFTA 19

CHAPTER 2:
ADDITIONAL DISPUTE RESOLUTION PROCEDURES 21
2.1 CHAPTER 5: CUSTOMS PROCEDURES 21
2.11 REDETERMINATION OF ORIGIN 21
2.2 CHAPTER 8: EMERGENCY ACTION 23
2.21 DEFINITION 23
2.22 PROVISIONS 24
2.23 PROCEDURAL MATTERS 25
2.24 CHAPTER 20 ALTERNATIVE 28
2.3 CHAPTER 10: GOVERNMENT PROCUREMENT 28
2.4 CHAPTER 15: COMPETITION POLICY, MONOPOLIES AND STATE ENTERPRISES 29
2.5 CHAPTER 16: TEMPORARY ENTRY 29
2.6 CHAPTER 20: DOMESTIC PROCEEDINGS AND PRIVATE COMMERCIAL DISPUTE SETTLEMENT 30
2.61 PRIVATE COMMERCIAL DISPUTES 30
2.7 AGREEMENT ON ENVIRONMENTAL COOPERATION 31
2.71 ADMINISTRATIVE STRUCTURE 31
2.72 PROCEDURAL MATTERS 32
2.73 CHOICE OF ALTERNATIVE FORUM 34
2.74 COMPLAINTS BY PRIVATE PARTIES 35
2.8 AGREEMENT ON LABOR COOPERATION 36
2.81 ADMINISTRATIVE STRUCTURE 36
2.82 PROCEDURAL MATTERS 37

CHAPTER 3:
INVESTOR–STATE ARBITRATION PROCEDURES 41
3.1 SCOPE AND COVERAGE 41
3.11 APPLICABLE PROVISIONS 42
3.12 EXCLUSIONS 42
3.13 CHAPTER 14: FINANCIAL SERVICES DISPUTES 43
3.2 WHO CAN INITIATE A CLAIM 44
3.3 SUBMITTING A CLAIM TO ARBITRATION 44
3.4 SYSTEMS OF ARBITRATION 45
3.5 CONDITIONS PRECEDENT TO SUBMITTING A CLAIM 48
3.6 ARBITRAL TRIBUNAL FORMATION 49
3.7 CONSOLIDATION OF CLAIMS 50
3.8 PROCEDURAL MATTERS 50
3.9 IMPLEMENTATION AND ENFORCEMENT 52

CHAPTER 4:
ANTIDUMPING AND COUNTERVAILING DUTY DISPUTE PROCEDURES: CHAPTER 19 55
4.1 DEFINITIONS 55
4.2 SCOPE AND COVERAGE 56
4.3 WHO CAN INITIATE A CLAIM 57
4.4 PANEL REVIEW OF DOMESTIC FINAL DETERMINATIONS 58
4.41 MAKING THE FINAL DETERMINATIONS 59
4.42 UNDERTAKINGS 71
4.43 REVIEW OF THE FINAL DETERMINATION 72
4.44 STANDARD OF REVIEW 75
4.45 INITIATING REVIEW BY A PANEL 76
4.46 PANEL FORMATION 77
4.47 PROCEDURES BEFORE PANELS AND PANEL DECISIONS 78
4.8 EXTRAORDINARY CHALLENGE PROCEDURES 80
4.9 SAFEGUARDING THE PANEL REVIEW SYSTEM 83
4.10 PANEL REVIEW OF STATUTORY AMENDMENTS 84
4.11 CONSULTATIONS 86

PART II
SOURCES AND CONTACTS 93

GENERAL CONTACT SOURCES 95

NAFTA CHAPTER 3:
NATIONAL TREATMENT AND MARKET ACCESS FOR GOODS 105
3.1 SCOPE AND COVERAGE 105
3.2 COMMITTEES AND WORKING GROUPS 105
3.21 COMMITTEE ON TRADE IN GOODS 105
3.22 COMMITTEE ON TRADE IN WORN CLOTHING 106
3.3 LONG-TERM REVIEW PROCESS 107
3.4 INFORMATION SOURCES 108

NAFTA CHAPTER 5:
CUSTOMS PROCEDURES 113
5.1 SCOPE AND COVERAGE 113
5.2 COMMITTEES AND WORKING GROUPS 113
5.21 WORKING GROUP ON RULES OF ORIGIN 113
5.22 CUSTOMS SUBGROUP 115
5.3 LONG-TERM REVIEW PROCESS 116
5.4 INFORMATION SOURCES 117

NAFTA CHAPTER 6:
ENERGY GOODS AND BASIC PETROCHEMICALS 123
6.1 SCOPE AND COVERAGE 123
6.2 INFORMATION SOURCES 123

NAFTA CHAPTER 7:
AGRICULTURE 125
7.1 SCOPE AND COVERAGE 125
7.2 COMMITTEES AND WORKING GROUPS 125

7.21 COMMITTEE ON AGRICULTURAL TRADE 125
7.22 WORKING GROUP ON AGRICULTURAL SUBSIDIES 127
7.23 ADVISORY COMMITTEE ON PRIVATE COMMERCIAL DISPUTES REGARDING AGRICULTURAL GOODS 129
7.24 COMMITTEE ON SANITARY AND PHYTOSANITARY MEASURES 130
7.25 WORKING GROUP ON AGRICULTURAL GRADING AND MARKETING STANDARDS [CANADA/MEXICO] 132
7.26 BILATERAL WORKING GROUP (U.S./MEXICO) TO REVIEW THE OPERATION OF GRADE AND QUALITY STANDARDS IN AGRICULTURE 133
7.27 CANADA/US/MEXICO WORKING GROUP ON GRADE AND QUALITY STANDARDS IN AGRICULTURE 134
7.28 CONTINUATION OF CANADA–U.S. FTA ARTICLE 708 WORKING GROUPS 134
7.29 WORKING GROUP ON TARIFF RATE QUOTE ADMINISTRATION 135
7.3 INFORMATION SOURCES 136

NAFTA CHAPTER 8: EMERGENCY ACTION 141
8.1 SCOPE AND COVERAGE 141
8.2 COMMITTEES AND WORKING GROUPS 141
8.21 WORKING GROUP ON EMERGENCY ACTION 141

NAFTA CHAPTER 9: STANDARDS-RELATED MEASURES 143
9.1 SCOPE AND COVERAGE 143
9.2 COMMITTEES AND WORKING GROUPS 143
9.21 COMMITTEE ON STANDARDS-RELATED MEASURES 143

9.22 LAND TRANSPORT STANDARDS SUBCOMMITTEE . . . 145
9.23 TRANSPORTATION CONSULTATIVE GROUP . . . 147
9.24 TELECOMMUNICATIONS STANDARDS SUBCOMMITTEE . . . 148
9.25 AUTOMOTIVE STANDARDS SUBCOMMITTEE . . . 149
9.26 SUBCOMMITTEE ON LABELING OF TEXTILE AND APPAREL GOODS . . . 151
9.3 LONG-TERM REVIEW PROCESS . . . 152
9.4 INFORMATION SOURCES . . . 153

NAFTA CHAPTER 10: GOVERNMENT PROCUREMENT . . . 157
10.1 SCOPE AND COVERAGE . . . 157
10.2 COMMITTEES AND WORKING GROUPS . . . 157
10.21 COMMITTEE ON GOVERNMENT PROCUREMENT AND SMALL BUSINESS . . . 157
10.3 INFORMATION SOURCES . . . 159

NAFTA CHAPTER 11: INVESTMENT . . . 163
11.1 SCOPE AND COVERAGE . . . 163
11.2 INFORMATION SOURCES . . . 163

NAFTA CHAPTER 12: CROSS-BORDER TRADE IN SERVICES . . . 165
12.1 SCOPE AND COVERAGE . . . 165
12.2 COMMITTEES AND WORKING GROUPS . . . 165
12.21 WORKING GROUP ON SERVICES AND INVESTMENT . . . 165
12.3 INFORMATION SOURCES . . . 167

NAFTA CHAPTER 13: TELECOMMUNICATIONS . . . 173
13.1 SCOPE AND COVERAGE . . . 173
13.2 INFORMATION AND SOURCES . . . 173

NAFTA CHAPTER 14:
FINANCIAL SERVICES 175
14.1 SCOPE AND COVERAGE 175
14.2 COMMITTEES AND WORKING GROUPS 175
14.21 FINANCIAL SERVICES COMMITTEE 175
14.3 INFORMATION SOURCES 177

NAFTA CHAPTER 15:
COMPETITION POLICY, MONOPOLIES AND STATE ENTERPRISES 181
15.1 SCOPE AND COVERAGE 181
15.2 COMMITTEES AND WORKING GROUPS 181
15.21 WORKING GROUP ON TRADE AND COMPETITION POLICY 181

NAFTA CHAPTER 16:
TEMPORARY ENTRY 183
16.1 SCOPE AND COVERAGE 183
16.2 COMMITTEES AND WORKING GROUPS 183
16.21 TEMPORARY ENTRY WORKING GROUP 183
16.3 LONG-TERM REVIEW PROCESS 184
16.4 INFORMATION SOURCES 185

NAFTA CHAPTER 17:
INTELLECTUAL PROPERTY 187
17.1 SCOPE AND COVERAGE 187
17.2 INFORMATION SOURCES 187

NAFTA CHAPTER 18:
PUBLICATION, NOTIFICATION, AND ADMINISTRATION OF LAWS 189
18.1 SCOPE AND COVERAGE 189
18.2 INFORMATION SOURCES 189

NAFTA CHAPTER 19:
REVIEW AND DISPUTE SETTLEMENT IN ANTIDUMPING AND COUNTERVAILING DUTY MATTERS 191
19.1 SCOPE AND COVERAGE 191
19.2 COMMITTEES AND WORKING GROUPS 191
19.21 SPECIAL SECRETARIAT SECTION 191
19.22 EXTRAORDINARY CHALLENGE COMMITTEE 191
19.23 SPECIAL COMMITTEE 192
19.3 LONG-TERM REVIEW PROCESS 192
19.4 INFORMATION SOURCES 192

NAFTA CHAPTER 20:
INSTITUTIONAL ARRANGEMENTS AND DISPUTE SETTLEMENT 197
20.1 SCOPE AND COVERAGE 197
20.2 COMMITTEES AND WORKING GROUPS 197
20.21 FREE TRADE COMMISSION 197
20.22 ADVISORY COMMITTEE ON PRIVATE COMMERCIAL DISPUTES 198
20.3 LONG-TERM REVIEW PROCESS 199
20.4 INFORMATION SOURCES 200

PART III
NAFTA DISPUTE RESOLUTION PROVISIONS 201

NAFTA PROVISIONS 203

CHAPTER 1:
OBJECTIVES 203

CHAPTER 5:
CUSTOMS PROCEDURES 206

CHAPTER 8:
EMERGENCY ACTION 207

CHAPTER 10:
GOVERNMENT PROCUREMENT 220

CHAPTER 11
INVESTMENT 224

CHAPTER 14:
FINANCIAL SERVICES 259

CHAPTER 15:
COMPETITION POLICY, MONOPOLIES AND STATE ENTERPRISES 268

CHAPTER 16:
TEMPORARY ENTRY FOR BUSINESS PERSONS 273

CHAPTER 18:
PUBLICATION, NOTIFICATION AND ADMINISTRATION OF LAWS 273

CHAPTER 19:
REVIEW AND DISPUTE SETTLEMENT IN ANTIDUMPING AND COUNTERVAILING DUTY MATTERS 277

CHAPTER 20:
INSTITUTIONAL ARRANGEMENTS AND DISPUTE SETTLEMENT PROCEDURES 317

CHAPTER 21:
EXCEPTIONS 338

RULES OF PROCEDURE FOR ARTICLE 1904 EXTRAORDINARY CHALLENGE COMMITTEES 340

RULES OF PROCEDURE FOR ARTICLE 1905 SPECIAL COMMITTEES 387

CODE OF CONDUCT FOR DISPUTE SETTLEMENT PROCEDURES UNDER CHAPTERS 19 AND 20 OF THE NORTH AMERICAN FREE TRADE AGREEMENT 403

INDEX 413

ABOUT THE AUTHORS

Leon Trakman is active as a commercial and trade arbitrator. He holds a doctorate in International Trade Law earned at the Harvard Law School and has served as a Chapter 19 panelist under the United States Free Trade Agreement and the NAFTA. Currently, a Professor of Law at the Dalhousie Law School, he is author of three books and a variety of articles on, among other topics, international trade law.

Kirti Jadeja is currently serving as an Assistant in a Chapter 19 dispute under the NAFTA. She is a law student at the Dalhousie Law school.

ACKNOWLEDGMENTS

Various individuals, governmental agencies and other organizations have provided invaluable assistance in developing this book. Particular thanks is owed to Cathy Beehan, James Holbein, Kirsten Crain, Katia Vila, Gary Horlick, Heather Grant, Gilbert Winham, Brian Russel and Gerardo Rodriguez Sanchez.

A special thanks is owed to Seema Monga who assisted in initiating this book.

Finally, we are indebted to the Foundation for Legal Research for providing partial funding in developing this study.

PREFACE

The purpose of this book is to provide government, business and students of the NAFTA with a working handbook of NAFTA procedures, practices and sources with a view to avoiding, or failing that, resolving disputes under the NAFTA. It addresses this purpose in three ways.

First, it serves as a procedural reference to dispute resolution procedures under Chapters 11, 19 and 20 of the North American Free Trade Agreement (NAFTA). Second, it outlines the activities of the different working groups and committees established under the NAFTA. Third, it provides key contact sources who have expertise on different aspects of the NAFTA.

The intention is to present the NAFTA as a living institution, with an ongoing history and changing practice. This involves familiarizing the reader with both the dispute resolution procedures set out in the Agreement, as well as information about important developments taking place before different working groups and committees established under the NAFTA to assist with consultation and dispute avoidance. The reader is also provided with detailed contact sources, including names, addresses, and telephone and facsimile numbers of organizations and functionaries appointed to administer the NAFTA.

The book is organized into three cross-referenced parts. Part I identifies dispute resolution procedures under the different chapters of the NAFTA. Part II provides contact sources under the NAFTA including information on the activities of various committees and working groups established since the implementation of the NAFTA. Part III, an appendix of documents, for convenience includes the actual text of provisions of the NAFTA referred to throughout the book.

PART I
DISPUTE RESOLUTION PROCEDURES

The North American Free Trade Agreement contains detailed procedures for the resolution of conflicting claims arising in trade activities between Canada, the United States and Mexico. The two central models of dispute settlement procedures employed are contained in Chapters 19 and 20 of the Agreement. Chapter 19 sets out a unique dispute settlement mechanism that applies only in respect of antidumping and countervailing duty matters; Chapter 20 applies to all other controversies arising under the Agreement, subject to modifications in individual sectors, particularly under NAFTA Chapter 11 (Investments).

Part I of this Book is divided into four chapters: Chapter 1 discusses NAFTA Chapter 20 procedures; Chapter 2 outlines additional procedures that arise under specific NAFTA provisions and their relationship to NAFTA Chapter 20; Chapter 3 covers NAFTA Chapter 11 investor-state dispute settlement procedures; and Chapter 4 describes NAFTA Chapter 19 provisions.

Only national governments can initiate dispute settlement procedures under Chapter 20. Therefore, if private parties consider themselves adversely affected by another party's interpretation or application of the NAFTA, they must approach officials of their government to persuade them to take action under Chapter 20. The initial vehicle for dispute resolution under Chapter 20 is consultation. The particular provisions of the NAFTA oblige the three NAFTA Parties to make their best effort to agree on the interpretation and application of the Agreement and to make every attempt through cooperation and consultation to arrive at a mutually satisfactory resolution of any matter that may affect its operation. Failure to settle a matter through consultation results in its referral to the Free Trade Commission for assistance. Subsequent failure permits any NAFTA Party to request the establishment of an arbitral panel for a final determination.

Chapter 20 procedures are supplemented by specific provisions that reflect the sensitivities and requirements of particular economic and business sectors. These specific provisions are found within the individual chapters of NAFTA. The most prominent provisions pertain to the financial services and investment sectors and are found in Section B of NAFTA Chapter 11 (discussed in Chapter 3, *infra*). It should be noted that investors can initiate dispute settlement proceedings under both NAFTA Chapters 11 and 14. The other supplements to NAFTA Chapter 20 procedures, concerning customs procedures, government procurement, emergency action situations, and environmental and labor cooperation disputes, are described in Chapter 2, *infra*.

As noted above, NAFTA Chapter 19 creates a separate and distinct process for disputes concerning antidumping and countervailing duty matters. The key feature of Chapter 19 is that it provides for binational panel review of final decisions of domestic administrative agencies concerning antidumping and countervailing duty matters. Such proceedings may be initiated by a private party adversely affected by a decision of the domestic agency. In conducting a review of an agency decision, a panel must consider whether the agency made its decision in accordance with the domestic law governing the particular proceedings in issue.

Binational panels can also review disputes over amendments to a NAFTA Party's antidumping and countervailing duty laws.

CHAPTER 1:
GENERAL DISPUTE RESOLUTION MEASURES: CHAPTER 20

1.1 Scope and Coverage

- ❑ NAFTA Chapter 20 Dispute Settlement Procedures [See Part III at p. 317] are provided for under Section B [See Part III at p. 320] of the Agreement. [For information on Chapter 20 contact sources see Part II, p. 93]

❑ 1.11 Applicable To

- ❑ Chapter 20 dispute resolution procedures can only be applied to matters involving:

  - Trade in Goods provided for under NAFTA Chapters 3 to 8, 9, 12, 17 (excluding automotive provisions under Annex 300 – A);
  - Energy investments under NAFTA Chapter 6;
  - NAFTA Chapters 10, 11, 13, 14, 15, 16 (but only where the actual or proposed measures themselves are inconsistent with the provisions in the NAFTA).

❑ 1.12 PROVISIONS THAT PRECLUDE THE APPLICATION OF CHAPTER 20

❑ NAFTA Chapter 20 dispute settlement procedures do **not** apply to:

- Matters covered under NAFTA Chapter 19 (Antidumping and Countervailing Duty Matters);

- Matters provided for under NAFTA 1501 [See Part III, at p. 268] (Competition Law).

❑ 1.13 ADDITIONAL DISPUTE RESOLUTION PROCEDURES AND THEIR RELATIONSHIP TO CHAPTER 20

❑ Chapter 20 **may** apply, subject to modifications or with the addition of specific provisions within each NAFTA chapter (these are dealt with in greater detail in Chapter 2, *infra*) and depending on the election of the NAFTA Parties involved in a dispute, to:

- Chapter 11, providing investors with access to remedies;
- Chapter 14, modifying procedures involving financial services;
- Chapter 5, with respect to issues of determination of origin;
- Chapter 8, on Emergency Action;
- Chapter 10, on Government Procurement;
- Chapter 16, on Temporary Entry;
- Chapter 20, on Private Commercial Disputes;
- Environmental Disputes;
- Labor Disputes.

❑ 1.14 ISSUES DEALT WITH

❑ The provisions apply to controversies arising under the Agreement:

1) respecting matters of interpretation and application;

2) where, under NAFTA 2004 [See Part III at p. 320] a NAFTA Party considers that an actual or proposed measure of another NAFTA Party is inconsistent with its NAFTA obligations;

3) where, under Annex 2004 [See Part III, at p. 337] , a NAFTA Party considers that a measure, while not inconsistent with its NAFTA obligations, has the **effect** of nullifying or impairing benefits it can expect to derive from the NAFTA.

1.2 WHO CAN INITIATE A CLAIM

❑ **Chapter 20 proceedings can only be initiated by governments at the federal level.**

❑ NAFTA 2021 [See Part III, at p. 335] prohibits NAFTA Parties from providing for private rights of action under domestic law against another NAFTA Party on grounds of a measure being inconsistent with a NAFTA obligation.

❑ Enterprises of NAFTA Parties, state and provincial governments, as well as nationals, have no standing at any stage of NAFTA Chapter 20 proceedings. Officially, their only recourse is to convince their own government to initiate a proceeding when a measure adversely affects them. In practice, however, private sector parties have been able to participate in limited ways. They work with government in writing briefs, in preparing arguments and in presenting those arguments orally.

1.3 Administrative Structure of the NAFTA

- The administrative structure of the NAFTA is provided for in NAFTA Chapters 18 and 20 [See Part III at p. 273 and p. 317]. Section A of Chapter 20 [See Part III at p. 317] establishes two institutions, the Free Trade Commission and the Secretariat. In addition, it sets up committees and working groups to facilitate joint administration of the Agreement and to avoid or settle disputes between the NAFTA Parties.

- Chapter 18 details general transparency requirements with regard to administration as well as due process requirements. It also establishes contact points on any matter covered by the Agreement to facilitate communications. On request, these contact points identify the office or official responsible for a matter and may assist in avoiding or resolving the dispute.

1.31 Free Trade Commission

- The Free Trade Commission is the central institution of the NAFTA, comprised of cabinet-level representatives of the three NAFTA Parties (the Canadian Minister of International Trade, the American Trade Representative, and the Mexican Secretary of the Secretariat of Commerce and Industrial Development (SECOFI)) or their designees.

- All decisions of the Commission are made by consensus, unless the Commission itself decides otherwise.
- The Commission is vested with broad authority to resolve disputes, oversee the implementation and further

elaboration of the Agreement, supervise the work of all NAFTA committees and working groups and consider any other matter relevant to the operation of the Agreement.

- ❑ The Commission will meet at least once a year in regular sessions to be chaired successively by each NAFTA Party.

❑ 1.32 SECRETARIAT

- ❑ The Secretariat is comprised of national sections in Canada, Mexico and the United States established, staffed and supported by each NAFTA Party.

- ❑ It provides administrative assistance to the Free Trade Commission, the panels and the committees established under NAFTA Chapters 19 and 20.

❑ 1.33 COMMITTEES AND WORKING GROUPS

- ❑ The NAFTA establishes eight Committees and six working groups listed under Annex 2001.2 [See Part III, at p. 336]:

- ❑ **A. Committees**

1. Committee on Trade in Goods (Article 316)
2. Committee on Trade in Worn Clothing (Annex 300–B, Section 9(1))
3. Committee on Agricultural Trade (Article 706)

    i) Advisory Committee on Private Commercial Disputes Regarding Agricultural Goods (Article 707)

4. Committee on Sanitary and Phytosanitary Measures (Article 722)
5. Committee on Standards-Related Measures (Article 913)

i) Land Transport Standards Subcommittee (Article 913(5))
ii) Telecommunications Standards Subcommittee (Article 913(5))
iii) Automotive Standards Subcommittee (Article 913(5))
iv) Subcommittee on Labeling of Textile and Apparel Goods (Article 913(5))

6. Committee on Small Business (Article 1021)
7. Financial Services Committee (Article 1412)
8. Advisory Committee on Private Commercial Disputes (Article 2022(4))

❑ B. **Working Groups**

1. Working Group on Rules of Origin (Article 513)
2. Customs Subgroup (Article 513(6))
3. Working Group on Agricultural Subsidies (Article 705(6))
4. Bilateral Working Group (Mexico–United States) (Annex 703(2a)(25))
5. Bilateral Working Group (Canada–Mexico) (Annex 703(2b)(13))
6. Working Group on Trade and Competition (Article 1504)
7. Temporary Entry Working Group (Article 1605)

❑ C. **Other Committees and Working Groups established under the NAFTA (since its coming into effect):**

1. Working Group on Emergency Action
2. Working Group on Government Procurement
3. Working Group on Services and Investment
4. Working Group on Subsidies and Countervailing Duties

5. Working Group on Dumping and Antidumping Duties
6. Under the authority of the Land Transport Standards Subcommittee:
   - Vehicle/Driver Compliance Subgroup
   - Vehicle Weight & Dimension Subgroup
   - Traffic Control Devices Subgroup
   - Rail Subgroup
   - Dangerous Goods Subgroup
7. Transportation Consultative Group
8. Under the authority of the Transportation Consultative Group:
   - Operations Subgroup
   - Border Facilities Subgroup
   - Automated Data Exchange Subgroup
   - Science and Technology Subgroup
   - Maritime Subgroup

❑ The committees are responsible for monitoring and reporting on the implementation of the NAFTA.

❑ The working groups provide additional functions to those of the committees. In particular, they elaborate the further development of the Agreement in select areas.

❑ The committees and working groups serve as useful vehicles for identifying disputes at the Consultation Stage and for resolving them on an informal basis, or at least making constructive proposals to the Commission for their resolution.

❑ None of the committees or working groups has authority on its own to resolve disputes, with the exception of the Financial Services Committee established under NAFTA Chapter 14. [For the NAFTA Committees and Working Groups, See Part II at p. 93]

❑ 1.34 TRANSPARENCY AND DUE PROCESS REQUIREMENTS

- ❑ The NAFTA requires that laws, regulations, procedures and administrative rulings regarding any matter covered by the Agreement are promptly published or otherwise made available to all NAFTA Parties.

- ❑ This involves notifying affected NAFTA Parties, or providing on request information regarding any proposed or actual measure that may materially affect either the operation of the Agreement or the interests of another NAFTA Party.

- ❑ NAFTA 1804 [See Part III, at p. 275] and 1805 [See Part III, at p. 275] set out basic due process requirements to be applied by each NAFTA signatory with regard to administrative proceedings that affect matters covered by the Agreement.

- ❑ Each NAFTA Party is required to establish and maintain judicial or quasi-judicial or administrative tribunals to allow prompt review of actions covered by the Agreement.

- ❑ The NAFTA requires that the NAFTA Parties establish Model Rules of Procedure to provide the framework for panels in the dispute resolution process in order to ensure the integrity of the process.

1.4 STAGES OF PROCEEDINGS

- ❑ The general dispute settlement procedures provided under NAFTA Chapter 20 involve three stages.

  1) Step I: Consultations.
  2) Step II: Review by the Free Trade Commission.
  3) Step III: Referral to an arbitral panel.

❑ 1.41 STEP I: CONSULTATIONS

- ❑ NAFTA 2003 [See Part III, at p. 320] stipulates that state-to-state consultations are the first and primary means of settling disputes under the Agreement. Any NAFTA Party may request consultations with other NAFTA Parties regarding any actual or proposed measure or other matter that may affect its interests.

- ❑ Formal dispute resolution begins when a NAFTA Party commences Chapter 20 procedures by delivering a request for consultation under NAFTA 2006(1) [See Part III, at p. 322] to the other NAFTA Parties and to the Secretariat.

- ❑ After the consulting NAFTA Parties have met, they are required to make every attempt to arrive at a mutually satisfactory resolution of any matter through consultations. The NAFTA Parties are required to provide all information necessary to make a full examination of the actual or proposed measure and to treat confidential information in the course of the consultation on the same basis as a NAFTA Party providing the information would have done. Resolutions that would adversely affect the interests of any other Party under the Agreement must be avoided.

- ❑ A NAFTA Party not directly involved can participate in consultations unless rules established by the Commission provide otherwise.

- ❑ Time Limitations

    - If consultations fail to yield a resolution in 30 days after their initiation, any consulting Party can request a meeting of the Free Trade Commission.

    - This time period is extended to 45 days when the third NAFTA Party participates in the consultations and reduced to 15 days when perishable agricultural products are involved.

❑ 1.42 STEP II: FREE TRADE COMMISSION

❑ A meeting of the Free Trade Commission can be requested after:

1) Consultations fail and the required time frame has lapsed;
2) In an environmental dispute under NAFTA 104 [See Part III, at p. 204], when the responding NAFTA Party requests that the dispute be heard under the NAFTA forum.

❑ The Free Trade Commission must convene within ten days of a request for it to meet and endeavor to resolve the dispute promptly.

❑ The Commission is authorized to employ a variety of alternative methods of dispute resolution (ADR) in an effort to bring about a negotiated settlement. It may act as a mediator and seek advice from technical advisors and experts; or it may convene working groups. The Commission may have recourse to good offices, conciliation, mediation or other dispute resolution procedures and make recommendations to the consulting NAFTA Parties. It may also refer a dispute to arbitration.

❑ The role of the Commission at this stage is to assist the NAFTA Parties and to facilitate the process of negotiation, rather than to act as a third-party arbiter of the dispute.

❑ The NAFTA provisions on ADR appear to be limited to this early stage of the process. This differs from the General Agreement on Trade and Tariffs (GATT) which provides that good offices, conciliation and mediation may be requested at any time by any party to a dispute.

- Time Limitations

  - If a dispute is not resolved in 30 days, any NAFTA Party can request the establishment of an arbitral panel.

1.43 STEP III: PANEL PROCEEDINGS

- The Free Trade Commission must establish an arbitral panel upon delivery of a written request from any consulting Party. The requesting NAFTA Party must notify the other NAFTA Party and each Section of the Secretariat. NAFTA panels operate in a manner similar to the panel dispute settlement process under the GATT [See *infra* at p. 19].

- Model Rules of Procedure for arbitral panels established by the Commission provide the NAFTA Parties with the right to at least one hearing and the opportunity to provide initial and rebuttal written submissions. They provide, further, for the confidentiality of panel proceedings, including all written submissions, hearings and communications with the panel, as well as deliberations and initial panel reports.

- Panels must adopt standard terms of reference, unless the NAFTA Parties agree otherwise. These terms of reference authorize the panel to make findings, determinations and recommendations after examining the matter and after taking relevant provisions of the NAFTA into consideration.

- Panel procedures permit reliance on a specially selected Scientific Review Board on any factual issue relating to environmental, health, safety or other scientific matters. NAFTA Parties must have notice and opportunity to comment on factual issues referred to by the Board and its report.

❑ Third Parties

- A third NAFTA Party may consider that it has a substantial interest in a NAFTA dispute and join as a complainant NAFTA Party before the panel by simply delivering notice at the earliest time possible after the request for establishment of a panel. Failure to join precludes a NAFTA Party from initiating or continuing a dispute settlement proceeding with respect to the same matter under either the NAFTA or the GATT, barring significant change in the economic or commercial circumstances surrounding the matter arising at a later date.

❑ Panel Formation

i) Roster

- Each NAFTA Party must establish a roster of ten people who have expertise in law, international trade or other matters covered by the Agreement, who are objective, reliable and possess sound judgment and who must comply with a code of conduct established by the Commission.

ii) Panel Selection

- Panels will consider of five members ordinarily chosen from the roster.
- Chair
    - The first step in panel formation requires the disputing NAFTA Parties to select a

Chair. This must be done within 15 days of delivery of a request for a panel.

- If this does not occur, one of the two disputing NAFTA Parties, (selected by lot) will choose the Chair within five days. If more than two NAFTA Parties are involved, the NAFTA Party selected by lot chooses the Chair within ten days.

- Each NAFTA Party involved in a dispute then selects two panelists from the rosters of the other disputing NAFTA Parties, rather than its own, within 15 days of the selection of the Chair. If no selection is made, then selection by lot is made from the roster. Where more than two NAFTA Parties are involved in a dispute, the NAFTA Party that is the subject of the complaint selects one panel member from each NAFTA Party.

- Any NAFTA Party may exercise a peremptory challenge against anyone chosen who is not on the roster, within 15 days of the naming of the person being proposed.

- If a panelist violates a code of conduct, the NAFTA Parties involved in the dispute can consult and on agreement, can remove and replace such a person [See Part III at p. 403].

❑ Initial and Final Reports

- A panel is required to issue initial and final reports evaluating the dispute, based on submissions, arguments, and the advice and reports of experts.

- A panel is required to provide its initial report to NAFTA Parties involved in a dispute 90 days after the last panelist is selected. It is required to include findings of fact, a determination of whether the measure at issue is inconsistent with the NAFTA obligations of one or more NAFTA Parties, and recommend resolution of the matter.

- Disputing NAFTA Parties have 14 days in which to submit written comments on the initial report. This allows the NAFTA Parties a final opportunity to present their positions.

- A panel must submit a final report within 30 days of the presentation of the initial report. This may include separate opinions on matters upon which the panelists disagree. Disputing NAFTA Parties are responsible for delivering the report to the Commission.

- The final report is required to be published within 15 days of its transmission to the Commission, unless the Commission decides otherwise.

1.5 POST-PANEL PROCEEDINGS

❑ Implementation and Enforcement of Determinations

- Panel determinations are not binding (although normally implemented), do not affect the domestic law of any NAFTA Party and cannot be enforced by domestic courts.

- At the implementation stage, the Commission provides that the NAFTA Parties resolve the matter on a bilateral or trilateral basis. On receipt of the final report, they are directed to agree upon a resolution of the dispute, which usually conforms with the determination of the panel.

- The resolution reached ordinarily involves the removal or non-implementation of the measure that does not conform with the Agreement, or causes nullification or impairment. Failing such a resolution, the nonconforming NAFTA Party may pay appropriate compensation in lieu of compliance.

- If agreement on a resolution is not reached in 30 days of receiving the final report, a complainant NAFTA Party may suspend equivalent NAFTA benefits to the nonconforming NAFTA Party. Suspension of benefits should be in the same sector as that affected by the inconsistent measure under dispute. If suspension in the same sector is not effective, suspension can be in a different sector. Special rules apply to suspending benefits related to financial services.

- On written request, a panel can be established by the Commission to determine whether the level of benefits suspended is excessive. [On Chapter 20 contact points, see Part II, at p. 197 and for Chapter 20 dispute provisions see Part III at p. 317]

1.6 CHOICE OF FORUMS: GATT V. NAFTA

❑ Many NAFTA provisions provide for the same or similar obligations as are required under the GATT. Therefore, at times, complainant governments can contend that both NAFTA and GATT obligations have been violated.

❑ NAFTA 2005 [See Part III, at p. 320] allows a complainant NAFTA Party to choose either the NAFTA or the GATT forum to resolve a dispute but not both. The choice of forum is at the discretion of the NAFTA Parties, subject to certain limitations.

- If the complainant Party chooses GATT procedures, the NAFTA Party that is not involved must be notified. If this third NAFTA Party wishes to join as a complainant as well and wants resolution under the NAFTA, there must be consultation to agree on the forum. Failure of the NAFTA Parties to reach agreement means that the issue must normally be settled under NAFTA dispute settlement procedures.

- If the GATT forum is chosen by both complainant NAFTA Parties, NAFTA 2005 [See Part III, at p. 320] states that the responding NAFTA Party can insist that the dispute be settled by a NAFTA Chapter 20 panel in situations involving factual issues on standards-related environmental, safety, health or conservation issues under Section B of NAFTA Chapter 7 or Chapter 9, or if the dispute arises under specific environmental agreements.

- Aside from factual differences, procedures, time frames, and personalities, the choice of a forum can be critical in circumstances involving Uruguay Round Agreements in which parallel NAFTA and GATT obligations are not the same and a complainant NAFTA Party has a stronger case under one set of obligations than the other.

[On institutional arrangements for dispute settlement, see generally, Part II, p. 197]

CHAPTER 2:
ADDITIONAL DISPUTE RESOLUTION PROCEDURES

2.1 CHAPTER 5: CUSTOMS PROCEDURES

❑ 2.11 REDETERMINATION OF ORIGIN

- ❑ NAFTA 510 [See Part III, at p. 206] gives a NAFTA Party the right to review, and subsequently appeal such review, of marking determinations of origin, NAFTA Party of origin determinations, and advance rulings by a customs administration that deny preferential NAFTA tariff treatment to goods of exporters or producers from another NAFTA Party. This is known as a **request for redetermination of origin**.

- ❑ Each NAFTA Party must provide substantially the same rights of review and appeal of determinations of origin and advanced rulings by its customs administration as it provides to importers within its territory. Appeal procedures are available to only those exporters and producers:

  1) who have completed a *Certificate of Origin* which states that the product is entitled to preferential tariff treatment under the NAFTA.

2) whose goods have been the subject of a country of origin marking determination pursuant to Article 311; or

3) who have received an advance ruling pursuant to Article 509(1).

- The rights of review and appeal must include access to:

1) at least one level of administrative review independent of the official or office responsible for the determination under review;

2) in accordance with the Party's domestic law, judicial or quasi-judicial review of the determination or decision taken at the final level of administrative review.

- When a NAFTA preferential tariff treatment request is denied a notice is sent to the individual who filed the *Certificate of Origin*.

- In Canada, either the importer or the exporter of a product may file a request for redetermination under either Section 60 or 61 of the *Customs Act*. If denial of tariff treatment is identified to be under Section 57 of the *Customs Act*, a request must fall under Section 60. If the denial of tariff treatment falls under Section 61, redetermination must be requested under Section 63.

- Requests for redetermination are filed using Form B226, *Request for Redetermination of the Origin of Goods Imported from a Country.* It may be obtained from any Canada Customs office and must be sent to the Chief of Rulings and Appeals at the Customs regional office which denied the NAFTA tariff treatment. The denial notice that is sent will provide the address.

❑ Notice of decision is sent by letter. The letter includes a technical reference number (TRS) to be used in correspondence with respect to the decision.

❑ In the U.S., Section 304 of the *Tariff Act of 1930* provides NAFTA exporters and producers with rights to challenge a NAFTA marking decision by the Customs Service denying preferential treatment. Section 1514 of the *Tariff Act* allows an exporter or producer to intervene in any protest proceeding initiated by the importer, or if no protest is filed, the exporter or producer may file a petition with the Customs Service. Section 514 allows Canadian and Mexican exporters and producers who have completed NAFTA certificates of origin to challenge a denial of preferential treatment.

❑ NAFTA 510 [See Part III, at p. 206] also provides for the appeal of the redetermination under the domestic law of the importing NAFTA Party. The right to appeal is indicated within the notice of decision.

[For information on customs procedures, see Part II, p. 113]

2.2 CHAPTER 8: EMERGENCY ACTION

❑ 2.21 DEFINITION

❑ An emergency (or safeguard) action is an action in which a NAFTA Party seeks temporarily to halt tariff reductions to protect a domestic industry that is being seriously injured by surges in imports resulting from the reductions.

- A safeguard action can be either:
  - a temporary suspension of further reductions of the tariffs for a particular good or goods;
  - an increase in the duty rate not greater than the lesser of the NAFTA Party's most-favored-nation rate for the good at the time, or the most-favored-nation rate in effect prior to the effective date of the NAFTA.

2.22 PROVISIONS

- NAFTA 804 [See Part III, at p. 213] prohibits NAFTA Parties from requesting the establishment of an arbitral panel under NAFTA Chapter 20 regarding a proposed emergency action.

- NAFTA 803 [See Part III, at p. 212] and Annex 803(3) [See Part III, at p. 214] establish a comprehensive code of requirements to be followed in emergency action proceedings. It requires that each NAFTA Party entrust the injury determination in an emergency action proceeding to a "competent investigating authority" defined in the Agreement as the U.S. International Trade Commission, the Canadian International Trade Tribunal and the Mexican Ministry of Trade and Industrial Development (SECOFI).

- Annex 803 defines specifications for ensuring correctness of the form and content of petitions for initiating such actions, the conduct of investigations and the provisions of public hearings and notification and publication of investigations and decisions.

❑ 2.23 PROCEDURAL MATTERS

❑ If a NAFTA Party chooses to take bilateral action against the imports of another NAFTA Party, it must proceed according to the guidelines under NAFTA 801 [See Part III, at p. 207]. If it chooses to take multilateral or global action against the other two Parties, GATT "escape clause" procedures must be employed.

❑ **Bilateral Action**

- A NAFTA Party can only initiate such an action during the NAFTA tariff reduction transition period, unless it receives the consent of the other NAFTA Party to the action. The injury must have been caused by the reduction or elimination of duties under the NAFTA and an action against the goods can only be taken once.

- An action can be maintained for a maximum of three years (four in the case of particularly sensitive goods with long tariff elimination periods). No action can be maintained after the expiration of the transition period.

- A NAFTA Party that begins a proceeding that could lead to a safeguard action must notify the affected NAFTA Party and request consultations. An emergency action must begin within one year after a proceeding is commenced.

- A NAFTA Party taking an emergency action must provide the NAFTA Party whose goods are affected with mutually agreed upon compensation. This compensation can take the form of trade concessions which have the equivalent trade effects or are equivalent in value to the additional duties that are expected to result from the duty action.

- If the NAFTA Parties cannot agree upon compensation, the affected NAFTA Party can take tariff action which has trade effects substantially equivalent to those of the safeguard action. This action can only be taken for the minimum period necessary to achieve effects substantially equivalent to the effects of the safeguard action.

- At the conclusion of the emergency action, the duty rate on the good will be the NAFTA rate that would have been in effect one year after the date the action was started.

- Canada opted out of the bilateral action provisions under Annex 801.1 [See Part III, at p. 214] and chose to maintain the Canada–U.S. Free Trade Agreement, Article 1101 [See Part III, at p. 224] provisions, which are similar.

- Article 1101 differs from NAFTA in that it strictly 1) restricts an emergency action to a period of three years; and 2) the rate of duty which is to be reimposed on the imported good at the conclusion of the emergency action is the duty that would have been in effect "but for the action."

❑ Global Action

- A NAFTA Party that initiates the GATT Article XIX "escape clause" proceedings (or in the U.S., proceedings under Section 201 of the Trade Agreements of 1974) can only do so where:

1) the imports of a NAFTA Party are a "substantial share of total imports"; and

2) the imports from that NAFTA Party, considered individually, "contribute importantly" to the serious injury caused by the imports of the merchandise. Imports can only be considered collectively to assess their impact on injury in exceptional circumstances.

- Imports cannot be considered to have a substantial share of total imports if the NAFTA Party is not among the top five suppliers of the goods by import share during the previous three-year period.

- Imports cannot be said to contribute importantly to serious injury if the growth rate of imports from that NAFTA Party is appreciably lower than the growth rate of total imports from all sources during the time of the import surge.

- A global action cannot be taken against a NAFTA Party when it would result in reducing imports of the good below the recent trend of imports from that NAFTA Party. The extent of imports is measured over a representative base-period and allows for reasonable growth.

❑ The NAFTA Party taking the emergency action must provide the other NAFTA Parties with mutually agreed upon compensation in the form of trade concessions that have substantially the same trade effects, or which are equivalent to the value of the additional duties expected to result from the emergency action. If the NAFTA Parties fail to agree, the affected NAFTA Parties are entitled to take tariff action which has the equivalent trade effects to those arising out of the emergency action.

❑ 2.24 CHAPTER 20 ALTERNATIVE

- ❑ Consultations and arbitral panel review under Chapter 20 can be requested to review the finding of injury in any emergency action that is taken.

[For contact points on emergency action see Part II, p. 141; For NAFTA provisions on emergency action see Part III at p. 207]

2.3 CHAPTER 10: GOVERNMENT PROCUREMENT

- ❑ In order to promote fair, open, and impartial procurement procedures, NAFTA 1017 [See Part III, at p. 220] provides that each NAFTA Party shall adopt and maintain bid-challenge procedures which are independent of NAFTA Chapter 20, which provide suppliers of each Party equal opportunity to compete with domestic suppliers for contracts involving specified classes of goods and services (including construction services).

- ❑ The Agreement guarantees national treatment and nondiscrimination toward goods originating in Canada, the United States and Mexico, as well as toward the suppliers of such goods and services suppliers in each NAFTA Party.

- ❑ Reports must be maintained by the NAFTA Parties for use in future proceedings under Chapter 20, if necessary. This means that the results of the process may be reviewed by the Free Trade Commission and, potentially, referred to binational panels.

[For contact points regarding government procurement see Part II at p. 157; For NAFTA provision see Part III, at p. 220]

2.4 CHAPTER 15: COMPETITION POLICY, MONOPOLIES AND STATE ENTERPRISES

- ❑ Issues related to competition law, enforcement and cooperation between the Parties under NAFTA 1501 [See Part III, at p. 268] are removed from the dispute settlement procedures of NAFTA Chapter 20 under NAFTA 1501(3) [See Part III, p. 269].

- ❑ Chapter 20 procedures do, however, apply to NAFTA 1502 [See Part III, at p. 268] and 1503 [See Part III, at p. 270] dealing with monopolies and state enterprises.

2.5 CHAPTER 16: TEMPORARY ENTRY

- ❑ NAFTA 1606 [See Part III, at p. 273] states that NAFTA Chapter 20 procedures cannot be invoked in a matter involving the refusal to grant temporary entry to a business person, unless the matter involves a pattern of practice and the business person has exhausted all available administrative remedies.

- ❑ Remedies are considered exhausted if a final determination has not been issued within one year of the initiation of the proceedings, where the business person has not caused the delay.

[For information sources see Part II at p. 183; For relevant provisions see Part III at p. 273]

2.6 CHAPTER 20: DOMESTIC PROCEEDINGS AND PRIVATE COMMERCIAL DISPUTE SETTLEMENT

❑ 2.61 PRIVATE COMMERCIAL DISPUTES

- ❑ The dispute settlement mechanism of NAFTA Chapter 20 is not accessible to private parties. Individuals and enterprises must rely on their respective governments to pursue their interests.

- ❑ NAFTA 2022 [See Part III, at p. 335], on Alternate Dispute Resolution (ADR), imposes an obligation on NAFTA Parties to encourage arbitration and alternative dispute resolution to the maximum extent possible for the settlement of international commercial disputes between private parties within NAFTA Parties. The purpose is to encourage the private parties to find solutions, primarily through commercial arbitration.

- ❑ NAFTA Parties are obliged to provide procedures for ensuring the observance of agreements to arbitrate and the recognition and enforcement of arbitral awards.

- ❑ To facilitate this, the Commission established the Advisory Committee on Private Commercial Disputes, comprised of people with expertise in resolving private international commercial disputes.

- ❑ The Committee is required to report on matters referred to it by the Commission regarding the availability and effectiveness of procedures for the resolution of such disputes in NAFTA Parties.

- ❑ NAFTA 2022 [See Part III, at p. 335] refers to the *United Nations Convention on the Recognition and Enforcement of Foreign Arbitral Awards* (the New York Convention) and the *Inter-American Convention on International Commercial Arbitration*. It provides that these Conventions may assist new exporters if appropriate arbitration clauses are included in contracts with NAFTA customers. The purpose is to ensure access to qualified arbitrators who will arrive at binding decisions and remedies in enforcing contract rights, in the event of a conflict.

- NAFTA 707 establishes an Advisory Committee on Private Commercial Disputes Regarding Agricultural Goods. The purpose is to assist in the prompt and effective resolution of phytosanitary and other agricultural disputes between private parties.

[On contact sources see Part II at p. 198; For relevant provisions see p. 335]

2.7 AGREEMENT ON ENVIRONMENTAL COOPERATION

- The *North American Agreement on Environmental Cooperation* (NAAEC) is one of the two supplemental agreements to the NAFTA. It establishes that a NAFTA Party may seek redress with respect to any environmental standards established by another NAFTA Party that:

  1) affect trade between the NAFTA Parties; and

  2) do not conform to the NAFTA's substantive rules with respect to the environment and conservation matters.

2.71 ADMINISTRATIVE STRUCTURE

- The Agreement establishes a separate administrative structure with its own Commission for Environmental

Cooperation, consisting of a Secretariat, Council and a Joint Public Advisory Committee.

- ❑ The Council is the governing body of the Commission. It is composed of cabinet-level or equivalent representatives of the NAFTA Parties and meets annually to discuss environmental matters, oversee implementation of the Supplemental Agreement and facilitate cooperation between the Parties.

- ❑ The Secretariat provides technical, administrative and operational support to the Council and its subcommittees. It is located in Montreal, Quebec, and has an Executive Director who is chosen by the Council for a three-year term.

❑ 2.72 PROCEDURAL MATTERS

- ❑ Environmental disputes are handled in a three-stage process similar to that of Chapter 20.

- ❑ Consultations

  - If any NAFTA Party believes that another NAFTA Party has failed **to enforce its environmental law effectively,** it can request consultations with the NAFTA Party by notifying the other NAFTA Parties and the Secretariat. The third NAFTA Party can join in at this stage unless the Council decides otherwise.

  - Failure to arrive at an agreement at this stage within 45 days allows a dissatisfied NAFTA Party to request a special session of the Council. The Council can employ technical advisers to provide advice to ensure that trade panelists have meaningful access to scientific and environmental expertise. It can also assist in settlement or make recommendations. If the dispute is not resolved before the Council, it must establish an arbitral panel.

❑ Panel

- A panel of five individuals must be selected from a roster maintained by the Council. The roster consists of 45 individuals appointed for a three-year term, who have expertise in environmental law, in the resolution of international disputes or other relevant expertise.

❑ Initial and Final Reports

- The panel makes an initial report which includes findings of fact, the panel's determination as to whether there has been a persistent failure to enforce environmental law and whether the action is inconsistent with NAFTA obligations, and the panel's recommendations for the resolution of the dispute.
- The panel must submit a final report in 60 days at which point the NAFTA Parties must agree on a plan to settle the dispute.

❑ Implementation and Enforcement

- If the NAFTA Parties cannot agree on the plan to implement the panel's recommendations, either NAFTA Party can request that the Panel be reconvened. The panel may order the enforcement of monetary assessments if it determines that the NAFTA Party complained against in the action has failed to fully implement the panel's recommendations.

- If the NAFTA Party fails to make payment in 180 days, a complainant NAFTA Party may suspend NAFTA benefits with effects equivalent to the monetary penalty being imposed. Where there is more than one complainant NAFTA Party suspending benefits, the combined suspension must be equivalent to the amount of the monetary enforcement assessment.

❑ 2.73 CHOICE OF ALTERNATIVE FORUM

❑ The NAFTA permits a special forum selection provision for environmental disputes under NAFTA Chapters 7 (Sanitary and Phytosanitary Measures), 9 (Standards-Related Measures) and those related to the mandatory trade provisions of specified international environmental agreements. A complainant Party may bring a challenge under the provisions of either the NAFTA or the GATT.

❑ NAFTA 104 [See Part III, at p. 204] states that if the dispute concerns environmental, health, safety, or conservation standards the defending Party may force the matter to be heard under the NAFTA forum.

❑ NAFTA 104, states, further, that the NAFTA takes priority over other international agreements to the extent that there is any conflict. This priority is excepted in situations involving existing mandatory trade provisions contained in:

1) the *Convention on the International Trade in Endangered Species*;

2) the *Montreal Protocol* (concerning ozone-depleting substances);

3) the *Basel Convention* (concerning hazardous substances);

4) two enumerated Basel-compatible bilateral waste agreements between the United States and Canada and Mexico, respectively.

- ❑ The NAFTA requires that Parties select the alternative least inconsistent with the NAFTA in implementing the trade-related provisions of the listed Agreements.

❑ 2.74 COMPLAINTS BY PRIVATE PARTIES

- ❑ The Secretariat can consider submissions by non-governmental organizations or other interested NAFTA Parties that a NAFTA Party is not enforcing its environmental laws.

- ❑ If the Secretariat determines that the submission merits requesting a response from the NAFTA Party subject to the complaint, it will request a response. The NAFTA Party must then advise the Secretariat if the matter is the subject of a pending judicial or administrative proceeding. If that is the case, the Secretariat will not take any further action.

- ❑ If the Secretariat feels that the submission warrants the development of a factual record, it will notify the Council. The record may be made public if the Council so decides.

[For information sources see p. 97]

2.8 AGREEMENT ON LABOR COOPERATION

- ❑ The second Supplemental Agreement to the NAFTA is the *North American Agreement on Labor Cooperation* (NAALAC).

The Agreement recognizes the right of each Party to establish its own labor laws and regulations. It enumerates principles that should underlie these laws and the steps a Party may take to enforce them.

❑ 2.81 ADMINISTRATIVE STRUCTURE

- ❑ This Agreement establishes the Commission for Labor Cooperation, consisting of a Ministerial Council and a Secretariat.

- ❑ The Council serves as the governing body of the Commission and is composed of the Ministers of the Parties who meet at least once a year to oversee the implementation of the Agreement and promote cooperation between the Parties regarding labor issues.

- ❑ The Secretariat assists the Council in implementing and administering the Agreement. In addition to other functions, it prepares background reports and studies on matters that the Council may request.

- ❑ National Administrative Offices are established by each NAFTA Party to act as focal points for the Parties. The Offices disseminate information on Commission activities, request consultations with other Offices and receive public complaints about the failure of a NAFTA Party to enforce labor law.

❑ 2.82 PROCEDURAL MATTERS

❑ The procedures established to resolve differences among Parties with respect to interpretation and application of the Agreement require that Parties first attempt to resolve the conflicts through consultation and evaluation.

❑ Cooperative Consultation

- Consultations can be initiated in two different ways.

- A National Administrative Office can request consultations with another Office with respect to a NAFTA Party's labor law, administration or other labor market conditions in its territory. Any National Administrative Office can participate in the consultations on notice to the Secretariat and the other Offices.

- A NAFTA Party can request consultations at the ministerial level.

❑ Evaluation Committee of Experts

- Any consulting NAFTA Party can request the establishment of an Evaluation Committee of Experts by the Ministerial Council if ministerial consultations fail to resolve an issue. However, the establishment of a committee can only be requested if the matter is trade-related and covered by mutually recognized labor laws.

- The Committee consists of three members who have expertise in labor matters or other appropriate disciplines.

- The Committee is required to analyse the practices of each NAFTA Party in enforcing its occupational safety and health or other technical labor standards as they apply to the particular matter.

- The Committee must present a draft report to the Council. Each NAFTA Party may submit written opinions which the Committee is required to take into consideration when preparing a final report. The report is not binding on the Parties.

❑ After the Evaluation Committee makes its final report, a NAFTA Party can request consultations with any other NAFTA Party regarding whether there has been a persistent pattern of failure by that NAFTA Party to effectively enforce the occupational safety and health, child labor, or minimum wage and technical labor standards.

❑ Special Council Session

- If the consulting Parties do not resolve the matter within 60 days, a NAFTA Party may request a special session of the Council in writing. The Council then decides if the matter is better covered in another Agreement, in which case the matter is referred, or if it will consider the matter. The Council may call experts and make recommendations to assist the Parties to reach a satisfactory resolution.

❑ Arbitral Panels

- If the matter is not resolved through consultations with the Council in 60 days, a NAFTA Party can request in writing that the Council convene an arbitral panel. This can only be done in relation to trade-related matters and those covered by mutually recognized labor laws.

- The panel consists of five individuals, selected from a roster of 45 individuals with expertise in labor law, or the resolution of disputes involving international agreements, or related expertise. Panelists must be independent of the Parties and the Secretariat.

❑ Initial and Final Reports

- The panel must submit a final report of its findings, determinations and recommendations within 60 days. The disputing Parties must then agree on an action plan to settle the dispute.

❑ Implementation and Enforcement

- If the Parties fail to agree, they can request that the panel be reconvened. The panel will then make a determination as to whether the NAFTA Party against whom the complaint is made has failed to fully implement recommendations. A monetary enforcement assessment, payable in 180 days, can be made. Failure to pay the penalty allows the complainant NAFTA Party to suspend NAFTA benefits equivalent to the monetary penalty that was determined.

- Where there is more than one complainant NAFTA Party suspending benefits, the combined suspension must be equivalent to the amount of the monetary enforcement assessment.

- In particular circumstances, Section 301 of the *Tariff Act of 1974* provides an alternative avenue for the U.S. to act against violations of internationally accepted labor standards. This may be employed in the event of Mexico's failure to enforce workers' rights.

[For information source on Labor Cooperation see p. 100]

CHAPTER 3:
INVESTOR–STATE ARBITRATION PROCEDURES

3.1 Scope and Coverage

- ❑ NAFTA Chapter 11, Section B [See Part III, at p. 237] outlines alternative dispute settlement provisions available to investors of one NAFTA Party to commence an action against another NAFTA Party for a breach of NAFTA obligations under this chapter and relevant sections of Chapter 14.

- ❑ NAFTA Chapter 11, Section A [See Part III, at p. 224] sets out the substantive standards for treatment of foreign investments with exceptions. It applies to all forms of investments, including minority equity interests, certain forms of debt security and tangible and intangible property. It provides that there must be free transfer of funds related to investments. Any expropriation must be for public purposes and must be applied on a nondiscriminatory basis in accordance with due process of law.

- ❑ NAFTA Chapter 14 applies to measures of NAFTA Parties that apply to the financial institutions of another NAFTA Party, cross-border trade in financial services, and investments made in financial institutions within one NAFTA Party by nationals of another NAFTA Party. Specific reference is made to provisions of NAFTA Chapter 11.

❑ 3.11 APPLICABLE PROVISIONS

❑ NAFTA Chapter 11, Section B, dispute settlement provisions apply to:

1) actions taken by federal, state and provincial governments;

2) certain actions taken by state enterprises;

3) actions taken by certain state-chartered monopolies when the actions are inconsistent with the NAFTA, with respect to their obligations under:

   i) Chapter 11, Section A;
   ii) NAFTA 1503(2) [See Part III, at p. 270] or 1502(3a) [See Part III, at p. 269] with respect to provisions relating to the exercise by state enterprises and monopolies of regulatory, administrative or other governmental authorities;
   iii) NAFTA 1109 through 1111 [See Part III, at p. 232], and NAFTA 1113 and 1114 [See Part III, at p. 236] as incorporated in NAFTA Chapter 14.

❑ 3.12 EXCLUSIONS

❑ Decisions of Investment Canada or the Mexico National Commission on Foreign Investment not to permit an acquisition under their national investment screening laws are not subject to the dispute settlement procedures available under either Sections B of Chapter 11 [See Part III, at p. 237] or Chapter 20 [See Part III, at p. 317].

- A decision of a NAFTA Party to prohibit or restrict the acquisition of an investment pursuant to NAFTA 2102 [See Part III, at p. 338] (National Security) is not subject to dispute settlement procedures under Section B of Chapter11 or Chapter 20.

3.13 CHAPTER 14: FINANCIAL SERVICES DISPUTES

- Disputes arising under Chapter 14 financial services provisions must be settled state-to-state (under Chapter 20) except where they involve those sections borrowed from Chapter 11. The most notable exceptions, here, deal with expropriation and transfers (e.g. foreign exchange restrictions). These may be resolved under either the investor-state arbitration procedures or under Chapter 20. Alternatively, the latter option may be employed prior to commencing a Chapter 11 review, to determine whether the action that was taken was for prudential reasons (as discussed below) and therefore not subject to further dispute resolution.

- Chapter 20 dispute settlement procedures are modified when applied to conflicts involving financial services obligations under Chapter 14. Special provisions are employed that take into consideration the particular sensitivities of the sector with respect to dispute settlement. These special provisions include the requirement that panelists be chosen from a special roster of individuals who have expertise in financial services law or practice. Furthermore, any retaliation taken for a dispute involving a sector other than financial services cannot result in suspension of benefits in the financial services sector.

3.2 WHO CAN INITIATE A CLAIM

- ❑ An investor can submit a claim for a breach of provisions (above) on its own behalf or on behalf of an enterprise the investor directly or indirectly controls.

- ❑ This avoids the international law problem that could arise where an investor does not suffer a loss or damage independent of its investment.

- ❑ The investor or enterprise on behalf of whom the claim is made must have suffered loss or damage as a result of the breach.

- ❑ A time limitation of three years on the submission of a claim is applied from the time the investor or enterprise knew or should have known of the breach and loss and the initiation of a claim.

- ❑ NAFTA 1118 [See Part III, at p. 239] proposes that disputing NAFTA Parties should first attempt to settle the problem through consultation or negotiation, but this is not mandatory.

3.3 SUBMITTING A CLAIM TO ARBITRATION

- ❑ A disputing investor must notify the NAFTA Party against whom a claim is being made 90 days before a claim is submitted to arbitration. That notice must specify the name and address of the disputing investor or enterprise, the NAFTA provisions allegedly breached, the issues, the factual bases, the relief sought and the approximate amount of damages.

- ❑ NAFTA 1120 [See Part III, at p. 240] provides that six months after the events giving rise to a claim took place, a disputing investor can opt to submit a claim to arbitration under:

1) The *Convention on the Settlement of Investment Disputes between Contracting States and Nationals of Other Contracting States* (ICSID Convention) provided that both the disputing NAFTA Party and the NAFTA Party of the investor are parties to the Convention.

2) The Additional Facility Rules of the ICSID, provided that either the disputing NAFTA Party or the NAFTA Party of the investor, but not both, is a party to the ICSID Convention.

3) The UN Commission on International Trade Law (UNCITRAL) Arbitration Rules.

- ❑ NAFTA Chapter 11, Section B also refers to the New York Convention and the Inter-American Convention. These Conventions form part of the mechanism set out in Section B for ensuring that arbitral awards are enforceable.

3.4 SYSTEMS OF ARBITRATION

- ❑ ICSID Convention

  - The ICSID Convention is the *Convention on the Settlement of Investment Disputes Between Contracting States and Nationals of Other Contracting States*. It is a facility of the World Bank and establishes the International Centre for the Settlement of Investment Disputes as an arbitration centre with its Secretariat in Washington. Neither Canada nor Mexico are signatories to the Convention. However

Canada is currently in discussion with its provinces, and considering whether to become a signatory.

- Arbitration procedures are not available for ordinary commercial transactions. Jurisdiction of the Centre is limited to "legal disputes" arising directly from an "investment."

- The Tribunal established under the Convention decides disputes in accordance with rules of law agreed on by the Parties. In the absence of agreement, the Tribunal applies the law of the contracting State-Party to the dispute and other applicable rules of international law.

- There is no judicial review. Courts of all States party to the Convention enforce awards as they would domestic judgments.

- Perceived advantages of ICSID Arbitration

    - The arbitrators and administrators are considered to be highly qualified.
    - Costs and fees are regarded as being relatively low.
    - The ICSID process is considered to be very helpful in bringing about settlements.

❑ Additional Facility Rules

- These rules were added to the ICSID Convention to handle disputes between investors of an ICSID Party and a non-ICSID member country, if the latter agrees.

- Proceedings for the purpose of fact-finding leading to a report are available.

- UNCITRAL Arbitration Rules

  - UNCITRAL Arbitration Rules are the *UN Commission on International Trade Law Arbitration Rules.* They can be used ad hoc or administered by an agency of the Parties' choice. Ad hoc arbitrations occur under rules especially adopted for a proceeding or under rules promulgated generally for application in ad hoc proceedings.

  - UNCITRAL is not an institution, but if the parties do not choose an institution, the rules provide that the Secretary-General of the Permanent Court of Arbitration at The Hague can designate an appointing authority upon the request of either party.

  - The UNCITRAL Rules are viewed as being flexible and sensible. They contain elements of civil law and common law arbitration traditions. They also have the UN imprimatur and are not viewed as especially slanted toward any national legal procedure.

  - The UNCITRAL Rules have been widely emulated in subsequent rules adopted by other organizations.

- The "New York Convention"

  - Known as the *United Nations Convention on Recognition and Enforcement of Arbitral Awards*, the New York Convention was created to aid in international award enforcement through national courts.

  - The U.S., Canada and Mexico are all parties to the Convention.

- The Convention is not limited to investment disputes, but applies to all commercial matters.

- The Convention allows for only limited judicial review.

3.5 CONDITIONS PRECEDENT TO SUBMITTING A CLAIM

❑ A disputing investor can submit a claim to arbitration under the investment chapter only if the investor and enterprise:

1) consent to the arbitration;

2) waive the right to commence or continue proceedings respecting the measure before a Tribunal or court under the domestic law of any NAFTA Party or other dispute settlement procedures (NAFTA Chapter 20 procedures are only available to NAFTA Parties and not to individual investors). The waiver of a right to commence or continue proceedings does not apply to proceedings for injunctive, declaratory or other extraordinary relief that does not involve the payment of damages before an administrative tribunal or court under the law of the disputing NAFTA Party. This is because tribunals, under Chapter 11, Section B, can only award monetary damages.

Consent must be in writing and delivered to the host-Party.

❑ A general rule of international law states that a person must exhaust all domestic remedies before resorting to international options. Given that there is no domestic remedy for persons in Canada or the U.S., arbitration under Chapter 11, Section B is the only recourse open to investors.

- In Mexico, NAFTA Annex 1120(1) [See Part III, at p. 257] gives rise to private rights of action. An investor, however, may commence an action only under Mexican domestic laws or in an arbitration under Chapter 11, Section B, but not both.

3.6 ARBITRAL TRIBUNAL FORMATION

- Panels are comprised of three arbitrators, one chosen by each disputing NAFTA Party, and a third presiding member, chosen by joint agreement.

- NAFTA 1414(3) [See Part III, at p. 262] requires each NAFTA Party to have a separate roster of 15 people to serve as financial service panelists. Individuals on the roster must have financial service expertise. Under a Chapter 20 procedure, normal panel selection procedures apply, except that disputing Parties may agree that the Panel be comprised entirely of individuals who are qualified to be members of the financial services rosters.

- If the issue involves a public retirement plan or statutory system of social security, the Chair of the panel must be on the financial services roster.

- NAFTA 1124 [See Part III, at p. 242] sets out procedures to be followed if a tribunal is not constituted within 90 days of the date when the claim is submitted. The ICSID Secretary-General acts as the appointing authority even if arbitration is not conducted under the ICSID Convention. On the request of either NAFTA Party, the ICSID Secretary-General chooses the remaining arbitrators. The presiding member must be one of the individuals on the roster but cannot be a national of either country. If no person is available from the roster, then the presiding member is chosen from the ICSID Panel of Arbitrators.

3.7 CONSOLIDATION OF CLAIMS

- ❑ NAFTA 1126 [See Part III, at p. 244] deals with the issue that arises when more than one investor submits a claim arising out of the same question of law or fact. The claims can be consolidated and heard by a tribunal established under the UNCITRAL Arbitration Rules, as modified by the NAFTA.

- ❑ Before the decision is made to consolidate, a hearing must take place to determine the question of whether the consolidation in a particular dispute meets the criteria of NAFTA 1126.

- ❑ The question of consolidation is heard by a tribunal comprising of three arbitrators appointed by the Secretary-General of the ICSID. The presiding member cannot be a national of either the Party of the disputing investor or the other disputing NAFTA Party.

- ❑ If the tribunal decides consolidation is appropriate, it may assume jurisdiction over and decide all or part of the claims, or one or more claims that it believes would help in the resolution of the others.

3.8 PROCEDURAL MATTERS

- ❑ A proceeding is governed by the applicable body of arbitration rules, except as modified by Section B. Issues in dispute must be decided in accordance with the NAFTA and the principles of international law.

- ❑ Unless decided otherwise by the parties, arbitration will be held in the territory of the NAFTA Party that is a party to the New York Convention in order to ensure enforceability under that Convention.

- Section B provides a number of provisions with respect to its interpretation by the Free Trade Commission which are binding on a tribunal. If requested by a tribunal, the Commission must provide an interpretation within 60 days. If it fails to do so, the tribunal may make its own decision. The third Party not involved in the dispute may make submissions on the question of NAFTA interpretation.

- The defending NAFTA Party must provide notice of a claim to other Parties and provide copies of pleadings filed.

- If a NAFTA Party invokes NAFTA 1410 [See Part III, at p. 259], (which states that a NAFTA Party can adopt or maintain reasonable measures with respect to financial services and investment for prudential reasons) as a defense to a claim, the tribunal must refer the question of whether the measure is prudential to the Financial Services Committee. Prudential reasons include:

  a) the protection of investors, depositors, financial-market participants, policyholders, policy-claimants, or persons to whom a fiduciary duty is owed by a financial institution or cross-border financial-service provider;

  b) the maintenance of the safety, soundness, integrity or financial responsibility of financial institution or cross-border financial-service providers; and

  c) ensuring the integrity and stability of a NAFTA Party's financial system.

  The Committee must provide an answer within 60 days. If it fails to do so, disputing NAFTA Parties may request the establishment of a panel under NAFTA 2008 [See Part III, at p. 325] to decide the issue in dispute. If this is not done within ten days of the lapse of the 60 day period, the tribunal may decide on its own initiative.

- A tribunal may, at the request of a disputing NAFTA Party, or on its own initiative, obtain expert reports.

- A tribunal may issue interim orders for the protection or preservation of evidence or to protect a tribunal's jurisdiction.

3.9 IMPLEMENTATION AND ENFORCEMENT

- A tribunal may only award monetary damages and applicable interest. It may order restitution of property, but the award must provide that the disputing NAFTA Party pay monetary damages and interest in lieu of restitution. A tribunal may not order punitive damages. Awards do not preclude recourse to domestic law for nonmonetary resolutions.

- Section B allows investors to employ the enforcement mechanisms provided by the ICSID Convention, the New York Convention and the Inter-American Convention on International Commercial Arbitration. This section also allows the NAFTA party of the investor to initiate an enforcement action.

- Each NAFTA Party has an obligation to abide by and comply with a final award and to provide for the enforcement of an award in its territory.

- Awards under the ICSID Convention may not be enforced until 120 days have elapsed, while UNCITRAL awards cannot be enforced until three months after the date of the award.

- ❑ On the failure of a NAFTA Party to comply with a decision of the tribunal, the Commission on the request of the NAFTA Party of the investor must establish an arbitral panel under Chapter 20. On the decision of the tribunal that there has been a failure to abide by or comply with the final award, the NAFTA Party may suspend benefits. NAFTA 1414(5) [See Part III, at p. 262] sets limits on the suspension of benefits.

    1) If the measure that is inconsistent affects only the financial-services sector, benefits may be suspended only in the financial-services sector.

    2) If the inconsistent measure affects other sectors, benefits cannot be suspended in the financial-services sector.

    3) If the inconsistent measure affects the financial-services sector of a NAFTA Party, that NAFTA Party may suspend benefits that it provides to the NAFTA Party that is not complying, in the same sector and to the equivalent extent.

[For contact points on Investment, see Part II at p. 163; For relevant provisions see Part III at p. 224.
For contact points on Financial Services see Part II at p. 175; For relevant provisions see Part III at p. 259]

CHAPTER 4:
ANTIDUMPING AND COUNTERVAILING DUTY DISPUTE PROCEDURES: CHAPTER 19

4.1 DEFINITIONS

❑ Countervailing Duties

- Countervailing duties are additional duties imposed by an importing NAFTA Party to offset government subsidies in the exporting NAFTA Party, where the subsidized imports cause material injury to a domestic industry in the importing NAFTA Party. Government subsidies may enable an industry to charge lower prices for its products sold abroad than would otherwise be possible, with a resulting competitive advantage in a foreign market.

❑ Dumping

- The sale of an imported good at a price lower than that which it is sold for in the exporting NAFTA Party or in a third country and which injures producers of competitive products in the importing NAFTA Party.

- Countervailing duty and antidumping laws are accepted to be those embodied in relevant statutes, legislative history, regulations, administrative practice and judicial precedent.

4.2 SCOPE AND COVERAGE

- Actions under NAFTA Chapter 19 may only commence as a review of a final determination. A petition to initiate an investigation into dumping and subsidization must first be filed under the domestic laws of each NAFTA Party.

- Chapter 19 [See Part III, at p. 277] includes all obligations owed by NAFTA Parties in respect to antidumping and countervailing duties. Each NAFTA Party must establish a division within its Secretariat (the national section established to provide assistance in administering the NAFTA), to facilitate the operation of Chapter 19. Each Secretary is required to perform specific responsibilities under Chapter 19.

- Under the Chapter 19 provisions each NAFTA Party can retain and apply its domestic antidumping and countervailing duty (AD/CVD) laws against goods imported from other NAFTA Parties. (However, common qualities sought in the administration of such laws are identified in Article 1907(3) [See Part III, at p. 291].)

- NAFTA 1904(1) [See Part III, at p. 280] requires that the NAFTA Parties replace domestic judicial review of final anti-dumping or countervailing duty determinations made under domestic laws with binational panel proceedings. These panel proceedings are an alternative avenue of appeal to the domestic judicial review of decisions of the importing state. **This applies only to goods that the competent**

investigating authority of an importing NAFTA Party determines emanate from another NAFTA Party.

- The process of review is essentially twofold, beginning with the issuance of a final determination made with respect to dumping, subsidization and material injury within a NAFTA Party under its domestic laws, and a subsequent assessment of CVD/AD duties. The affected NAFTA party, then, has the right to request a review of the decision through the binational panel proceedings established under Chapter 19.

- Chapter 19 reviews are permitted for two purposes:

  1) to challenge whether an amendment to antidumping and countervailing duty laws of a NAFTA party:

     1) conforms to the norms established by NAFTA 1902(2) [See Part III, at p. 277], or

     2) such an amendment has the effect of overturning a prior decision of a panel and does not conform to NAFTA 1902(2); and

  2) to review final determinations made under domestic antidumping and countervailing duty laws.

4.3 WHO CAN INITIATE A CLAIM

- A complaint can be made by or on behalf of an industry by an interested party with the support of producers whose collective production of the goods in question represents 25% or more of the total national production of the goods. In Mexico, SECOFI may also initiate an investigation on its own initiative. In Canada, there must be more support than opposition to the complaint. In the U.S., the Assistant

Secretary of Commerce may, on his/her own initiative or in response to a complaint or petition, initiate an investigation when there is evidence of dumping or subsidizing of goods causing or likely to cause material injury to an established domestic industry, or retarding the establishment of a domestic industry.

- Interested parties can include:

  1) a manufacturer, producer, or wholesaler of a domestic-like product;

  2) a certified or recognized union of group-workers that is representative of the industry;

  3) a trade or business association, a majority of whose members manufacture, produce, or wholesale a domestic-like product;

  4) a coalition of firms, unions or trade associations.

- Access to the Chapter 19 process by private parties enables them to choose to litigate in instances in which a government declines to act for political or economic reasons.

4.4 PANEL REVIEW OF DOMESTIC FINAL DETERMINATIONS

- Final determinations are lists of specific orders and determinations made under the domestic antidumping and countervailing duty laws of the NAFTA Party, specifically, the *Special Import Measures Act* (SIMA) in Canada, the *Tariff Act of 1930* in the U.S., or Article 131 of the Mexican Constitution and certain other laws in Mexico.

❑ 4.41 MAKING THE FINAL DETERMINATIONS

CANADA

❑ In Canada, decisions with respect to dumping and subsidization are performed by the Deputy Minister of National Revenue for Customs and Excise (Deputy Minister). Material injury is established by the Canadian International Trade Tribunal (CITT).

❑ The *Special Import Measures Act* (SIMA) provides protection to Canadian producers who are being harmed by the dumping or subsidizing of goods imported into Canada. The Deputy Minister of National Revenue and the Canadian International Trade Tribunal (CITT) are responsible for its administration.

❑ Making the Complaint

- If a Canadian producer has evidence that the dumping or subsidizing of imported goods is injuring Canadian production, a complaint can be submitted to the Antidumping and Countervailing Directorate of Revenue Canada [See Part II, at NAFTA Chapter 19, Sources of Information]. The Directorate conducts investigations and determines whether goods imported into Canada are dumped or subsidized. The Tribunal decides whether the dumped or subsidized goods have caused material injury or threaten to cause injury.

- A petition for a dumping or countervailing investigation must include:

  1) A description of the imported goods, including country of export of the goods, names and

addresses of known foreign producers, exporters and Canadian importers;

2) Names and addresses of Canadian producers of the goods in question, total estimated Canadian production and total Canadian market (including imports);

3) Evidence of dumping, including the estimated price at which goods are being sold to Canadian importers, the estimated price at which goods are sold in the domestic market of the exporter or the estimated cost of imported goods; or evidence of subsidizing, including a description of the subsidy program and supporting details of the subsidy and the estimated amount of subsidy;

4) Evidence of injury such as increased market penetration achieved by the imports allegedly dumped or subsidized, sales lost to dumped or subsidized imports, depressed market prices, decline in profitability of the Canadian producers, loss of market share, and other such evidence where present.

❑ The Preliminary Determination [Note Chart p. 87]

- After the initial receipt of a written complaint from a party, Revenue Canada has 21 days to examine the documents and request any additional information necessary. After the completion of all documentation, Revenue Canada has 30 days to decide to initiate an investigation.

- Within 90 days of the commencement of the investigation, Revenue Canada will:

1) terminate the investigation if no injurious dumping or subsidizing is found; or

2) issue a preliminary determination of dumping or subsidizing.

- In situations which are particularly complex, the 90-day deadline may be extended to 135 days.

- If there is an affirmative preliminary determination, provisional duties will be levied on dumped or subsidized goods pending the completion of the investigation.

- A complete investigation takes 210 days from its initiation by Revenue Canada to the decision of material injury by the CITT.

❑ Material Injury

- Once there has been an affirmative preliminary determination of dumping or subsidization, the Canadian International Trade Tribunal must be notified to commence an inquiry to determine if dumping or subsidizing is causing material injury. This must be completed within 120 days of the preliminary determination.

- If material injury is found, SIMA duties are levied on all goods imported on and after the date of the preliminary determination. Where injury is not found, but there is a potential threat of future injury, SIMA duties are applied to goods imported after the date of the Tribunal's decision. Duties paid prior to that time are refunded. Where no injury is found, all SIMA duties are refunded and all proceedings in the case are terminated.

❑ The Final Determination

- Under SIMA Section 41, a final determination must be issued within 90 days of the date of the preliminary determination. Interested parties are notified and provided with a *Statement of Reasons* which states the Department's decisions.

- In Canada, if there is an affirmative final determination on subsidization or dumping and material injury, the Deputy Minister requests that a customs appraiser determine the normal value and export price of goods released before the final determination by the CITT to help to assess CVD/AD duties. Once the duty is paid, an importer may request that the appraiser redetermine that duty. The Deputy Minister may review these determinations, or be requested to do so.

❑ The Review of the Final Determination

- Governments, manufacturers, producers and exporters may appeal to Revenue Canada for a review of the final decision. The grounds of appeal include:

  1) the goods in question do not fit the product description of the CITT injury decision;

  2) disagreement as to the normal value, export price of the goods or the amount of subsidy.

- Parties have the right to appeal final decisions of Revenue Canada or CITT in a AD/CVD action to the Federal Court of Appeal.

- NAFTA Parties have the further option of seeking review under Chapter 19 procedures instead of the Federal Court.

- In Canada, the CITT may review any order or finding made by it on its own initiative, or at the request of the Deputy Minister, or an interested person or government. It may then rescind the order or finding, or continue it, with or without amendment.

United States

❑ In the U.S., determination of dumping and subsidization is a function of the International Trade Administration of the U.S. Department of Commerce (Commerce). Material injury is determined by the International Trade Commission (ITC).

❑ The Preliminary Determination [Note Charts at p. 88]

- An interested party must file an antidumping or countervailing duty petition with both Commerce and the Commission, simultaneously. Commerce then has 20 days to determine if an investigation will be initiated to determine if dumping or subsidies exist. A negative determination will terminate the process.

- The ITC must make a preliminary determination as to whether there is reasonable indication of material injury within 45 days of the filing of a petition or receiving notice from Commerce that it has initiated an investigation.

- A six-person team consisting of an investigator, an industry analyst, an economist, an accountant/auditor, an attorney, and a supervisory investigator are assigned by ITC to investigate the petition. A notice of the institution of investigation must be filed with the *Federal Register* and a work schedule must be prepared.

- Any party other than the petitioner who wishes to participate in the preliminary investigation must file an "entry of appearance" with the Secretary to the Commission within seven days after the publication of notice in the *Federal Register.*

- Questionnaires are sent to U.S. importers and U.S. and foreign producers to gather the information necessary for the investigation to make the preliminary determination. These are generally mailed within one to three business days after receipt of the petition.

- Public conferences are held approximately three weeks into the preliminary investigation, chaired by the Commission's Director of Investigations. Parties supporting and opposing the petition are each given one hour to present legal and factual arguments and testimony in support of their position. Other parties can request to present a brief statement of their position. Presiding officials may question witnesses but cross-examination by opposing parties is not permitted. Ten-minute rebuttal time is allowed for each side. A court reporter must transcribe the conference and transcripts are available. Parties are encouraged to file postconference briefs three days after the conference. These can be up to 50 double-spaced pages of text. Other parties are also permitted to submit a brief written statement.

- Information collected through the statistical data, questionnaires, public documents, field visits, telephone interviews and other sources are compiled and presented in a staff report. The report does not contain any recommendations regarding determinations that the Commission must make. It is provided to the Commission five weeks after the investigation is initiated. A memoranda is then submitted on the next business day, prepared by the General Counsel, to the Commission. This provides a summary of the arguments on both sides and provides legal advice.

- Four business days after the submission of the staff report, the Commission must have a public meeting to vote on the investigation. Each Commissioner announces his/her vote and the majority vote constitutes the determination of the Commission.

- The Commission must, one day after the public briefing and vote, transmit its views to Commerce explaining its decision in a brief. A public version of the report is subsequently published in the *Federal Register* and the determination and the views of the Commission are made available to the public electronically through the Internet. A publication is also made available by the Commission's Publishing Division. If the determination is negative the process is terminated.

- In the U.S., a decision by the ITC with respect to a countervailing action normally must be rendered within 85 days. An antidumping action must take place 160 days from the initiation of the investigation, but not prior to the ITC making a preliminary determination on material injury. Commerce must make a preliminary determination based on the information available.

- If Commerce's preliminary determination is affirmative, it can order the suspension of liquidation of all entries of the subject imports on or after the date of the publication of the notice of determination in the *Federal Register*. Importers must also put up a cash bond for each entry of the subject merchandise. A negative determination terminates the process.

- Provisional duties may be levied on the basis of an affirmative preliminary determination.

❑ The Final Determination

- In the U.S., a final determination must be made under the *Tariff Act of 1930* (Section 705 for countervailing duties and Section 735 for antidumping actions), within 75 days of a preliminary determination of subsidization/dumping. This must be done within 235 days after the date on which the petition is filed in antidumping cases, or 160 days in countervailing duty cases.

- A final determination with respect to material injury must be made by the ITC within 280 days following the filing of the petition or an affirmative final determination on subsidization or dumping.

- An assessment of the final determination begins on the Commission's receipt of notice of the affirmative preliminary determination from Commerce. Notice of the initiation of this investigation is then published in the *Federal Register*.

- The investigation is conducted by, again gathering information through questionnaires, a prehearing staff report, briefs filed four days before the hearing, and the public hearing which takes place two-and-a-half months after Commerce submits its final determination. Posthearing briefs are encouraged. A final staff report is submitted to the Commission two weeks after the posthearing briefs are due. A legal memorandum is submitted two days later, including the statement of issues and opinions of the staff involved. The record is closed five days after the staff report is issued. Parties are then permitted to inspect the public information. After a further three days, parties are allowed to make final comments. Other parties are permitted to submit information and participate. Notice must be provided within 21 days of the filing of the Notice in the *Federal Register.*

- A public hearing and vote is held approximately six days after the completion of the investigation. A further public briefing and vote is then conducted by the Commission.

- The final determination is then submitted to Commerce within 45 days of notification of Commerce's final determination (or 120 days after the preliminary determination, whichever is longer). Official notice of the final determination is published in the *Federal Register.*

❑ Assessing Duties

- In the U.S., after an affirmative final determination on subsidization or dumping and material injury, Commerce publishes the CVD/AD duty order which directs customs officers to assess the appropriate duty on the class of goods prescribed in that order.

- CVD/AD orders may be reviewed by Commerce at least once annually after the first year of the request for review is received. This review is intended to determine whether CVD/AD orders warrant revocation in the event of changed circumstances. A review must be made within five years of the issuance of the antidumping and countervailing duty order.

MEXICO

- ❑ In Mexico, the authority to take action against unfair trade practices is contained in Article 131 of the Mexican Constitution. CVD/AD matters are administered by the Secretariat for Commerce and Industrial Development (SECOFI) and investigations are undertaken by the SECOFI office. In general, SECOFI has been much less active in pursuing countervailing duty matters than its counterparts in Canada and the U.S. It is important to note that Mexico does not have a bifurcated system as in Canada and the United States; SECOFI makes both the determinations with respect to dumping and subsidizing and injury.

- ❑ NAFTA 1907(3) [See Part III, at p. 291] outlines desirable standards for the administration of antidumping and countervailing duty laws. This provision was included, in part, to ensure that Mexico's system of trade remedies was sufficiently similar to that of Canada and the U.S., given the requirement that Chapter 19 binational panels apply the domestic law of the NAFTA Party whose agency's determination is being challenged. This seeks to ensure that all interested NAFTA Parties have resort to similar standards of due process.

- ❑ Preliminary Determination

    - The Foreign Trade Law authorizes SECOFI to initiate an antidumping or countervailing duty investigation on its own or on the filing of a written petition by a Mexican interested party.

- Thirty days after the filing of a written petition, SECOFI must determine whether there is sufficient cause to initiate an investigation.

- Written notice of the initiation of an investigation must be provided to interested NAFTA Parties, including the relevant foreign exporters and governments, and Mexican importers. Notice must also be published in the *Diario Oficial de la Federacion.*

- Questionnaires are sent to foreign entities and Mexican importers requesting trade data on sales, prices, costs, government subsidy programs, import volume, production capabilities, and shipments to be completed within 30 days.

- Within 130 working days after the publication of the initial determination, SECOFI must publish its preliminary determination in *Diario Oficial de la Federacion*. Provisional duties can be levied at this point provided that 45 working days have elapsed since the publication in the *Diario Oficial* of the determination to initiate the antidumping or countervailing duty proceeding.

- At the same time as the issuance of the affirmative preliminary determination, SECOFI must direct the Secretariat of Treasury and Public Credit, Customs Administration, to impose preliminary or provisional antidumping or countervailing duties starting on the day after the publication of the preliminary determination in the *Diario Oficial*.

❑ The Final Determination

- Following the issuance of the preliminary determination, SECOFI must verify all information gathered from the questionnaire responses obtained through site visits. This is part of a verification process that takes place prior to the issuance of the final determination.

- A public hearing must also be held prior to the issuance of the final determination. Parties are provided with the opportunity to file written briefs and to present oral arguments on the preliminary determination.

- The final determination must be published within 260 days of the publication of the *Diario Oficial*. Administrative authorities must maintain a record and the final determination must be based on that record. Recommendations must be recorded and made available to NAFTA Parties to the proceedings.

- SECOFI must direct the Secretariat of Treasury and Public Credit, Customs Administration, to subsequently collect final antidumping and countervailing duties if there is an affirmative final determination.

- Final determinations must be accompanied by detailed reasons enabling interested NAFTA Parties to make informed decisions as to whether to seek review. Immediate access to a binational panel for review of a final determination of dumping or subsidization must be provided without having to exhaust the domestic administrative appeal procedure.

- A right to annual review of dumping margins and countervailing duties is provided under Article 68 of the Foreign Trade Law.

- The Foreign Trade Law establishes two separate appeal tracks for purposes of challenging a final SECOFI antidumping or countervailing duty determination. It allows the traditional Mexican domestic appeal process and the Chapter 19 NAFTA binational panel review mechanism.

❑ 4.42 UNDERTAKINGS

- In Canada, pursuant to Section 49 of the *Special Import Measures Act* (SIMA), an undertaking to eliminate dumping, subsidization, or material injury may be accepted from a NAFTA Party or private parties within 60 days of a preliminary determination. These undertakings suspend the investigation of dumping or subsidization, although such investigations may continue on request of the NAFTA parties involved.

- As long as undertakings are in force and complied with, no duties are collected.

- Investigations that are not suspended as a consequence of such undertakings will continue until a final decision is reached.

- Each NAFTA Party provides for the periodic review of undertakings to determine if they continue to serve their purposes in changed circumstances.

- In the U.S., a request by a NAFTA Party will not terminate an undertaking, but the investigation will continue concurrently. If the ITC finds that the undertaking will not completely eliminate injury, a full investigation may resume.

- Legislation in each NAFTA Party provides remedies for violating undertakings that eliminate dumping or subsidization.

❑ 4.43 REVIEW OF THE FINAL DETERMINATION

❑ A NAFTA Party may request binational panel review of a domestic final determination to establish whether it was in accordance with the antidumping or countervailing duty law of the importing NAFTA Party. The implementing legislation within each NAFTA country provides that private parties can initiate proceedings by filing requests with their NAFTA Secretariat.

❑ If no binational panel review is sought, domestic judicial review of the determination may proceed. Any revised final determination arising from judicial review is not subject to binational panel review. Once a NAFTA Party has requested a NAFTA panel review, a final determination may not be reviewed by any domestic court.

❑ Types of Final Determinations Subject to Review

- The types of final determination decisions that are subject to panel review are listed in NAFTA Annex 1911 [See Part III, at p. 312].

❑ Canada (listed under subparagraph (a))

1) Clause (i): An order or finding by the Canadian International Trade Tribunal (CITT) arising from its inquiry as to material injury under *Special Import Measures Act* (SIMA), Section 43(1).

2) Clause (ii): An order by the CITT arising from a review of its own prior order or finding of material injury under SIMA, Section 76(4).

3) Clause (iii): A final determination of the Deputy Minister of National Revenue as to whether there has been dumping or subsidization under SIMA, Section 41.

4) Clause (iv): A decision of the Deputy Minister arising from his/her redetermination of the determination or redetermination of a customs appraiser under SIMA, Section 59.

5) Clause (v): A decision by the CITT under SIMA, Section 76(3), not to review an order or finding of material injury.

6) Clause (vi): A reconsideration by the CITT of a decision as to which of two or more persons is an importer under SIMA, Section 91(3).

7) Clause (vii): A decision of the Deputy Minister arising from the periodic review of undertakings under SIMA, Section 53(1).

8) The decisions of the CITT referred to in clauses (i), (ii), (v) and (vi) are all subject to judicial review by the Federal Court of Appeal.

9) The decision of the Deputy Minister referred to in clause (iv) is subject to review by the CITT and an appeal from the CITT to the Federal Court of Appeal may be made on a question of law only.

10) Decisions of the Deputy Minister referred to in clauses (iii) or (vii) are reviewable by the Federal Court of Appeal.

- United States (listed under subparagraph (b))

  1) Clauses (i) and (ii): Refers to final determinations made by the Department of Commerce as to the occurrence of subsidization or dumping and the International Trade Commission (ITC) as to material injury under Sections 705 and 735 of the *Tariff Act of 1930*.

  2) Clause (iii): Refers to Commerce's review of antidumping and countervailing duty orders under Section 751 of the Tariff Act of 1930.

  3) Clause (iv): Refers to determinations of the ITC under Section 751(b) of the *Tariff Act of 1930* not to review a determination based on changed circumstances.

  4) Clause (v): Refers to a determination by Commerce as to whether a particular type of merchandise is within a class or kind that is subject to an existing finding of antidumping or countervailing duty order.

  5) Each of these determinations is subject to judicial review by the U.S. Court of International Trade.

- Mexico (listed under subparagraph (c))

  1) Clause (i): Refers to a final resolution by SECOFI respecting dumping, subsidization, or injury.

  2) Clause (ii): Refers to a final resolution in an annual application for review of antidumping or countervailing duty rates created by the amendments required by NAFTA, Annex 1904(15) [See Part III, at p. 314].

  3) Clause (iii): Refers to a final resolution by SECOFI as to whether a particular type of merchandise is within

the class or kind of merchandise described in an existing antidumping or countervailing duty resolution.

4.44 STANDARD OF REVIEW

- Binational panels must apply the standard of review and general legal principles that a court of the importing state otherwise would apply in reviewing a final AD/CVD determination.

- Canada

  - The standard of review to be applied is set out in Section 18.1(4) of the *Federal Court Act*. Grounds for review are:

    1) Acting without jurisdiction;
    2) Acting beyond its jurisdiction or refusing to exercise jurisdiction;
    3) Failing to observe a principle of natural justice;
    4) Erring in law in making a decision or order;
    5) Basing a decision on an erroneous finding of fact made in a perverse or capricious manner, or without regard for the evidence presented;
    6) Acting or failing to act by reason of fraud or perjured evidence;
    7) Acting in any other way contrary to law.

- United States

  - The standard of review to be applied in proceedings in the U.S. is that applied by the United States Court of International Trade.

  - The standard of review concerning a final determination of the ITC not to review a determination because of changed circumstances under Section

751(b) of the Tariff Act of 1930 is that the decision is arbitrary, capricious, an abuse of discretion, unsupported by substantial evidence, or otherwise not in accordance with law.

❑ Mexico

- In Mexico the standard of review is set out in Article 238 of the *Federal Fiscal Code*, or successor statutes based solely on the administrative record.

- The standard used is lack of competence of the administrator issuing the decision or conducting the proceeding, omission of legal requirements, procedural defects in the proceeding, incorrect or misunderstood facts, improper issuance or enforcement of the decisions, or an exercise of discretionary authority that is inconsistent with the objectives of the law granting the authority.

❑ 4.45 INITIATING REVIEW BY A PANEL

❑ Request for a Panel

- A NAFTA Party must request a panel review of a final determination upon request of any person entitled to commence judicial review procedures of that determination under domestic law.

- A request for panel review may also be made by a NAFTA Party of its own volition. The request must be made in writing to the importing NAFTA Party within 30 days of publication of the final determination.

- If provisional remedies are imposed, the exporting NAFTA Party may notify the importing NAFTA Party of its intention to request a panel.

- The importing NAFTA Party must inform the NAFTA Party whose goods are affected by the final determination of its intention to make such a request. A request for panel review may be made within 30 days of receipt of that notice.

- Failure to make a timely request will preclude panel review.

4.46 PANEL FORMATION

❑ Panels are always binational, not trinational as under NAFTA Chapter 20. This is regardless of whether an amendment to a law governing duties or a final determination affects goods of both the other NAFTA Parties. In the event of a dispute involving more than two NAFTA Parties, two separate binational panels have to be constituted.

❑ Panelists

- Panels consist of five members chosen from a roster of 75 people (25 selected by each member NAFTA Party). Panelists must be of high standing, good character, objective, reliable, and have sound judgment and general familiarity with international trade law. Individuals on the rosters must also be citizens of the member NAFTA Party from which they are chosen. The rosters are required to include judges or former judges to the greatest extent practicable.

- The majority of members of a panel must be lawyers and the Chair must be chosen from the lawyers on the panel.

❑ Selection

- Each NAFTA Party chooses two members. Each is permitted four peremptory challenges, disqualifying proposed candidates. If a panelist becomes unable to fulfill his/her obligations, the panel will be suspended pending a new selection. If appointment is not complete within 30 days, selection of a panelist proceeds by lot.

- The fifth member of the panel is chosen by agreement of both NAFTA Parties. This must be done within 55 days of a request for a panel. Again, failure to decide results in selection by lot.

- Panelists choose a Chair promptly from among the lawyers on the panel, by majority vote. Failing a majority, a lawyer on the panel is chosen by lot.

- Panelists must not be affiliated with or take instructions from any NAFTA Party.

❑ 4.47 PROCEDURES BEFORE PANELS AND PANEL DECISIONS

❑ The authority that issued the final determination under review has the right to appear before the panel, as does any other person who would have been allowed to participate in a review before a domestic court. These parties may be represented by counsel.

❑ The jurisdiction of a panel is unequivocally restricted to applying the CVD/AD duty laws of the importing NAFTA Party. This includes applying relevant statutes, legislative history, regulations, administrative practices, and judicial precedents to the extent that the courts of the importing NAFTA Party would have relied on them.

- ❑ Such panels are required to apply the domestic law of the NAFTA Party whose agency's determination is being challenged. Unlike Chapter 20, Chapter 19 panel decisions are binding on the NAFTA Parties involved.

- ❑ Review is to be based on the administrative record, consisting of all documentary or other information presented to, or obtained by an investigating authority. This includes government memoranda and records of *ex parte* proceedings unless otherwise agreed upon, reasons and transcript records of conferences, hearings and all published notices in an official journal of the importing NAFTA Party.

- ❑ Panel Decisions

  - A panel can uphold a final determination or remand it back to the investigating authority for action not inconsistent with the panel's decision.

  - Where the final decision is remanded, a panel must establish as brief a time as is reasonable for compliance with the remand by the investigating authority. The period for review cannot be longer than the time it took to make the final determination.

  - An investigating authority shall report on the action that it took on remand by filing a Determination on Remand with the responsible Secretariat. A participant can challenge the action taken by filing a written submission within a prescribed time period. If the action must be reviewed, the same panel must do so and issue a final decision within 90 days.

❑ Rules of procedure

- The Panel Review process is governed by Chapter 19 Rules of Procedure [See Part III, at pp. 340, 387] and the NAFTA Code of Conduct [See Part III, at p. 387].

- The Rules govern the content and service of panel requests, transmission of the administrative record, protection of confidential information, participation by private persons in panel proceedings, the filing, service, form and content of briefs, the limitation of review of alleged error and the conduct of hearings and timing.

- Final panel decisions shall be made within 315 days of a request for a panel.

❑ Time Limitations

- The complaint must be filed within 30 days of receipt of a final determination.
- 30 days is provided for filing the designated or certified administrative record with the panel.
- 60 days is provided for the complainant to file its brief.
- 60 days is provided for the respondent to file its brief.
- 15 days is provided for the filing of reply briefs.
- 15 to 30 days is provided for the panel to convene and hear oral argument.
- 90 days is provided for the panel's written decision.

4.8 EXTRAORDINARY CHALLENGE PROCEDURES

❑ Unlike Chapter 20, Chapter 19 panel decisions are binding on the NAFTA Parties involved. This obliges them to give effect to the panel decisions respecting the particular matter in question under their domestic law.

- NAFTA Parties are prohibited from providing for an appeal of panel decisions to domestic courts. NAFTA also does not provide for routine appeal procedures from decisions of binational panels.

- NAFTA 1904(13) [See Part III, at p. 283], however, allows an Extraordinary Challenge Procedure set out in Annex 1904(13) [See Part III, at p. 301], which may be invoked by a NAFTA Party only and not by other interested persons.

- Grounds for challenge

  - The grounds for an Extraordinary Challenge are set out in NAFTA 1904(13).

  - An Extraordinary Challenge can be invoked if it is alleged within a reasonable time that one of the actions listed in 1904(13a) has materially affected the panel's decision and threatens the integrity of the binational panel review process. These actions are:

    1) A member of the panel was guilty of gross misconduct, bias, a serious conflict of interest, or otherwise materially violated the rules of conduct.

    2) The panel seriously departed from a fundamental rule of procedure.

    3) The panel manifestly exceeded its powers, authority or jurisdiction set out in NAFTA 1904 [See Part III, at p. 280].

- Procedures

  - Procedures are set out in NAFTA Annex 1904(13).

  - Thirty days are allowed for requesting an Extraordinary Challenge Committee (ECC), from the Notice of Final Panel Action, or after a NAFTA Party finds out about a panelist's misconduct if that occurs after the Notice of Final Panel Action.

  - The ECC is to be established within 15 days of request.

  - The Committee is to be comprised of three members, selected from a roster of 15 judges or former judges of a federal judicial court of the U.S. or Mexico, or a court of superior jurisdiction of Canada. Each involved NAFTA Party elects one member from the roster and then they decide by lot which of them is entitled to select the third member.

  - A decision must be rendered within 90 days of the appointment of panelists and that decision is binding on Parties involved in the matter.

- Decisions

  - If the ECC finds that one of the grounds for an Extraordinary Challenge exists, the panel decision will be vacated or remanded back for action which is not inconsistent with the ECC decision.

  - A three-prong test must to be satisfied to sustain an Extraordinary Challenge:

    1) the panel or member was guilty of an action listed; and

2) that action materially affected the panel's decision; and
3) that action threatened the integrity of the panel process.

4.9 SAFEGUARDING THE PANEL REVIEW SYSTEM

- ❑ A state-to-state dispute settlement mechanism is designed to safeguard the functioning of the binational review system.

- ❑ If any NAFTA Party's domestic law interferes with the proper functioning of the panel system by:

  1) preventing the establishment of a panel;
  2) interfering with the panel decision-making process;
  3) preventing the implementation of a panel decision;

  another NAFTA Party may request consultations and the establishment of a Special Committee to address the matter.

- ❑ Consultations must begin within 15 days of the request for consideration. If the matter is not resolved in 45 days, the complainant NAFTA Party may request the establishment of a Special Committee. This must be done within 15 days of the date of the request.

- ❑ The Special Committee consists of three members drawn from a roster, selected in accordance with procedures for Extraordinary Challenges.

- ❑ If the Special Committee makes an affirmative finding on any ground described above, consultation must begin within 10 days with a view to resolution of the matter within 60 days.

- If the matter is not resolved within 60 days, or if the NAFTA Party that is the subject of the complaint has not demonstrated to the Special Committee that it has corrected the problem, the Complainant NAFTA Party may suspend the operation of NAFTA 1904 with respect to the offending NAFTA Party and may also suspend other NAFTA benefits it deems appropriate. The NAFTA Party that is the subject of the complaint may ask for a review as to whether the suspension of benefits is excessive, or whether it has corrected the problem.

- The Special Committee has 45 days in which to make its decision and decide if the problem has been corrected. If it is decided that it has been corrected, the suspension is terminated.

4.10 PANEL REVIEW OF STATUTORY AMENDMENTS

- Amending Countervailing Duties and Antidumping Laws

    - Each NAFTA Party has the right to amend its AD/CVD laws subject to requirements respecting statutory amendments. NAFTA 1902(2) [See Part III, at p. 288] provides the norms to which such amendments must conform. Amendments must be consistent with GATT provisions, including the Antidumping and Subsidies Codes and with the object and purpose of the NAFTA.

    - Parties must notify and, at times, consult with other NAFTA Parties to which such a statutory amendment would apply. An amendment will only apply to other NAFTA Parties if it is specified explicitly in the amending statute.

- ❑ If consultations between disputing NAFTA Parties fail to settle a dispute with respect to an amendment to antidumping and countervailing duty provisions of the NAFTA, the matter can be referred to a binational panel for a declaratory opinion as to whether:

  1) the amendment is inconsistent with the object and purpose of the NAFTA and the provisions of the GATT; or

  2) the amendment has the effect of overturning a prior decision made by a panel with respect to a final determination and the measure is inconsistent with the GATT or NAFTA.

- ❑ Procedures for Making Declaratory Opinions

  - A panel may establish its own rules of procedure, but these must provide for at least one hearing.

  - An initial opinion by the panel must be rendered within 90 days of the selection of the Chair. That opinion must be based solely on submissions and arguments. It becomes final unless written objections are presented to the panel by a disputing NAFTA Party within 14 days. All decisions are based on votes by all members.

  - On objection, the panel may take 30 days in which to conduct such further examinations as it deems appropriate in reconsidering its opinion.

  - The panel's final declaratory opinion, including any dissents or concurring opinions, must be published, unless the NAFTA Parties agree otherwise.

- If a statutory amendment is found to be inconsistent with the NAFTA, a panel may recommend appropriate modifications. In such a case, affected Parties shall immediately consult to reach a mutually satisfactory solution in light of the recommendations within 90 days of issuance of the final panel determination. If the modification arrived at involves passing corrective legislation, that legislation must be passed within nine months.

- If no corrective legislation is enacted or if consultations to implement recommendations of the panel fail, the NAFTA Party that requested the panel can enact comparable legislation, or executive action, or terminate the NAFTA on 60 days' written notice of that intention.

4.11 CONSULTATIONS

- NAFTA 1907 [See Part III, at p. 290] requires that member Parties consult annually, or on request in respect of problems that may arise in implementing Chapter 19. The purpose is to develop more effective rules to limit the use of subsidies and to establish a system of dealing with unfair transborder price subsidization.

[On review of dispute settlement in antidumping and countervailing duty matters under Chapter 19, see Part II, at p. 191 and Part III at p. 277]

SIMA PROCESS

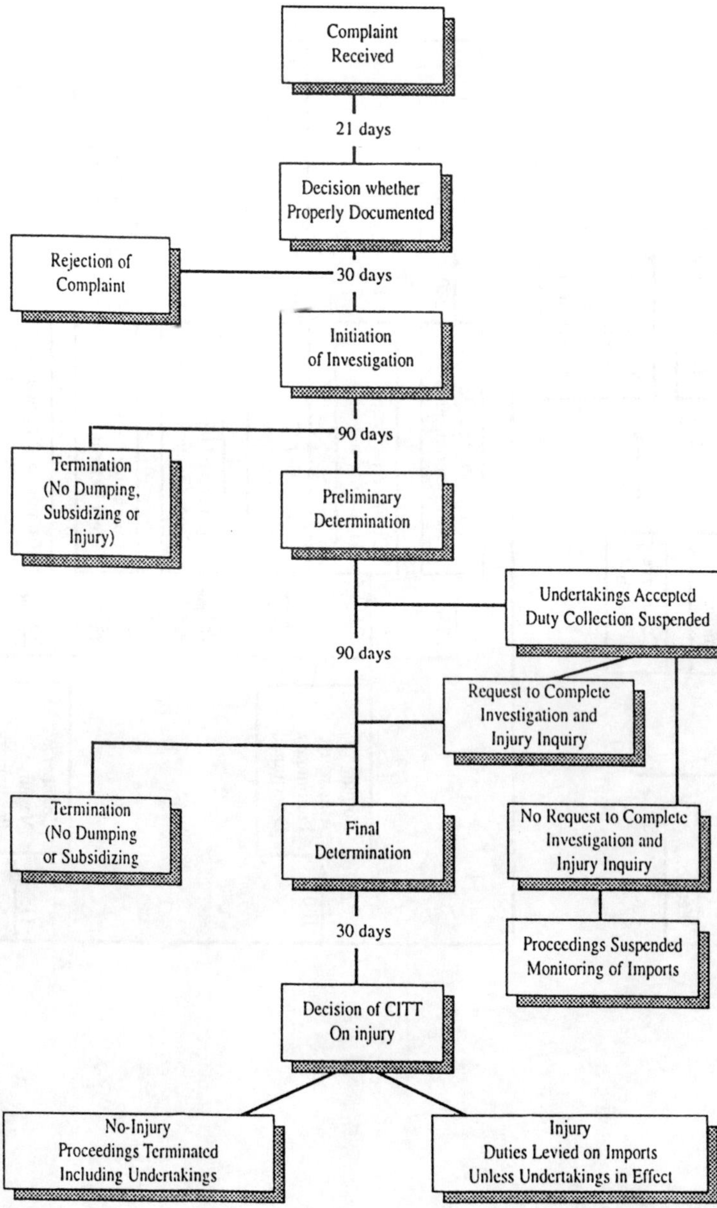

Figure 1

Statutory Timetable for Autidumping Investigations

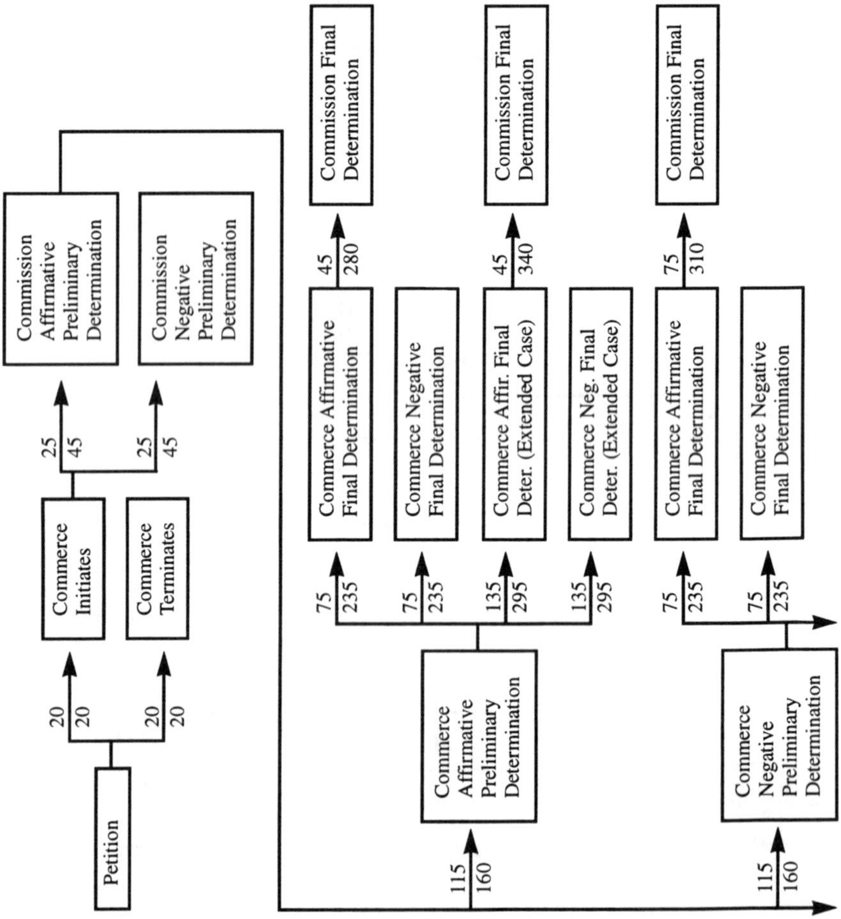

match to next page

Figure 1 continued

Statutory Timetable for Autidumping Investigations

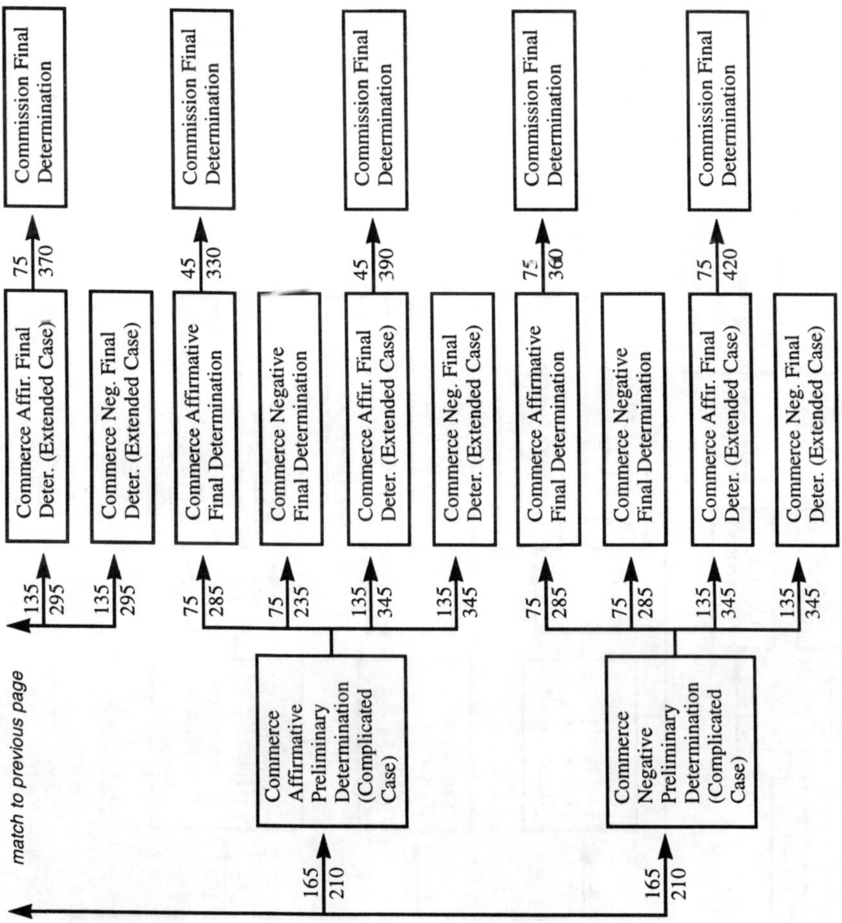

Note: --Days between events are shown above arrows: cumulative days from the date of filing of the petition are shown below arrows. Commerce may also postpone its initiation determination by up to 20 days in order to poll the industry to determine support for the petition.

Statutory Timetables

Figure 2

Statutory Timetable for Countervailing Duty Investigations

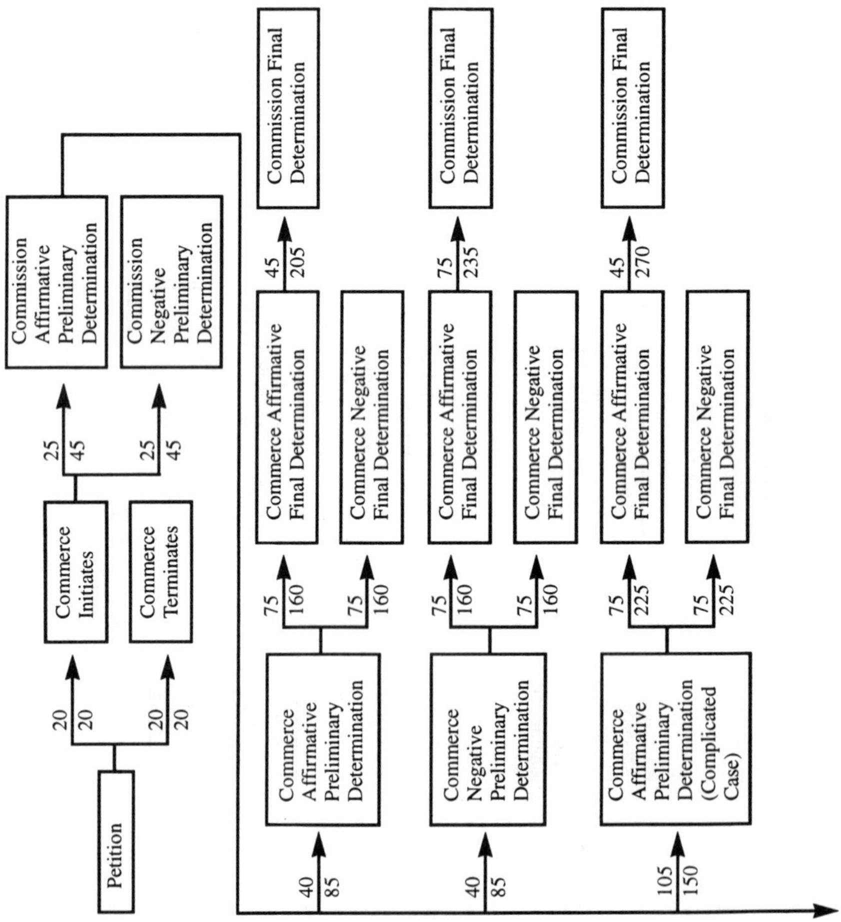

match to next page

Figure 2 continued

Statutory Timetable for Countervailing Duty Investigations

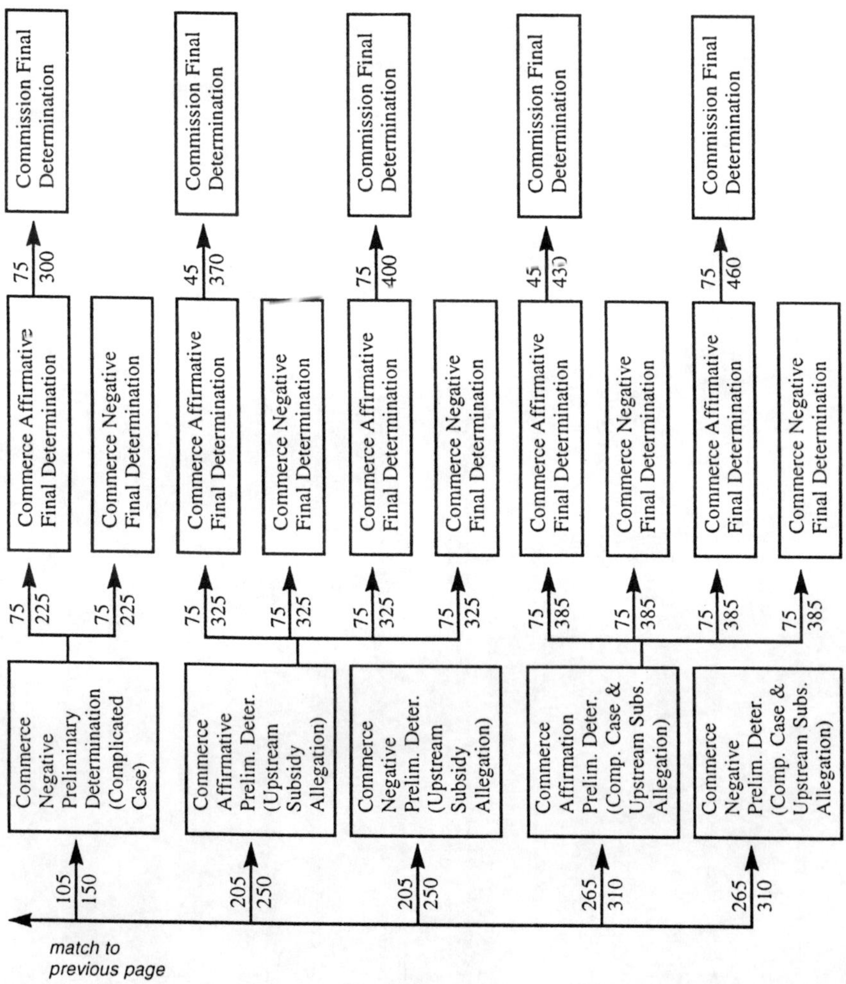

Note: --Days between events are shown above arrows: cumulative days from the date of the petition are shown below arrows. Commerce may also postpone its initiation determination by up to 20 days in order to poll the industry to determine support for the petition, and may, at the request of petitioners, postpone the date for its final subsidy determination to conform with the date of its final dumping determination in simultaneously filed cases.

Statutory Timetables

PART II
SOURCES AND CONTACTS

This part of the book contains data on essential contact and information sources within various government departments and agencies, for referral by those seeking to obtain answers to queries relating to NAFTA and dispute avoidance or resolution. The chapters in this section correspond to NAFTA chapters and include data on the committees and working groups, contact and inquiry points, as well as general industry-related contact sources.

Parties may gather answers to preliminary questions and narrow their investigation by calling the general numbers provided on pp. 95-103. Contact and Inquiry points, established for NAFTA Chapters 7, 9, 10, 12, 17, 18 and 20, may also provide further information and guidance. Contact points facilitate communication on any matter covered by the Agreement. On request, they can identify the office or official responsible for a matter and can sometimes assist in dialogue in avoiding or resolving a dispute. Inquiry points have been established as contacts for trade-related standards and other information, in recognition of the fact that lack of information about a NAFTA Partie's trade standards can act as a barrier to trade. In Canada, for example, trade standards are under the management of the Standards Council of Canada and have strategic information with respect to design, manufacture, marketing, export and import of products and services.

The committees and working groups established, and continuing to be established under the Agreement, to facilitate implementation, communication and the gathering of information, are listed under their respective promulgating NAFTA chapters. They can provide more technical information in their target areas and assist by providing answers to technical questions. Each has a central representative (referred to as the "Lead") in Canada, the U.S. and Mexico. Leads act as their Parties' point of contact for matters dealt with under the committee or working group. Each is also responsible to attend all scheduled trilateral meetings and work toward accomplishing the terms of reference of the committee or working group.

Given the fluidity in the operation of the NAFTA at this time, some specific contact and inquiry points are likely to change over time. However, general contact and inquiry points ordinarily remin constant; and NAFTA offices usually provide referrals in the event of staff and other changes.

GENERAL CONTACT SOURCES

CANADA

NAFTA Secretariat, Canadian Section

Cathy Beehan
The Secretary, Canadian Section
NAFTA Secretariat
Royal Bank Centre
Ste. 705, 90 Sparks St.
Ottawa, Ontario K1P 5B4
Tel: (613) 992-9388
Fax: (613) 992-9392

General NAFTA Information (for referral)

1-800-267-8376

Export and Services Information

Info Export
External Affairs and International Trade Canada
(Industry Canada)
125 Sussex Dr.
Ottawa, Ontario K1A 0G2
InfoEx: 1-800-267-8376
(613) 944-4000
Fax: (613) 996-9709

Copy of guide for temporary entry of businesspersons under NAFTA

Citizenship and Immigration Canada
Ottawa, Hull K1A 1L1

NAFTA Customs Enquiry Line (tariff and border administration issues)

NAFTA Information Desk
Revenue Canada Customs, Excise and Tax
1st Fl., 555 Mackenzie Ave.
Ottawa, Ontario K1A 0L5
Tel: 1-800-661-6121
(613) 941-0965
Fax: (613) 941-8138
(613) 952-0022

NAfFTA Customs Help Line in Spanish

NAFTA Spanish Help Desk
Revenue Canada Customs (Spanish)
Tel: (613) 941-0965

Electronic Bulletin Board

Computer Info. on NAFTA
1-800-267-5979

Information on how to access NAFTA/ Inquiry Point resources

WTO/NAFTA Enquiry Point
Standards Council of Canada
1200 – 45 O'Connor St.
Ottawa, Ontario K1P 6N7
Tel: (613) 238-3222
Fax: (613) 995-4564

For information on the role of the Canadian International Trade Tribunal

The Secretary
Canadian International Trade Tribunal
333 Laurier Ave., W.
Ottawa, Ontario K1A 0G7
Tel: (613) 993-4601
Fax: (613) 998-4783

Department of Foreign Affairs and International Trade InfoCentre

Tel: (613) 267-8376
Tel: 1-800-267-8376
Fax: (613) 996-9709
Interactive FaxLink:(613) 944-4500
Bulletin Board: (613) 944-1581
Website: http:\www.dfait-maeci.gc.ca

Canada – Mexico Trade

Latin America and Caribbean Trade Division
Department of Foreign Affairs and International Trade
125 Sussex Dr.
Ottawa, Ontario K1A 0G2
Tel: (613) 996-5547
Fax: (613) 996-6142

Canada – U.S. Trade

U.S. Trade, Tourism and
Investment Bureau (UTD)
Department of Foreign Affairs
and International Trade
Lester B. Pearson Building
125 Sussex Dr.
Ottawa, Ontario K1A 0G2
Tel: (613) 944-5726
Fax: (613) 944-9119

Responsibility for the management and coordination of Canadian participation in the NAFTA and NAFTA implementation

Dexter Bishop, Deputy Director
Multilateral Trade Institutions
Department of Foreign Affairs
and International Trade
125 Sussex Dr.
Ottawa, Ontario K1A 0G2
Tel: (613) 995-7523

Contact for referral (For issues unrelated to dispute settlement)

Henri Jarque
Department of Foreign Affairs
and International Trade
Multilateral Trade Institutions
125 Sussex Dr.,
Ottawa, Ontario K1A 0G2
Tel: (613) 944-4955

General
Information: 1-800-267-8376 for referral

- Mr. Jarque has a list of officials to whom he redirects calls

Information on the dispute resolution process

Peter Iakat
Tel: (613) 992-4841

Canadian Embassies in the U.S. and Mexico

The Embassy of Canada in Mexico
Commercial Division
Schiller No. 529
Col. Polanco
Apartado Postal 105-5
11560 Mexico, D.F.
Tel: (525) 724-9000
Fax: (525) 724-7982

Canadian Consulate
Edificio Kalos, Piso C-1
Local 108A
Zaragoza y Constitucion
64000 Monterrey
Mexico
Tel: (525) 443-200
Fax: (525) 443-048

Canadian Embassy
501 Pennsylvania Ave., N.W.
Washington, D.C.
Tel: (202) 682-1740
Fax: (202) 682-7689

NAFTA Trilateral Cooperation (to arrange conferences and presentations)

Tel: (613) 952-3483

Publications on NAFTA

InfoEx: 1-800-267-8376
(613) 944-4000
Fax: (613) 996-9709

Canada Communications Group
Publications
Ottawa, Ontario
K1A 0S9

Agreement on Environmental Cooperation

Secretariat of the Commission for Environmental Cooperation
393 Rue St. Jacques Ouest,
Bureau 200
Montreal, Que H2Y 1N9
Tel: (613) 350-4300

Linda Duncan
Division Head
Law and Enforcement Division
Tel: (613) 350-4334

UNITED STATES

NAFTA Secretariat, American Section

James R. Holbein
U.S. Secretary
NAFTA Secretariat, U.S. Section
14th & Constitution Aves., N.W.
Room 2061
Washington, D.C. 20230
Tel: (202) 482-5438
Fax: (202) 482-0148

For technical assistance on U.S. Customs law and NAFTA

NAFTA Help Desk
U.S. Customs Service
1301 Constitution Ave., N.W.
Room 1325
Washington, D.C. 20229
Tel: (202) 927-0066
Fax: (202) 927-0097

Office of International Affairs
U.S. Customs Service
Department of the Treasury
1301 Constitution Ave., N.W.
Washington, D.C. 20229-0001

For U.S. Customs Information and Mexican Customs Information

Enquiry Desk
Tel: (214) 574-4061

DEPARTMENT OF COMMERCE

Information on exporting from U.S. to Mexico

U.S. Dept. of Commerce
Office of Mexico, Room 3022
14th St. & Constitution Ave., NW
Washington, D.C. 20230
Tel: (202) 482-0300

Information on exporting from U.S. to Canada

U.S. Dept. of Commerce
Office of Canada,
14th St. & Constitution Ave., NW
Room 3033
Washington, D.C. 20230
Tel: (202) 482-3101

NAFTA Trade Promotion and Business
(202) 482-0305

UNITED STATES TRADE REPRESENTATIVES OFFICE

Office of North American Affairs
Office of the United States Trade Representative
600 17th St., N.W.
Washington, D.C. 20506

USTR Inquiry Line
Tel: (202) 395-3412

Trade Policy and Trade Negotiation Issues

Tel: (202) 395-3412

Kenneth P. Freiberg, Esq.
Deputy General Counsel
Office of U.S. Trade Representative
Winder Building
600 17th St., N.W.
Washington, D.C. 20506
Fax: (202) 395-3639

Office of GATT Affairs
Office of the United States
Trade Representative
600 17th St., N.W.
Washington, D.C. 20506

Agreement on Labor Cooperation

Secretariat of the Commission
for Labor Cooperation
350 North St. Paul St.
Suite 2424
Dallas, TX 75201

John McKennirey
Secretariat Executive Director
Tel: (214) 754-1103

MEXICO

NAFTA Secretariat, Mexican Section

Rafael Figueroa Serrano
Coordinadora General de la
Seccion Mexicana del TLCAN
Boulevard Adolfo Lopez Mateos
No. 3025 piso 2
Col. Heroes de Padiema
CP 10700 Mexico, D.F.
Tel: (525) 629-9630
Fax: (525) 629-9637

SECOFI
130 Albert St., Ste. 1700
Ottawa, ON K1P 5G4
Tel: (613) 235-7782
Fax: (613) 235-1129

Embassy of Mexico
Trade Office/SECOFI
45 O'Connor St.
Ste. 1500
Ottawa, Ontario K1P 1A4

Secretariat of Budget and Programming
Secretaria de Programacion y
Presupuesto
Palacio Nacional Patio de
Honor, Piso 4
Col. Centro
06740 Mexico, D.F.
Tel: (542) 8762/ 8763
Fax: (542) 1209
Information
Dept: 286-1000/1900

Secretariat for Commerce and Industrial Promotion

Secretaria de Comercio y
Fomento Industrial
(SECOFI)
Direccion General de Servicios
al Comercio Exterior
Alfonso Reyes No. 30 Piso 10
Col. Hipodromo de la Condesa
06170 Mexico, D.F.
Tel: (525) 286-1757
Fax: (525) 286-1543

SECOFI
Subsecretaria de Negociaciones
Comerciales Internacionales
Calle Alfonso Reyes No. 30
Colonia Condesa
C.P. 06140 Mexico, D.F.
Tel: (525) 211-3545/3405
Fax: (525) 224-3000

SECOFI
Licenciado Hector Rafael Perez
Partida
Delegacion Jalisco
Avenida Mariano Otero 3431
Colonia Valle Verde
Guadalajara, Jalisco
Tel: (523) 621-0694/1642
Fax: (523) 621-1360/0534

For information on exporting from Mexico to the United States

SECOFI
Delegacion Nuevo Leon
Licenciado Carlos Alberto
Garcia Triana
Edificio Cintermex, Local 88
Avenida Fundidora y Adolfo P.
Monterrey, N.L.
Tel: (528) 696-480/481
Fax: (528) 696-487

For Import requirements related to NAFTA

Secretariat of Finance and Public Credit
Secretaria de Hacienda y
Credito Publico
Direccion General Tecnica de
Ingresos
Palacio Nacional
1er. Patio Mariano
Col. Centro
06066 Mexico, D.F.
Tel. (525) 518-5420
Fax: (525) 542-2821

Secretaria de Hacienda y
Credito Publico
Subsecretaria de Ingresos
Direccion General Fiscal
Internacional
Avenida Hidalgo #77, Modulo 1
Planta Baja, Colonia Guerrero
Delegacion Cuauhtemoc
06300 Mexico, D.F.

National Bank of Exterior Commerce

Banco Nacional de Comercio
Exterior, S.N.C.
Camino a Sta. Teresa 1679
01900 Mexico, D.F.
Tel: (525) 227-9078

Director General of International Business

Lic. Javier Bonilla
Director General
Direccion General de Asuntos Internacionales
Secretaria de Agricultura y Recursos Hidraulicos
Benjamin Franklin 146
Mexico, D.F. 11800

Director General of Standards

Lic. Luis Guillermo Ibarra
Director General
Direccion General de Normas
Secretaria de Comercio y Fomento Industrial
Puente de Tecamachalco No. 6
Colonia Lomas de Tecamachalco
Estado de Mexico

Director General of Normative and Management Development

Lic. Javier Lozano Alarcon
Director General
Direccion General de Normatividad y Desarrollo Administrativo
Secretaria de Hacienda y Credito Publico
Av. Constituyentes 1001, Edif. B, 3er. piso
Col. Belen de las Flores
Mexico, D.F. 01110

Director General of Ground Transport

C.P. Alejandro Peniche Alvarez
Director General
Direccion General de Transporte Terrestre
Calzada de las Bombas 411-9o piso
Mexico, D.F. 04920

Director General of Technological Development

Lic. Jorge Amigo, Dir. General
Direccion General de Desarrollo Tecnologico
Secretaria de Comercio y Fomento Industrial
Azafran 18, 2o. piso
Mexico, D.F. 08400

Subsecretariat of International Commerce Relations

Ms. Katyia Valia
Subsecretaria de Negociaciones
Comerciales Internacionales
Secretaria de Comercio y
Fomento Industrial
Alfonso Reyes No. 30 piso 16
Mexico, D.F. 06179
Tel: (525) 286-0276
Fax: (525) 729-9307

Karla Pina Kurczyn
Executive Assistant
Instituto Mexicano de la
Propiedad Industrial (IMPI)
Mexico City
Fax: (525) 624-0406

NAFTA CHAPTER 3:
NATIONAL TREATMENT AND MARKET ACCESS FOR GOODS

3.1 SCOPE AND COVERAGE

- Chapter 3 deals with the central objective of trade in goods between Canada, the U.S. and Mexico, to eliminate import duties on goods that originate within North America. This Chapter also deals with the removal of nontariff restrictions.

- Annex 300-A deals with Trade and Investment in the Automotive Sector.

- Annex 300-B deals with Textile and Apparel Goods.

3.2 COMMITTEES AND WORKING GROUPS

❑ 3.21 COMMITTEE ON TRADE IN GOODS
Chapter 3, Article 316

TERMS OF REFERENCE:

- To convene meetings of officials responsible for customs, immigration, inspection of food and agricultural products, border inspection facilities and transportation regulations for the purposes of addressing issues related to the movement of goods through each NAFTA Party's ports of entry.

LEADS:

CANADA

Patricia Close, Director,
Tariffs Division
International Trade and Finance Branch
Department of Finance,
14th Floor, East Tower,
140 O'Connor St.
Ottawa, Ontario K1A 0G5
Tel: (613) 992-6881

Assistant:
Denise Climenhage
Officer (Responsible for Coordinating NAFTA Accelerated Tariff Elimination)
Tel: (613) 992-2518

MEXICO

COMITE SOBRE COMERCIO DE BIENES
Responsable y Enlace

Lic. Humberto Jasso Torres
Director de Negociaciones de Acceso a Mercados
Subsecretaria de Negociaciones Comer-ciales Internacionales
SECOFI
Alfonso Reyes N° 30, piso 18,
Col. Condesa, 06140,
México, D.F.
Tels: 7 29 91 46, 7 29 91 47
Fax: 7 29 93 52

UNITED STATES

John Melle
The Director of Mexican Affairs
Executive Office of President
Office of U.S. Trade Representative
600 17th St. Northwest
Washington, D.C., 20508
Tel: (202) 395-3412

❑ 3.22 COMMITTEE ON TRADE IN WORN CLOTHING
Chapter 3, Annex 300-B, Section 9(1)

TERMS OF REFERENCE:

- To review manufacturing and retailing issues pertaining to the trade in worn clothing, including assessing the potential benefits and risks for business and employment opportunities that arise from the elimination of existing trade restrictions. The Committee attempts to consult with or include representatives drawn from the manufacturing and retail sectors of each NAFTA Party for the purposes of making recommendations to the Commission.

LEADS:

CANADA

c/o Catherine McClymont
Industry Canada
10th Floor, 235 Queen St.
Ottawa, Ontario K1A 0H5
Tel: (613) 954-3104

UNITED STATES

M. Walsh
International Trade Representative
Office of Textiles and Apparels
US Department of Commerce
14th and Constitution, Rm. 3100
Washington, D.C., 20230
Tel: (202) 482-3400

MEXICO

COMITE SOBRE COMERCIO DE ROPA USADA
Responsable y Enlace

Dr. Hector Marquez Solis
Director General de Analisis y Seguimiento a Tratados Comerciales Internacionales
Subsecretaria de Negociaciones Comerciales Internacionales
SECOFI
Alfonso Reyes N° 30, piso 16, Col. Condesa, 06140, Mexico, D.F.
Tels: 729 91 19, 729 91 20 Fax: 729 93 08

Otros Participantes

Lic. Susana Gomez Ramirez
Directora de Bienes de Capital y de Consumo
Subsecretaria de Industria
SECOFI
Insurgentes Sur N° 1940, piso 6, Col. Florida, 01030, Mexico, D.F.
Tels: 229 61 23, 229 61 00 exts. 4305, 4306
Fax: 229 65 05

3.3 LONG-TERM REVIEW PROCESS

CHAPTER 3, Annex 300-D, Section 7(3)

TERMS OF REFERENCE:

- To review the rules of origin, taking into consideration the effect of global competition and the implications of GATT developments within five years of the implementation of the NAFTA.

Chapter 3, Annex 300-A, Paragraph 2

TERMS OF REFERENCE:

- To review the North American Automotive Sector and effectiveness of the measures to strengthen the integration and global competitiveness of the sector within ten years of the NAFTA' s implementation.

3.4 INFORMATION SOURCES

❑ ***General Trade Information Sources***

Latin America and Caribbean Trade Division
Department of Foreign Affairs and International Trade
125 Sussex Drive
Ottawa, Ontario K1A 0G2
Tel: (613) 996-5547 Fax: (613) 996-6142

U.S. Trade, Tourism and Investment Bureau (UTD)
Department of Foreign Affairs and International Trade
Lester B. Pearson Building
125 Sussex Drive
Ottawa, Ontario K1A 0G2
Tel: (613) 944-5726 Fax: (613) 944-9119

Secretariat for Commerce and Industrial Promotion
Secretaria de Comercio y Fomento Industrial (SECOFI)
Direccion General de Servicios al Comercio Exterior
Alfonso Reyes No. 30, Piso 10
Col. Hipodromo de la Condesa
06170 Mexico, D.F.
Tel: (525) 286-1757 Fax: (525) 286-1543

TEXTILES AND APPAREL

- ***For information on importing textiles and apparel to Canada***

  Textiles, Apparel Export and Import Permits Bureau
  Canadian Department of External Affairs
  Tel: (613) 996-3711

- ***For information on importing and exporting textiles and apparel to the United States***

  Office of Textiles and Apparel
  U.S. Department of Commerce
  Washington, D.C. 20230
  Tel: (202) 482-3400 Fax: (202) 482-2331

  Customs Flash Facts
  Tel: (202) 927-1692
  Tel: (202) 927-1694

  U.S. Customs Importers' Help Desk
  Tel: (202) 927-0066

- ***For NAFTA textiles and apparel tariffs for Mexico and NAFTA rules of origin for textiles***

  Tel: (202) 482-4464
  Fax: (202) 482-4464

AUTOMOTIVE TRADE

- ***For information on the NAFTA Automotive Standards Council***

  Director of International Harmonization
  National Highway Traffic Safety Administration
  U.S. Dept. of Transportation, 400 7th St., S.W., Room 5220
  Washington, D.C. 20590
  Tel: (202) 366-2114
  Fax: (202) 366-2106

- ***For information on international automotive trade policy***

  Director of Aerospace and Automotive Trade Policy
  Office of the United States Trade Representative
  Executive Office of the President
  600 17th Street, N.W.
  Washington, D.C. 20506
  Tel: (202) 395-4946
  Fax: (202) 395-3911

- ***For information on importing vehicles into Canada***

  Revenue Canada Customs and Excise
  Tel: (613) 993-0534

- ***For information on Mexican automotive policy issues, Mexican Automotive Decree and NAFTA automotive provisions***

  Office of NAFTA,
  U.S Department of Commerce
  Room 3022,
  Washington, D.C. 20230
  Tel: (202) 482-0305 Fax: (202) 482-5865

- ***For auto parts and motor vehicle industry information, Mexican automotive commercial issues and assistance for U.S. exporters, information on NAFTA Automotive Provisions on auto parts and motor vehicles, and the Automotive Standards Council***

Parts Division,
Office of Automotive Affairs,
U.S Department of Commerce, Room 4036,
Washington, D.C. 20230
Tel: (202) 482-5784 Fax: (202) 482-0674

Motor Vehicle Division,
Office of Automotive Affairs,
U.S. Department of Commerce,
Room 4036,
Washington, D.C. 20230
Tel: (202) 482-0669 Fax: (202) 482-3864

NAFTA CHAPTER 5:
CUSTOMS PROCEDURES

5.1 SCOPE AND COVERAGE

- Chapter 5 establishes safeguards to ensure that only goods satisfying the NAFTA Rules of Origin qualify for preferential tariff treatment. They include verifications and advance rulings, as well as record-keeping requirements and cooperation between the NAFTA Parties on customs-related matters.

5.2 COMMITTEES AND WORKING GROUPS

❑ 5.21 WORKING GROUP ON RULES OF ORIGIN

Chapter 5, Article 513

TERMS OF REFERENCE:

- To ensure effective implementation and administration of, and endeavor to agree on any proposed modification to Articles 303 (Restriction on Drawback and Duty Deferral Programs), 308(Most-Favored Nation Rates of Duty on Certain Goods), and 311, as well as Chapters 4 and 5 with respect to

Marking Rules and the Uniform Regulations and the customs-related aspects of Chapter Three. The Working Group shall also consider any matter referred to it by a NAFTA Party or by the Customs Subgroup. If it fails to resolve such matter within 30 days of a referral, any NAFTA Party may request a meeting of the Commission under Article 2007 (Commission–Good Offices, Conciliation and Mediation).

LEADS:

CANADA

John Masswhol
Dept. of Foreign Affairs and International Trade
L.B. Pearson Building
125 Sussex Drive
Ottawa, Ontario K1A 0G2
Tel: (613) 992-7109

UNITED STATES

Timothy Skud
U.S. Department of Treasury
Office of Tariff and Trade Affairs
1500 Pennsylvania Av. Northwest
Washington, D.C. 20220
Tel: (202) 622-0220

MEXICO

GRUPO DE TRABAJO SOBRE REGLAS DE ORIGEN

Responsable

Lic. Jose Guadalupe Saenz Solis
Director General de Politica de Ingresos y Asuntos Fiscales Internacionales
Subsecretaria de Ingresos
Secretaria de Hacienda y Credito Publico
Av. Hidalgo N° 77, Modulo 4, piso 4, Col. Guerrero, 06300,
Mexico, D.F.
Tels: (525) 228 31 92, 228 39 53
Fax: (525) 512 11 29, 228 21 15

Enlace

Lic. Adalberto Gonzalez
Director do Negociaciones de Reglas de Origen
Sulesecretaria de Negociaciones Comerciales Internacionales
Secretaria de Comercio y Fomento Industrial
Alfonso Reyes N 30, piso 18, Col. Condesa, 06140, Mexico, D.F.
Tels: 729 91 43, 729 91 44, 729 91 00 exts. 6046. 6048
Fax: 729 93 52

❑ 5.22 CUSTOMS SUBGROUP
Chapter 5, Article 513(6)

TERMS OF REFERENCE:

- Established by the Working Group on Rules of Origin to endeavor to agree on the uniform interpretation, application and administration of Articles 303, 308 and 311, Chapter 4, 5, the Marking Rules and Uniform Regulations. The Customs Subgroup shall work to simplify customs procedures for importers and exporters under the provisions of the North American Free Trade Agreement.

LEADS:

CANADA

W. A. Claypole
Origin Determination Directorate
Trade Administration Branch
Revenue Canada
Connaught Building
Floor 6, 555 MacKenzie Ave.
Ottawa, Ontario K1A 0L5
Tel: (613) 954-6980
Fax: (613) 954-2224

UNITED STATES

Joyce Metzger
Special Assistant for NAFTA
Dept of Treasury, US Customs Services
Headquarters
1301 Constitution Ave.
Franklin Court
Washington, D.C. 20229
Tel: (202) 927-0792
Fax: (202) 927-0097

MEXICO

SUBGRUPO DE ADUANAS

Responsable

Mauricio Martinez
Representative - Revenue and Customs Affairs
Embassy of Mexico
1911 Pennsylvania Ave., N.W.
Washington, D.C. 20006
Tel: (202) 728-1621
Fax: (202) 728-1664

Enlace

Lic. Adalberto Gonzalez
Director de Negociaciones de Reglas de Origen
Subsecretaria de Negociaciones Comerciales Internacionales
Secretaria de Comercio y Fomento Industrial
Alfonso Reyes N 30, piso 18, Col. Condesa, 06140, México, D.F.
Tels: 729 91 43, 729 91 44 exts. 6046, 6048
Fax: 729 93 52

Otros Participantes

Lic. Norma A Ramirez Hinojosa
Directora General de la Comision Mixta para la Promocion de las Exportaciones
Subsecretaria de Comercio Exterior e Inversion Extranjera
Secretaria de Comercio y Fomento Industrial
Insurgentes Sur N° 1940, piso 9, Col. Florida
01030, Mexico, D.F.
Tel. 229 61 73, 229 65 78, 229 61 00 ext. 3700, 3815, 6173
Fax: 229 61 60, 229 61 61

5.3 LONG-TERM REVIEW PROCESS

WORKING GROUP ON RULES OF ORIGINS

STATUS:

- This Working Group has discussed and agreed upon amendments to Chapters 4 and 5, Uniform Regulations, two sets of technical rectifications to Annex 401, proposals to amend the rules of origin for chemical goods, and proposals to amend the rules of origin for certain other products. The Working Group also has agreed to discuss further revisions to Chapter 5, Uniform Regulations, dealing with issues such as: advance rulings, Certificates of Origin and drawback implementation. The Co-Chairs have recommended to the Free Trade Commission that the amendments to the Uniform Regulations be approved and implemented by each signatory to the Agreement. The Working Group has discussed the rectification that will be required to Annex 401 in order to incorporate the 1996 changes to the Harmonized Tariff System under the World Customs Organization. The Working Group has reached an agreement on proposals to amend the chemical rules of origin that are to be published by each signatory for public comment. The Working Group has also briefly discussed country of origin marking, Marking Rules, used car imports, and questions of rules of origin from the WTO/GATT Working Group in the NAFTA.

CUSTOM SUBGROUP

STATUS:

- The agenda for the Customs Subgroup has recently included classification issues, such as those affecting both prepared meat and single-substance chemicals for photographic uses. Discussions will also include improvements to the *Certificate of Origin*, origin determination for used goods and implementation of NAFTA 504(2) and 512(2b) on textile production verification.

5.4 INFORMATION SOURCES

❑ ***Canadian Customs and NAFTA issues Enquiry Line***

NAFTA Information Desk
Revenue Canada Customs, Excise and Tax
1st Floor
555 Mackenzie Avenue
Ottawa, Ontario K1A 0L5
Tel: (613) 941-0965
Fax: (613) 941-8138

❑ ***NAFTA Spanish Help Desk***

Revenue Canada Customs (Spanish)
Tel: (613) 941-0965

- ***For information regarding Mexican import requirements under NAFTA***

  Government of Mexico's NAFTA Help Desk
  Tel: (525) 211-3545 Fax: (525) 224-3000
  (525) 211-3405
  (525) 211-0872

- ***For U.S. Customs Information–Enquiry Line***

  Tel: (202) 927-0066

- ***Advance Rulings on Customs Classifications***

  Mexican Customs Service
  Secretaria de Hacienda y Credito Publico
  Direccion General de Aduanas
  Departamento de Consula
  Av. 20 de Noviembre 195
  C.P. 06090 Mexico D.F.
  Tel: (525) 709-6365 Telex: (022) 1774-303

  Ministry of Finance and Public Credit
  Av. Hidalgo No 77 Modulo IV, 4 piso
  Col. Guerro, Delegacion Cuauhtemoc
  Mexico, D.F. C.P. 06300 Tel: (202) 482-4464

- ***For advanced ruling on tariffs from Canadian Customs on exporting to Canada***

  Tel: (202) 482-4464

- ***Information on the marking program (Origin Determination)***

Chief, Interdepartmental Programs
Commercial Operations
Revenue Canada, Customs, Excise and Tax
5th Floor, 555 Mackenzie Avenue
Ottawa, Ontario K1A 0L5
Tel: (613) 954-7129 Fax: (613) 952-1698

Manager of Origin Audits
6th Floor, Sir Richard Scott Building
191 Laurier Avenue, W.
Ottawa, Ontario K1A 0L5

- ***NAFTA Rules of Origin Regulations copies***

Canada Communications Group
Ottawa, Ontario K1A 0S9
Tel: (819) 956-4802 Fax: (819) 956-4800

- ***Trilateral Customs Guide to NAFTA***

Superintendent of Documents
U.S. Government Printing Office
Washington, D.C. 20402-9328
Attn: Order Desk
Tel: (202) 783-3238

Instituto Nacional de Capacitacion Fiscal
Allende Sur No. 8
Col. Centro
Queretaro, Qro. 76000, Mexico
Tel: (5242)14 28 86 Fax: (5242)12 54 53
(5242)12 60 93

Transportation Services Division
External Affairs and International Trade Canada
Lester B. Pearson Building
125 Sussex Drive
Ottawa, Ontario K1A 0G2
Tel: (613) 996-0245 Fax: (613) 996-1225

The Commercial Division
Canadian Embassy
Calle Schiller No. 529
Col. Polanco
11560 Mexico, D.F.
Tel: (525) 254-3288 Fax: (525) 545-1769

- ***Appeal of seizure of goods***

Revenue Canada
Trade Administration Branch
Adjudications Division
Ottawa, Ontario K1A 0L5
Tel: (613) 941-6144

- ***For information regarding Canadian import requirements from the U.S. under NAFTA***

Government of Canada's Customs Help Desk
Office of NAFTA
U.S. Department of Commerce
Washington, D.C. 20230
Tel: (613) 941-0965 Fax: (202) 482-5865
(202) 482-0305

Mexico Free Trade Office, Mexican Embassy
1777 I Street, N.W.
Washington, D.C. 20006
Tel: (202) 728-1774 Fax: (202) 296-4904

- ***For information on U.S. importing requirements under the NAFTA***

  U.S. Customs Flash Facts
  Tel: (202) 927-1692 Tel: (202) 927-1694

  U.S. Customs Importers' Help Desk
  Tel: (202) 927-0066

- ***For additional information regarding NAFTA Customs Procedures***

  Tel: (202) 783-3238

NAFTA CHAPTER 6:
ENERGY GOODS AND BASIC PETROCHEMICALS

6.1 Scope and Coverage

- Chapter 6 deals with the energy provisions of the NAFTA, especially relating to the petroleum, electricity and natural gas sectors, general guidelines on the energy-related government procurement provisions and central investment provisions relating to energy and petrochemicals

6.2 Information Sources

❑ ***For information on energy in Canada***

Energy, Mines, and Resources Canada
580 Booth Street
Ottawa, Ontario K1A 0E4
Tel: (613) 995-4037

- ***For information on energy in the U.S.***

U.S. Department of Energy
International Energy Assessments
Room 7G090
1000 Independence Avenue, S.W.
Washington, D.C. 20585
Tel: (202) 586-6832 Fax: (202) 586-6148

Energy Division
Room 4413
U.S. Department of Commerce
Washington, D.C. 20230
Tel: (202) 482-1466 Fax: (202) 482-0170

Chemicals Division
Room 4059
U.S. Department of Commerce
Washington, D.C. 20230
Tel: (202) 482-0128 Fax: (202) 482-2565

- ***For information on NAFTA and chemicals in the U.S.***

Chemicals Division
U.S. Department of Commerce
Room 4053
Washington, D.C. 20230
Tel: (202) 482-0128 Fax: (202) 482-2565

NAFTA CHAPTER 7:
AGRICULTURE

7.1 Scope and Coverage

- The chapter deals with trade in agricultural goods and sanitary and phytosanitary measures with the purpose of eliminating nontariff barriers to agricultural trade; eliminating many tariff barriers; encouraging the NAFTA Parties to eliminate export subsidies; ensuring common application of agricultural classification, grading or marketing standards and avoiding trade barriers resulting from certain sanitary or phytosanitary measures.

7.2 Committees and Working Groups

❑ 7.21 Committee on Agricultural Trade
Chapter 7, Article 706

Terms of Reference:

- To monitor and promote cooperation in the implementation and administration of Chapter 7, to provide a forum to consult on issues and to report annually to the Commission.

LEADS:

CANADA

Terry Norman, Director Western
HemisphereTrade Policy Division,
International Trade Policy Directorate
Market and Industry Service Branch
Agriculture and Agri-Food Canada
Room 1089, Sir John Carling Bldg.
Ottawa, Ontario, K1A 0C5
Tel: (613) 759-7663
Fax: (613) 759-7503

Claude Carriere, Director
Tariffs and Market Access Division
Dept. of Foreign Affairs and Int'l Tarde
Lester B. Pearson Building
125 Sussex Drive
Ottawa, Ontario, K1A 0G2
Tel: (613) 996-8190
Fax: (613) 992-6002

General Contact:
Glyn Chancey, Deputy Director
Western Hemisphere Trade Policy
Division
International Trade Policy Directorate
Market and Industry Services Branch
Agriculture and Agri-food Canada
Room 1089, Sir John Carling Building
Ottawa, Ontario, K1A 0C5
Tel:(613) 759-7657
Fax: (613) 759-7503

UNITED STATES

Richard Schroeter, Deputy Administrator
International Trade Policy
Foreign Agricultural Service
Rm. 5057 South Building
14th and Independence Avenue
Southwest
Washington, D.C., 20250
Tel: (202) 720-6887
Fax: (202) 720-0069

Leonard W. Condon, Deputy Assistant
US Trade Rep. for Agricultural Affairs
US Trade Representative
Room 415, 600 17th St., N.W.
Washington, D.C., 20508
Tel: (202) 395-5006
Fax: (202) 395-4579

General Contact:
Carol Goodloe
Western Europe and Inter-America
Division
Foreign Agricultural Service
United States Department of Agriculture
South Building
14th and Independence Ave., S.W.
Washington, D.C., 20250
Tel: (202) 720-1325
Fax: (202) 690-2079

MEXICO

COMITE SOBRE COMERCIO AGRICOLA

Responsables

Lic. Humberto Jasso Torres
Director de Negociaciones de Acceso a Mercados
Subsecretaria de Negociaciones Comerciales Internacionales
Secretaria de Comercio y Fomento Industrial
Alfonso Reyes N° 30, piso 18, Col.
Condesa 06140, Mexico, D.F.
Tels: 7 29 91 46, 7 29 01 47
Fax: 7 29 93 52

❑ 7.22 WORKING GROUP ON AGRICULTURAL SUBSIDIES
Chapter 7, Article 705(6)

TERMS OF REFERENCE:

- To work toward the elimination of all export subsidies affecting agricultural trade between the NAFTA Parties including: monitoring the volume and price of imports into the territory of any NAFTA Party of agricultural goods that have benefited from export subsidies; providing a forum for the NAFTA Parties to develop mutually acceptable criteria and procedures for reaching agreement on the limitation or elimination of export subsidies for imports of agricultural goods into the territories of the NAFTA Parties; and reporting annually to the Committee on Agricultural Trade, established under Article 706, on the implementation of this Article.

LEADS:

CANADA

Terry Norman, Director Western HemisphereTrade Policy Division,
International Trade Policy Directorate
Market and Industry Service Branch
Agriculture and Agri-Food Canada
Room 1089, Sir John Carling Bldg.
Ottawa, Ontario, K1A 0C5
Tel: (613) 759-7663
Fax: (613) 759-7503

Claude Carriere, Director
Tariffs and Market Access Division
Dept. of Foreign Affairs and Int'l Tarde
Lester B. Pearson Building
125 Sussex Drive
Ottawa, Ontario, K1A 0G2
Tel: (613) 996-8190
Fax: (613) 992-6002

General Contact:
Glyn Chancey, Deputy Director
Western Hemisphere Trade Policy Division
International Trade Policy Directorate
Market and Industry Services Branch
Agriculture and Agri-food Canada
Room 1089, Sir John Carling Building
Ottawa, Ontario, K1A 0C5
Tel:(613) 759-7657
Fax: (613) 759-7503

MEXICO

GRUPO DE TRABAJO SOBRE SUBSIDOS AGRICOLA

Responsables
Lic. Humberto Jasso Torres
Director de Negociaciones de Acceso a Mercados
Subsecretaria de Negociaciones Comerciales Internacionales
Secretaria de Comercio y Fomento Industrial
Alfonso Reyes N° 30, piso 18, Col. Condesa, 06140, México, D.F.
Tels: 7 29 91 46, 7 29 91 47
Fax: 7 29 93 52

Jose Luis Verdin
Director de Negociaciones de Acceso a Mercados
Subsecretaria de Negociaciones Comerciales Internacionales
Secretaria de Comercio y Fomento Industrial
Alfonso Reyes N° 30, piso 18, Col. Condesa, 06140, México, D.F.
Tels: 7 29 91 46, 7 29 91 47
Fax: 7 29 93 52

UNITED STATES

Richard Schroeder, Deputy Administrator International Trade Policy
Foreign Agricultural Service
Rm. 5057 South Building
14th and Independent Avenue, S.W.
Washington, D.C., 20250
Tel: (202) 720-6887
Fax: (202) 720-0069

Leonard W. Condon, Deputy Assistant US Trade Representative for Agricultural Affairs
US Trade Representative
Room 415, 600 17th St., N.W.
Washington, D.C., 20508
Tel: (202) 395-5006
Fax: (202) 395-4579

❑ 7.23 ADVISORY COMMITTEE ON PRIVATE COMMERCIAL DISPUTES REGARDING AGRICULTURAL GOODS

Chapter 7, Article 707

TERMS OF REFERENCE:

- To be established by the Committee on Agriculture Trade comprising individuals with expertise or experience in the resolution of private commercial disputes in agriculture trade. It shall report and provide recommendations, to the Committee on Agricultural Trade, the development of systems to achieve prompt and effective resolution of disputes, taking into account special circumstances such as the perishability of goods.

LEADS:

CANADA

Robert Carberry, Director
Dairy, Fruit and Vegetable Division, Food Inspection Directorate,
Food Production and Inspection Branch
Agriculture and Agri-Food Division
59 Camelot Drive
Nepean, Ontario, K1A 0Y9
Tel: (613) 952-8000
Fax: (613) 995-8511

Glyn Chancey, Deputy Director
Western Hemisphere Trade Policy Div.
International Trade Policy Directorate
Market and Industry Services Branch
Agriculture and Agi-food Canada
Room 1089, Sir John Carling Building
Ottawa, Ontario, K1A 0C5
Tel: (613) 759-7657
Fax: (613) 759-7503

Contacts:

Geoff Adams, Deputy Director
Technical Barriers and Regulations Div.
Dept. of Foreign Affairs and Int'l Trade
Lester B. Pearson Building
125 Sussex Drive
Ottawa, Ontario, K1A 0G2
Tel: (613) 995-3273
Fax: (613) 943-0346

MEXICO

COMITE ASESOR EN MATERIA DE CONTROVERSIAS COMERCIALES PRIVADAS SOBRE PRODUCTOS AGROPECUARIOS

Responsable

Lic. Humberto Jasso Torres
Director de Negociaciones de Acceso a Mercados
Subsecretaria de Negociaciones Comerciales Internacionales
Secretaria de Comercio y Fomento Industrial
Alfonso Reyes N° 30, piso 18, Col. Condesa, 06140, México, D.F.
Tels: 7 29 91 46, 7 29 91 47
Fax: 7 29 93 52

UNITED STATES

Dr. Kenneth Clayton
Deputy Administrator for Marketing Programs
AMS, USDA
Rm. 3069 South
P.O. Box 96456
Washington, D.C., 20090-6456
Tel: (202) 720-4276
Fax: (202) 720-8477

Assistant:
David Priester
Tel: (202) 720-2184

❑ 7.24 COMMITTEE ON SANITARY AND PHYTOSANITARY MEASURES
Chapter 7, Article 722

TERMS OF REFERENCE:

- To facilitate technical cooperation (including consultation and cooperation in the development, application and enforcement of sanitary and phytosanitary measures) for the enhancement of food safety, and improvement of sanitary and phytosanitary conditions. The Committee shall, to the extent possible, in carrying out its function seek the assistance of relevant international and North American standardizing organizations to obtain available scientific and technical advice. It may, as it considers appropriate, establish and determine the scope and mandate of working groups.

LEADS:

CANADA
Randy Benoit, Director
Policy Coordination and Analysis Division
Food Production and Inspection Branch
Agriculture and Agri-food Canada
59 Camelot Drive
Nepean, Ontario, K1A 0Y9
Tel: (613) 952-8000
Fax: (613) 995-8511

Contacts:

Geoff Adams, Deputy Director
Technical Barriers and Regulations Div.
Dept. of Freign Affairs and Int'l Trade
Lester B. Pearson Building
125 Sussex Drive
Ottawa, Ontario, K1A 0G2
Tel: (613) 995-3273
Fax: (613) 943-0346

Glyn Chancey, Deputy Director
Western Hemisphere Trade Policy Div.
International Trade Policy Directorate
Market and Industry Services Branch
Agriculture and Agi-food Canada
Room 1089, Sir John Carling Building
Ottawa, Ontario, K1A 0C5
Tel: (613) 759-7657
Fax: (613) 759-7503

MEXICO

COMITE SOBRE MEDIDAS SANITARIAS Y FITOSANITARIAS

Responsables

Lic. Humberto Jasso Torres
Director de Negociaciones de Acceso a Mercados
Subsecretaria de Negociaciones Comerciales Internacionales
Secretaria de Comercio y Fomento Industrial
Alfonso Reyes N° 30, piso 18, Col. Condesa, 06140, Mexico, D.F.
Tels: 7 29 91 46, 7 29 91 47
Fax: 7 29 93 52

UNITED STATES

Lloyd Harbert, Director
OFSTS
1400 Independence Ave., Southwest
Rm 5545 South
Washington, D.C., 20250
Tel: (202) 720-1301
Fax: (202) 690-0677

Leon W. Condon
Deputy Assistant
US Trade Rep. for Agricultural Affairs
US Trade Representative
Rm 415, 600 17th St, NW
Washington, D.C., 20508
Tel: (202) 395-5006
Fax: (202) 395-4579

❑ 7.25 WORKING GROUP ON AGRICULTURAL GRADING AND MARKETING STANDARDS [CANADA/MEXICO]

Chapter 7, Annex 703(2) Section B, Paragraph 13

TERMS OF REFERENCE:

- Comprised of representatives of Canada and Mexico to review, in coordination with the Committee on Standards-Related Measures established under Article 913, the operation of agricultural grade and quality standards as they affect trade, and resolve issues regarding the operation of these standards. This Committee shall report to the Committee on Agriculture Trade. The Group has not met as yet and discussion of grade and marketing standards issues among the NAFTA parties is now centered in the newly formed trilateral working group discussed below.

LEADS:

CANADA

Robert Carberry, Director
Dairy, Fruit & Vegetable Div.
Food Inspection Directorate
Food Production and
Inspection Branch
Agriculture & Agri-Food Div.

Assistant:
Glen Chancey, Deputy Dir.
Latin American and
Caribbean Section
Room 1089,
Sir John Carling Building
Ottawa, Ontario, K1A 0C5
Tel: (613) 759-7657
Fax: (613) 759-7503

MEXICO

Lic. Humberto Jasso Torres
Director de Negociaciones de
Acceso a Mercados
Subsecretaria de
Negociaciones Comerciales
Internacionales
Secretaria de Comercio y
Fomento Industrial
Alfonso Reyes N° 30, piso
18, Col. Condesa, 06140,
México, D.F.
Tels: 7 29 91 46, 7 29 91 47
Fax: 7 29 93 52

UNITED STATES

Dr. Kenneth Clayton
Deputy Administrator for
Marketing Programs
AMS, USDA
Rm. 3069 South
P.O. Box 96456
Washington, D.C.
20090-6456
Tel: (202) 720-4276
Fax: (202) 720-8477

Assistant:
David Priester
Tel: (202) 720-2184

❑ 7.26 BILATERAL WORKING GROUP (U.S./MEXICO) TO REVIEW THE OPERATION OF GRADE AND QUALITY STANDARDS IN AGRICULTURE

Chapter 7, Annex 703.2(A)25

TERMS OF REFERENCE:

- Comprised of representatives of the U.S. and Mexico, to review in coordination with the Committee on Standards-Related Measures under Article 913, and resolve issues regarding the operation of grade and quality standards as they affect trade. The Groups shall report annually to the Committee on Agricultural Trade. The group has not met and discussion is now centered in the newly formed trilateral working group (7.27).

LEADS:

MEXICO

Lic. Humberto Jasso Torres
Director de Negociaciones de Acceso a Mercados
Subsecretaria de Negociaciones Comerciales Internacionales
Secretaria de Comercio y Fomento Industrial
Alfonso Reyes N° 30, piso 18, Col. Condesa, 06140, México, D.F.
Tels: 7 29 91 46, 7 29 91 47
Fax: 7 29 93 52

UNITED STATES

Dr. Kenneth Clayton
Deputy Administrator for Marketing Programs, AMS, USDA
Rm. 3069 South
P.O. Box 96456
Washington, D.C., 20090-6456
Tel: (202) 720-4276
Fax: (202) 720-8477

Assistant:
David Priester
Tel: (202) 720-2184

❑ 7.27 CANADA/US/MEXICO WORKING GROUP ON GRADE AND QUALITY STANDARDS IN AGRICULTURE (NEWLY FORMED, NO DIRECT REFERENCE IN THE NAFTA AGREEMENT)

STATUS:

- At the November 15, 1994 meeting of the Committee on Agricultural Trade, a trilateral Working Group on Agricultural Grading and Marketing Standards was formed. The Working Group met on June 18, 1996 at which time possible future roles for the group were discussed.

❑ 7.28 CONTINUATION OF CANADA–U.S. FTA ARTICLE 708 WORKING GROUPS

TERMS OF REFERENCE:

- Through an exchange of letters dated January 15, 1993, Canada and the United States agreed that, following the entry into force of the NAFTA, the bilateral technical working groups established under FTA Article 708 (Technical Regulations and Standards for Agricultural, Food, Beverage and Certain Related Goods) shall continue to meet and work toward the implementation of the provisions of Article 708. The exchange of letters also indicated that any disputes arising out of Article 708 would be adjudicated under the dispute settlement provisions of Chapter 20 of the NAFTA. This understanding was agreed to by Mexico.

- Discussions have taken place on issues such as: meat border inspection, UHT milk, and the importation of table eggs. The Pesticides Technical Working Group has discussed issues including: the harmonization of specific Maximum Residue Levels

(MRLs) (stakeholders were invited to submit and prioritize the current trade irritants); minor use program; a pilot project for the Parallel registration process; the level of FDA sampling of Canadian products; and the trilateralization of the Pesticides Technical Working Group. A meeting of the Dairy, Fruit and Vegetable Technical Working Group has - discussed issues of licensing and arbitration regulations, import requirements and border activities for potatoes.

❑ 7.29 WORKING GROUP ON TARIFF RATE QUOTE ADMINISTRATION

TERMS OF REFERENCE:

- A Working Group on Tariff Rate Quote Administration has now been formed, pursuant to a proposal made at the first meeting of the NAFTA Committee on Agricultural Trade on November 15, 1994. This Working Group has met on several occasions. Its purpose is to facilitate the exchange of information on the operation of the respective parties NAFTA tariff rate quota regimes for trade between the parties in certain agricultural products. It reports to the Committee on Agricultural Trade.

LEADS:

<u>CANADA</u>

Terry Norman, Director Western
HemisphereTrade Policy Division,
International Trade Policy Directorate
Market and Industry Service Branch
Agriculture and Agri-Food Canada
Room 1089, Sir John Carling Bldg.
Ottawa, Ontario, K1A 0C5
Tel: (613) 759-7663
Fax: (613) 759-7503

Claude Carriere, Director
Tariffs and Market Access Division
Dept. of Foreign Affairs and Int'l Tarde
Lester B. Pearson Building
125 Sussex Drive
Ottawa, Ontario, K1A 0G2
Tel: (613) 996-8190
Fax: (613) 992-6002

UNITED STATES

Richard Schroeter, Deputy Administrator
International Trade Policy
Foreign Agricultural Service
Rm. 5057 South Building
14th and Independent Avenue Southwest
Washington, D.C., 20250
Tel: (202) 720-6887
Fax: (202) 720-0069

Leonard W. Condon, Deputy Assistant
US Trade Rep. for Agricultural Affairs
US Trade Representative
Room 415, 600 17th St., N.W.
Washington, D.C., 20508
Tel: (202) 395-5006
Fax: (202) 395-4579

General Contact:
Carol Goodloe
Western Europe and Inter-America Division
Foreign Agricultural Service
US Dept. of Agriculture, South Bldg
14th and Independence Ave., S.W.
Washington, D.C., 20250
Tel: (202) 720-1325
Fax: (202) 690-2079

MEXICO

COMITE SOBRE COMERCIO AGRICOLA

Responsables

Lic. Humberto Jasso Torres
Director de Negociaciones de Acceso a Mercados
Subsecretaria de Negociaciones Comerciales Internacionales
Secretaria de Comercio y Fomento Industrial
Alfonso Reyes N° 30, piso 18, Col. Condesa
06140, Mexico, D.F.
Tels: 7 29 91 46, 7 29 91 47
Fax: 7 29 93 52

7.3 INFORMATION SOURCES

- ❑ **CONTACT POINTS**
  Articles 718 and 719 (notification and inquiry point for sanitary and phytosanitary measures)

United States

Office of Standards Code and Information
TRF Building, Room A-163
National Institute of Standards and Technology
Department of Commerce
Gaithersburg, MD 20899
Tel: (301) 975-4037 Fax: (301) 963-2871

Mexico

Humberto Jasso, Dir. General
Direccion General de Asuntos Internacionales
Secretaria de Agricultura y Recursos Hidraulicos
Benjamin Franklin 146
Mexico D.F. 11800
Tel: (525) 523-4775 Fax: (525) 523-5563
543-7019

Canada

Inquiry Point:
Randy Benoit, Director
Policy Coordination and Analysis Div.
Food Production and Inspection Branch
Agriculture and Agri-food Canada
59 Camelot Drive
Nepean, Ontario, K1A 0Y9
Tel: (613) 952-8000
Fax: (613) 995-8464

Contact Point:
Geoff Adams, Deputy Director
Technical Barriers and Regulations Div.
Dept. of Freign Affairs and Int'l Trade
Lester B. Pearson Building
125 Sussex Drive
Ottawa, Ontario, K1A 0G2
Tel: (613) 995-3273
Fax: (613) 943-0346

- ***For information regarding NAFTA agriculture provisions***

Mexico Desk/Foreign Agriculture Service
U.S. Department of Agriculture
14th & Independence Ave. S.W. South Bldg.
Washington, D. C. 20250
Tel: (202) 720-1340 Fax: (202) 690-2079

Canada Desk/Foreign Agricultural Service
U.S. Department of Agriculture
14th & Independence Ave. S.W. South Bldg.
Washington, D. C. 20250
Tel: (202) 720- 1336 Fax: (202) 690-2079

❑ ***For information regarding the export services of USDA, including commodity fact sheets, state fact sheets, and business guide***

AGEXPORT Services
U.S. Department of Agriculture
14th & Independence Ave. S.W. South Bldg.
Washington, D. C. 20250
Tel: (202) 720-6343 Fax: (202) 720-4374

❑ ***For information on importing requirements for agriculture products into Mexico and general assistance to U.S. exporters to Mexico***

Agricultural Trade Office
U.S. Embassy
Mexico City, Mexico
Tels: (525) 202-0168
(525) 202 0212
(525) 202-0434

❑ ***For NAFTA tariff phaseout for agricultural products exported to Mexico and NAFTA Rules of Origin***

Tel: (202) 482-4464

- ***For information on Canada's Agricultural Products Standards Act***

Agriculture Canada
Food Protection and Inspection Branch
930 Carling Avenue
Ottawa, Ontario KIA 0C5
Tel: (613) 998-8784

- ***For information on the registration of food products in Mexico***

Dirrecion General de Regulacion Sanitaria de Alimentos
Secretaria de Salud Donceles 39, Centro
06000 Mexico D.F.
Tel: (525) 518-3696

- ***The primary Canadian government contact for matters related to Chapter 7B***

Michele Marquardt
The Food Production and Inspection Branch (FPIB of Agriculture and Agri-Food Canada (SPS))
Sir John Carling Building
930 Carling Avenue
Ottawa, Ontario K1A 0C5

- ***For information on importing agricultural products into the U.S. under NAFTA, excluding phytosanitary norms***

U.S. Department of Agriculture
The Interamerica Group
South Building, Room 5506
14th Street and Independence Avenue, SW
Washington, D.C. 20250
Tel: (202) 720-1340

- ***For information on phytosanitary norms affecting agricultural imports into the United States***

  U.S. Department of Agriculture
  Animal and Plant Health Inspection Service
  Trade Support Group
  South Building, Room 1128
  14th Street and Independence Avenue, SW
  Washington, D.C. 20250

  U.S. Department of Agriculture
  Foreign Agriculture Service
  International Trade Policy
  Western Europe and Inter-America Division
  Room 5506, South Building
  Washington, D.C. 20250
  Tel: (202) 720-1340 Fax: (202) 690-2079

NAFTA CHAPTER 8: EMERGENCY ACTION

8.1 SCOPE AND COVERAGE

- This chapter establishes the provisions for situations in which a NAFTA Party seeks to halt tariff reductions temporarily to protect an industry that is being seriously injured by surges in imports resulting from the tariff reductions.

8.2 COMMITTEES AND WORKING GROUPS

❑ **8.21 WORKING GROUP ON EMERGENCY ACTION**

(Established by the Supplemental Agreement on Import Surges under NAFTA Article 2001(2d))

TERMS OF REFERENCE:

- To consider any issue related to recourse to Chapter 8, any recourse to Article XIX of the GATT, to serve as a forum for consultations and to make recommendations to the Free Trade Commission.

LEADS:

CANADA

Terry Collins-Williams, Director,
International Economic Relations Division
Department of Finance
14th Floor, 140 O'Connor St.
Ottawa, Ontario, K1A 0G5
Tel: (613) 996-8650

Assistant:
Arlene Turner
Tel: (613) 996-0620

UNITED STATES

John Melle
Office of the USTR
Executive Office of the President
Washington, D.C. 20508
Tel: (202) 395-9675
Fax: (202) 395-3911

Assistant John Hunemann
(202) 395-5190

MEXICO

GRUPO DE TRABAJO SOBRE MEDIDAS DE EMERGENCIA

Responsable
Dr. Alvaro Baillet
Jefe de la Unidad de Practicas, Comerciales Internacionales
Subsecretaria de Industria , SECOFI
Insurgentes Sur 1940, piso 11, Col. Florida
01030, Mexico
Tels: 229 61 52, 229 61 53, exts. 3100, 3101
Fax: 229 65 02, 229 65 03

Enlace

Dr. Hector Marquez Solis
Director General de Analisis y Seguimiento a Tratados Comerciales Internacionales
Subsecretaria de Negociaciones Comerciales Internacionales
SECOFI,
Alfonso Reyes N° 30, piso 16, Col. Condesa
06140, Mexico,
Tels: 729 91 19, 729 91 20 Fax: 729 93 08

NAFTA CHAPTER 9:
STANDARDS-RELATED MEASURES

9.1 SCOPE AND COVERAGE

- This chapter deals with technical standards (which are a traditional nontariff barrier to trade) that directly or indirectly affect trade in goods or services between the NAFTA Parties. NAFTA Parties have agreed not to use standards-related measures as obstacles to trade. The Chapter does not apply to standards-related matters covered by Section B of Chapter 7 (Sanitary and Phytosanitary Measures).

9.2 COMMITTEES AND WORKING GROUPS

❑ **9.21 COMMITTEE ON STANDARDS-RELATED MEASURES**
Chapter 9, Article 913

TERMS OF REFERENCE:

- To monitor the implementation and administration of Chapter 9. The Committee is responsible for facilitating the process by which NAFTA Parties make compatible their standards-related measure providing a forum for consultation and cooperation. It shall consider nongovernmental, regional and multilateral developments in standards-related measures and report annually to the Commission. The Committee shall establish and determine the scope and mandate of working groups and subcommittees it considers appropriate to address issues pertaining to standards-related measures.

LEADS:

CANADA

Earl Weeybrecht
Trade and Economic Policy Branch
Dept. of Foreign Affairs and
International Trade Building
125 Sussex Dr.
Ottawa, Ontario K1A 0G2
Tel: (613) 992-1617
Fax: (613) 943-0346

UNITED STATES

Suzanne Troje
Director for Standards
US Trade Representative
600 17th St. N.W.
Washington, D.C. 20508
Tel:(202) 395-3063
Fax: (202) 395-5674

MEXICO

COMITE DE MEDIDAS RELATIVAS A LA NORMALIZACIOIN

Responsables

Dr. Hector Marquez Solis
Director General de Analisis y
Seguimiento a Tratados Comerciales
Internacionales
Subsecretaria de Negociaciones
Comerciales Internacionales

(SECOFI)
Alfonso Reyes N° 30, piso 16, Col.
Condesa, 06140, Mexico, D.F.
Tels: 729 91 19, 729 91 20
Fax: 729 93 08

Lic. Maria Eugenia Bracho
Directora General de Normas,
Subsecretaria de Industria
Secretaria de Comercio y Fomento
Industrial Av. Puente de Tecamachalco
N° 6, piso 3, Col. Lomas de
Tecamachalco, Seccion Fuentes, 53950,
Naucalpan de Juarez, Estado de Mexico
Tel. 729 94 75, 729 94 76
Fax: 729 94 84

❑ 9.22 LAND TRANSPORT STANDARDS SUBCOMMITTEE
Chapter 9, Article 913(5a)(I), Annex 913(.5a-1)

TERMS OF REFERENCE:

- To make compatible the NAFTA Parties' relevant standards-related measures on bus, truck and rail operations, and transportation of dangerous goods.

LEADS:

CANADA

Christine Burr, Director General
Surface Policy and Program, Transport Canada
Rm. 2766 Tower C, Place de Ville
Ottawa, Ontario K1A 0N5
Tel: (613) 998-2689
Fax: (613) 998-2686

General Contact:
Emille de Sanza
(613) 998-1914

UNITED STATES

David DeCarme
Office of the International Transportation and Trade
400 7th St. Southwest, Rm. 10300
Washington, D.C., 20590
Tel: (202) 366-4368
Fax: (202) 366-7417

MEXICO

SUBCOMITE DE NORMAS SOBRE TRANSPORTE TERRESTRE

Responsable

Ing. José Aguilar Alcerreca
Director General de Transporte Terrestre
Subsecretaria de Transporte
Secretaria de Comunicaciones y Transportes
Calzada de las Bombas N° 411, piso 11,
Col. Los Girasoles, Del. Coyoacan 04920,
Mexico, D.F.
Tel. 684 07 57, 684 06 38
Fax: 684 07 21

Enlace

Dr. Fernando de Mateo V.
Director General de Negociaciones de Servicios y Coordinacion con Europa
Subsecretaria de Negociaciones Comerciales Internacionales

SECOFI
Alfonso Reyes N° 30, piso 18, Col. Condesa. 06140, Mexico, D.F.
Tels: 729 91 40, 729 91 41 ext. 6043, 6044
Fax: 729 93 81

❑ **VEHICLE/DRIVER COMPLIANCE SUBGROUP**

TERMS OF REFERENCE:

- The Subgroup functions to harmonize technical and safety standards (driver, vehicles and compliance).

❑ **VEHICLE WEIGHT & DIMENSION SUBGROUP**

TERMS OF REFERENCE:

- The purpose of the Subgroup is to harmonize regulations relating to commercial vehicle weights and dimensions.

❑ **TRAFFIC CONTROL DEVICES SUBGROUP**

TERMS OF REFERENCE:

- The purpose of the Subgroup is to harmonize regulations related to traffic control devices for highways.

❑ **RAIL SUBGROUP**

TERMS OF REFERENCE:

- The purpose of the Subgroup is to harmonize rail standards regulations related to operating personnel, locomotive and railcar standards.

❑ DANGEROUS GOODS

TERMS OF REFERENCE:

- The purpose of the Subgroup is to harmonize regulations related to transportation of dangerous goods.

❑ 9.23 TRANSPORTATION CONSULTATIVE GROUP

TERMS OF REFERENCE:

- This group is not specifically prescribed for in the NAFTA. It was established to deal with broader questions of a "facilitation" nature.

❑ OPERATIONS SUBGROUP

TERMS OF REFERENCE:

- The purpose of the Subgroup is to deal with the operational aspects of transborder transportation (including operating authorities, vehicle registrations, licensing and taxation, insurance and bill of lading).

❑ BORDER FACILITIES SUBGROUP

TERMS OF REFERENCE:

- The purpose of the Subgroup is to deal with border facilitation issues in order to maximize efficiencies at the border, identify point-of-entry inconsistencies including border clearance procedures, border agency coordination, immigration and temporary entry, customs, and planning of border infrastructure facilities.

❑ **AUTOMATED DATA EXCHANGE SUBGROUP**

TERMS OF REFERENCE:

- The Subgroup is concerned with automated data exchange including the exchange of driver-related information and linking licensing information systems among the three Parties.

❑ **SCIENCE AND TECHNOLOGY SUBGROUP**

TERMS OF REFERENCE:

- The Subgroup is working to establish paperless clearance procedures, electronic vehicle identification and global satellite systems.

❑ **MARITIME SUBGROUP**

TERMS OF REFERENCE:

- The Subgroup is concerned with port facilities, standards and safety, maritime traffic systems and naval engineering.

❑ **9.24 TELECOMMUNICATIONS STANDARDS SUBCOMMITTEE**
Chapter 9, Article 913(5a)(ii), Annex 913(5a)(2)

TERMS OF REFERENCE:

- To develop a program for making compatible, to the greatest extent practicable, the standards-related measures of the NAFTA Parties for authorized telecommunication equipment under Chapter 13 and other work carried on by the NAFTA Parties in other forums, and that of nongovernmental standardizing bodies.

LEADS:

CANADA

Keith Chang, Director,
International Business Development
Industry Canada
300 Slater St.
Ottawa, Ontario K1A 0C8
Fax: (613) 990-3858

General Contact:
Dan Byron
Tel: (613) 991-4903
Fax: (613) 990-3858

UNITED STATES

Mr. Jim McGlinchey
Director, Telecommunication Trade Policy
USTR
600 17th St. N.W.
Washington, D.C. 20508
Tel: (202) 395-6160
Fax: (202) 395-9674

MEXICO

SUBCOMITE DE NORMAS SOBRE TELECOMUNICACIONES

Responsable
Dr. Enrique Melrose, Commissioner,
Commision Federal De Telecomunicaciones
Secretaria de Comunicaciones y Transportes
Centro Nacional de la SCT, Cuerpo C, ler piso, Xola y Av. Universidad, 03020
Tels: 530 3514, 538 78 43
Fax: 530 0089

Enlace
Dr. Fernando de Mateo V.
Director General de Negociaciones de Servicios y Coordinacion con Europa
Subsecretaria de Negociaciones Comerciales Internacionales
SECOFI
Alfonso Reyes N° 30, piso 18, Col. Condesa. 06140, México, D.F.
Tels: 729 91 40, 729 91 41, ext. 6043, 6044
Fax: 729 93 81

❑ 9.25 AUTOMOTIVE STANDARDS SUBCOMMITTEE
Article 913(5a)(iii), Annex 913(5a)(3)

TERMS OF REFERENCE:

- To facilitate the attainment of compatibility among, and review the implementation of, national standards-related measures of the NAFTA Parties that apply to automotive goods and to address other related matters. To facilitate its objectives, the Council may establish subgroups, consultation procedures and other appropriate operational mechanisms. On the agreement of the NAFTA Parties, the Council may include state and provincial government or private sector representatives in its subgroups. Any recommendations by the Council shall require agreement of the NAFTA Parties and recommendations, not involving laws, shall be implemented by the NAFTA Party within a reasonable time. Where recommendations involve the adoption of law, the NAFTA Party shall use its best efforts to do so in a reasonable time.

LEADS:

CANADA

Nicole Pageot, Director General
Road Safety and Motor Vehicle Regulation
Transport Canada
13th Floor, Canada Building
344 Slater St.
Ottawa, Ontario K1A 0N5
Tel: (613) 993-6735
Fax: (613) 990-2914

UNITED STATES

Frank Turpin, Director
International Harmonization
400 7th St. SW Rm. 5220
Washington, D.C. 20590
Tel: (202) 366-2114
Fax: (202) 366-2106

Tom Baines
Environmental Protection Agency
Tel: (313) 668-4366

MEXICO

CONSEJO DE NORMAS AUTOMOTRICES

Responsable

Dr. Hector Marquez Solis
Director General de Analisis y Seguimiento a Tratados Comerciales Internacionales
Subsecretaria de Negociaciones Comerciales Internacionales
Secretaria de Comercio y Fomento Industrial
Alfonso Reyes N° 30, piso 16, Col. Condesa, 06140, Mexico, D.F.
Tels: 729 91 19, 729 91 20
Fax: 729 93 08

Lic. Gustavo Saavedra Ordorika
Director General de Fomento Industrial
Subsecretaria de Industria
Secretaria de Comercio y Fomento Industrial
Insurgentes Sur N 1940, piso 6, Col. Florida, 01030, Mexico, D.F.
Tels: 229 61 19, 229 61 19
Fax: 229 65 05

Otros Participantes

Lic. Ana Maria Camacho Carranza
Directora de la Industria Automotriz y del Transporte
Subsecretaria de Industria
Secretaria de Comercio y Fomento Industrial
Insurgentes Sur N° 1940, piso 6, Col. Florida, 01030, Mexico, D.F.
Tels: 229 61 24, 229 61 00, exts. 4307, 4308
Fax: 229 65 05

❑ 9.26 SUBCOMMITTEE ON LABELING OF TEXTILE AND APPAREL GOODS

Chapter 9, Article 913(5a)(iv), Annex 913(5a)(4)

TERMS OF REFERENCE:

- To develop and pursue a work program on the harmonization of labeling requirements to facilitate trade in textile and apparel goods between the NAFTA Parties through the adoption of uniform labeling provisions. The Subcommittee shall consult with technical experts, as well as a broadly representative group from the manufacturing and retailing sectors in the territory of each NAFTA Party.

LEADS:

CANADA

Mr. M. Zane Brown
Director General
Consumer Products Directorate
Competition Bureau
Industry Canada
16th Floor, Zone 8
Place de Portage, Phase 1
50 Victoria Street
Hull, Quebec, K1A 0C9
Tel: (613) 953-3187
Fax: (819) 953-4792

General Contact:
Diane Carmanico
Tel: (613) 953-3187

UNITED STATES

Carol Miller
Deputy Chief Textile Negotiator
Office of the U.S. Trade Representative
600 17th St. Northwest, Room 300
Washington, D.C., 20508
Tel: (202) 395-3026
Fax: (202) 395-5639

MEXICO

SUBCOMITE DE ETIQUETADO DE PRODUCTOS TEXTILES Y DEL VESTIDO

Responsable y Enlace

Hector Marquez Solis
Subsecretaira de Negociaciones Commerciales Internacionales
SECOFI
Alfonso Reyes #30 piso 16, Col. Condesa
Mexico, D.F. CP06140
Tel: (525) 729-9119
Fax: (525) 729-9308

Otros Participantes

Lic. Susana Gomez Ramirez
Directora de Bienes de Capital y de Consumo
Subsecretaria de Industria
Secretaria de Comercio y Fomento Industrial
Insurgentes Sur N° 1940, piso 6,
Col. Florida, 01030, México, D.F.
Tels: 229 61 23, 229 61 00, exts. 4305 y 4306
Fax: 229 65 05

9.3 LONG-TERM REVIEW PROCESS

COMMITTEE ON STANDARDS-RELATED MEASURES (CSRM)
Chapter 9, Article 913

STATUS:

- This Committee has met in the past to discuss reports from the four Subcommittees, as well as a number of implementation issues including those relating to a recently formed Subcommittee on generic labeling issues. The Trilateral Standardization Forum (TSF) was established in the spirit of the NAFTA to facilitate harmonization in the voluntary standards area. It is sponsored by the Standards Council of Canada (SCC), the American National Standards Institute (ANSI), Direction General de Normas (DGN) of the Mexican government and the Mexican National Chamber of Industry and Transformation (CANACINTRA). It met for the first time in Mexico City in October of 1994. Some of the areas being pursued by the TSF are: conformity assessment, building codes and toy standards.

LAND TRANSPORT STANDARDS SUBCOMMITTEE
Chapter 9, Article 913(5a)(i), Annex 913(5a)(1)

STATUS:

- This Subcommittee has met to develop procedures and work plans for its five Subgroups: Drivers and Vehicle Standards and Compliance; Vehicle Weights and Dimensions; Road Signs; Rail Standards; and Hazardous Materials Standards. Each Subgroup now has its work plan in place.

TELECOMMUNICATIONS STANDARDS SUBCOMMITTEE
Chapter 9, Article 913(5a)(ii), Annex 913(5a)(2)

STATUS:

- This Subcommittee has met to discuss Mexico's regulations and product standards. The Consultative Committee on Telecom (CCT) is the industry advisory group to the Telecom Subcommittee.

9.4 INFORMATION SOURCES

- **CONTACT AND INQUIRY POINTS**
  Article 910 (inquiry point for standards-related measures and technical regulations)

United States
Office of Standards Code and Information
TRF Building, Room A-163
National Institute of Standards & Technology
Department of Commerce
Gaithersburg, MD 20899
Tel: (301) 975-4037 Fax: (301) 963-2871

Mexico
Lic. Luis Guillermo Ibarra, Director General
Direccion General de Normas
SECO FI
Puente de Tacamachalco No.6
Colonia Lomas de Tecamachalco
Estado de México
Tel: (525) 520-8493
(525) 520-8494

Canada

Inquiry Point:
Sandra E. Watson,
Standards Council of Canada
Standards Information Service
45 O'Connor Street, Suite 1200
Ottawa, Ontario K1P 6N7
Tel: (613) 238-3222 Fax: (613) 995-4564

Contact Point:
Ron Davidson, Acting Director
Technical Barriers and Regulations Division (EAS),
Trade and Economic Policy Branch
Department of Foreign Affairs and International Trade
L. B. Pearson Building
125 Sussex Drive
Ottawa, Ontario K1A 0G2
Tel: (613) 995-2807 Fax: (613) 944-0756

❑ ***For information on Canadian Standards System***

Standards Council of Canada
Tel: (613) 238-3222

Canadian Standards Association
Tel: (416) 747-4000

- ***For information on how to obtain Mexican Standards***

The Mexican Bureau of Standards
Director General de Normas, SECOFI
Av. Puente de Tecamachalco
53950 Naucalpan, Edo. De Mexico
Tel. (525) 520-8493

- ***Standards Related Measures Provisions***

Office of Standards Code and Information
TRF Building, Room A-163
National Institute of Standards and Technology
Department of Commerce, Gaithersburg, MD 20899

NAFTA CHAPTER 10: GOVERNMENT PROCUREMENT

10.1 Scope and Coverage

- This chapter imposes requirements of openness, transparency, and competitive bidding to procurement activity on federal government agencies and government-owned enterprises. Detailed rules for conducting procurements and reviewing protests by disappointed procurers from other NAFTA Parties are set out to be implemented by each NAFTA Party.

10.2 Committees and Working Groups

❑ 10.21 Committee on Government Procurement and Small Business

Chapter 10, Article 1021

Terms of Reference:

- This Committee is responsible for identifying and promoting small business and government procurement opportunities. It shall work to facilitate the identification of available opportunities for the training of small business personnel in government procurement procedures, the identification of small businesses interested in becoming trading partners of other small business, the development of databases of small businesses in the territory of each NAFTA Party for use by entities of another NAFTA Party, consultations regarding the factors that each NAFTA Party uses in establishing its criteria for eligibility for any small business programs and activities related to such matters.

LEADS:

CANADA

David Devine
Tariffs & Market Access Division
Trade and Economic Policy Branch
Dept. of Foreign Affairs and Int'l Trade
L.B. Pearson Building
125 Sussex Drive
Ottawa, Ontario K1A 0G2
Tel: (613) 995-3921
Fax: (613) 992-6002

UNITED STATES

Mark Linscott
Director, Government Procurement
U.S. Trade Representatives
600 17th St. NW, Rm. 511
Washington, D.C. 20508
Tel: (202) 395-3063
Fax: (202) 395-5674

William Craft
Director, Office of Multilateral Trade Affairs
U.S. Department of State, 2201 "C" St., N.W.
Washington, D.C. 20520
Tel: (202) 647-8958
Fax: (202) 647-6540

MEXICO

COMITE SOBRE LA PEQUENA Y MEDIANA INDUSTRIA

Responsable

Dr. Gerardo Traslosheros
Director General de Organismos Internacionales
Subsecretaria de Negociaciones Comerciales Internacionales, SECOFI
Alfonso Reyes N° 30, piso 1, Col. Condesa, 06140, Mexico,
Tels: 729 91 58, 729 9159, exts. 6061, 6062
Fax: 729 93 13

10.3 INFORMATION SOURCES

- ❑ **CONTACT AND INQUIRY POINTS**
  Article 1019(2c) (contact point for information on government procurement)

United States
Office of GATT Affairs
Office of the United States
Trade Representative
600 17th Street, N.W.
Washington, D.C. 20506
Tel: (202) 395-3063
Fax: (202) 395-3911

Mexico
Lic. Javier Lozano Alarcon
Director General
Direccion General de
Normatividad y Desarrollo
Administrativo
Secretaria de Hacienda y
Credito Publico
Av. Constituyentes 1001, Edif.
B. 3er. piso
Col. Belen de las Flores
Mexico D.F. 01110
Tel: (525) 228-5053
Fax: (525) 228-5177

Canada
David Devine
Tariffs & Market Access Div.
Trade & Economic Policy
Branch
Department of Foreign Affairs &
Internationall Trade
L. B. Pearson Building
125 Sussex Drive
Ottawa, Ontario K1A 0G2
Tel: (613) 995-3921
Fax: (613) 992-6002

- ❑ ***For Canadian Government bid request line***

  Information Systems Management Corporation
  Open Bidding Service
  PO Box 22011
  Ottawa, Ontario, K1V 0C2
  Tel: (613) 737-3374

- ***For information on Mexican and Canadian Government procurement policy and procedures, Mexican procurement opportunities for U.S. business, and NAFTA Government Procurement Provisions***

  Office of NAFTA, Room 3022
  U.S. Department of Commerce
  Washington, D.C. 20230
  Tel: (202) 482-0305 Fax: (202) 482-5865

- ***For information regarding NAFTA Government Procurement Provisions***

  Special Trade Activities Division
  Bureau of Economic and Business Affairs
  U.S. Department of State
  Washington, D.C. 20520
  Tel: (202) 647-6683 Fax: (202) 647-6540

  Director of International Procurement Policy
  Office of the United States Trade Representative
  Executive Office of the President
  600 17th Street, N.W.
  Washington, D.C. 20506
  Tel: (202) 395-3063 Fax: (202) 395-5674

- ***For information on U.S. implementation of NAFTA obligations, general policy questions, procurement process questions, how procurements are conducted and items procured***

  Office of Acquisition Policy
  General Services Administration
  18th & F Streets, N.W.
  Washington, D.C. 20405
  Tel: (202) 501-1224 Fax: (202) 501-3341

Acquisitions/Foreign Contracting
Office of the Secretary
U.S. Department of Defense
OUSD (A) DP/FC
3060 Defense Pentagon (Room 3C762)
Washington, D.C. 20301
Tel: (703) 697-9351 Fax: (703) 693-9616

Office of Procurement
National Aeronautics and Space Administration
Washington, D.C. 20546
Tel: (202) 358-2090 Fax: (202) 358-3082

Deputy Associate Administrator
Office of Federal Procurement Policy
Office of Management and Budget
New Executive Office Building, Room 9025
Washington, D.C. 20503
Tel: (202) 395-6167 Fax: (202) 395-5150

Office of Federal Procurement Policy
Procurement Law and Legislation
New Executive Office Building, Room 9025
Washington, D.C. 20503
Tel: (202) 395-3501 Fax: (202) 395-5105

NAFTA CHAPTER 11: INVESTMENT

11.1 Scope and Coverage

- This chapter deals with the establishment of an open investment regime. Section B of the chapter provides elaborate subchapters directed at settling disputes between a NAFTA Party and an investor of another NAFTA Party either through arbitration in accordance with ICSID Convention or UNCITRAL Arbitrations Rules.

11.2 Information Sources

❑ ***For information on investing in Mexico***

Mexican Investment Board (Mexico)
Tel: (525) 328-9929 Fax: (525) 328-9930

Mexican Investment Board U.S. Fax Line
Fax: (602) 930-4802

1-800-MIB-2434 TEL
Mexican Investment Board Hot Line

American Chamber of Commerce for Mexico,
Lucerna No. 78, Colonia Juarez, 06600 Mexico, D.F.
(703) 487-4650
(525) 724-3800

❑ ***For information on investing in Canada***

Investment Canada
240 Sparks Street
PO Box 2800, Postal Station D
Ottawa, Ontario K1P 6A5
Tel: (613) 995-0465 Fax: (613) 996-2515

❑ ***For questions on investing in the U.S.***

Office of NAFTA
U.S. Department of Commerce
Washington, D.C. 20230
Tel: (202) 482-4305 Fax: (202) 482-5865

Office of International Investment
U.S. Department of the Treasury
15th Street and Pennsylvania Avenue, NW.
Tel: (202) 622-1860 Fax: (202) 622-0391

NAFTA CHAPTER 12:
CROSS-BORDER TRADE IN SERVICES

12.1 SCOPE AND COVERAGE

- This chapter establishes provisions which apply to measures adopted by a NAFTA Party relating to cross-border trade in specific services by service providers of another NAFTA Party.

12.2 COMMITTEES AND WORKING GROUPS

❑ **12.21 WORKING GROUP ON SERVICES AND INVESTMENT**
Chapters 11 and 12, Article 1210(4) and Annex 1210(5)

TERMS OF REFERENCE:

- This Working Group was established by the NAFTA Trade Ministers at their meeting of January 14, 1994, in Mexico City. The Group is focusing its work on the implementation of Chapters 11 (Investment) and 12 (Trade in Services).

LEADS:

CANADA

Steve Brerton
Director of Services
Investment and Intellectual Property Division
Dept. of Foreign Affairs and Int'l Trade
125 Sussex Drive
Ottawa, Ontario, K1A 0G2
Tel: (613) 995-0990
Fax: (613) 995-0679

and

Andrea Lyon
Director of Services, Trade Policy Division
Tel: (613) 995-0990

UNITED STATES

Bernie Ascher
United States Trade Representative
600 17th St. Northwest
Washington, D.C., 20508
Tel: (202) 395-4510
Fax: (202) 395-3891

Mr. B. Barreda
Deputy Assistant Secretary for Trade and Investment
Rm. 3208
Main Treasury
1500 Pennsylvania Ave.
Washington, D.C., 20220
Tel: (202) 622-0168
Fax: (202) 622-5304

MEXICO

GRUPO DE TRABAJO DE INVERSION Y SERVICIOS

Responsables

Lic. Carlos Garcia Fernandez
Director General de Inversion Extranjera
Subsecretaria de Negociaciones Comerciales Internacionales
Secretaria de Comercio y Fomento Industrial
Insurgentes Sur 1940, piso 8, Col. Florida, 01030, Mexico, D.F.
Tels: 229 61 63, 229 61 64, exts. 3500, 350l
Fax: 229 65 07

Dr. Fernando de Mateo V.
Director General de Negociaciones de Servicios y Coordinacion con Europa
Subsecretaria de Negociaciones Comerciales Internacionales
Secretaria de Comercio y Fomento Industrial
Alfonso Reyes N 30, piso 18, Col. Condesa, 06140, México, D.F.
Tels: 729 91 40, 729 91 41, ext. 6043
Fax: 729 93 81

Otros Participantes

Dr. Ignacio Navarro Zermeno
Director General de Politica Industrial
Subsecretaria de Comercio Exterior e Inversion Extranjera
Secretaria de Comercio y Fomento Industrial
Insurgentes Sur 1940, piso 3, Col. Florida, 01030, Mexico, D.F.
Tels: 229 61 36, 229 61 37, exts. 4800 y 4801
Fax: 229 65 09, 229 65 34

12.3 INFORMATION SOURCES

- **CONTACT AND INQUIRY POINT**
  Annex 1212 (contact point for information on land transportation services)

United States
Office of International
Transportation and Trade
Department of Transportation
400 Seventh Street, S.W.
Washington, D.C. 20590
Tel: (202) 366-4368
Fax: (202) 366-7417

Mexico
C.P. Alejandro Peniche Alvarez
Director General
Direccion General de
Transporte Terrestre
Calzada de las Bombas 411 -
90 piso
México, D.F. 04920
Tel: (525) 684-0806
Fax: (525) 684-2586

Canada
John Hill, Director
Services Industries and
Transportation Division (TPS)
Department of Foreign Affairs
and International Trade
L.B. Pearson Building
125 Sussex Drive
Ottawa, Ontario K1A 0G2
Tel: (613) 996-2964
Fax: (613) 996-1225
(613) 996-1267

❑ ***For information on providing financial services in Mexico and Canada***

International Affairs
U.S. Department of the Treasury
15th Street and Pennsylvania Avenue NW
Washington, D.C. 20220
Tel: (202) 622-1986 Fax: (202) 622-1956

Office of NAFTA, Room 3022
U.S. Department of Commerce
Washington, D.C. 20230
Tel: (202) 482-0305 Fax: (202) 482-5865

Office of Service Industries
U.S. Department of Commerce
Tel: (202) 482-5261 Fax: (202) 482-4775

- ***For information on obtaining professional licenses in Mexico***

  Lic. Antonio Montes Pena
  Director General de Professionistas
  Insurgentes Sur 2387, 2 piso
  Mexico, DF Mexico
  Tel: (525) 550-8762

TRANSPORTATION

Office of International Transportation and Trade
Department of Transportation
400 Seventh St., S.W.
Washington, D.C. 20590

- ***For information on international transportation policy***

  Service Industry Affairs
  Office of the United States Trade Representative
  Executive Office of the President
  600 17th Street, N.W.
  Washington, D.C. 20506
  Tel: (202) 395-4510 Fax: (202) 395-3640

- ***For information on Mexican land transportation policy issues and NAFTA Land Transportation Provisions***

  Office of NAFTA
  U.S. Department of Commerce, Room 3022
  Washington, D.C. 20230
  Tel: (202) 482-0305 Fax: (202) 482-4865

- ***For information on Mexican land transportation commercial issues and commercial assistance for U.S. exporters***

  Office of NAFTA
  U.S. Department of Commerce
  Tel: (202) 482-0305

- ***For information on U.S.-Mexico cargo facilitation***

  Maritime and Surface Division
  Office of the Secretary
  U.S. Department of Transportation
  P-20/Room 10300
  400 7th Street, S.W.
  Washington, D.C. 20590
  Tel: (202) 366-2892 Fax: (209) 366-7417

- ***For information on passenger and charter/tour bus issues, ongoing U.S.-Mexico transportation-related activities and Land Transport Standards Subcommittee***

  Senior International Policy Analyst
  U.S. Department of Transportation
  Tel: (202) 366-2892 Fax: (209) 366-7417

- ***For information on Land Transportation Investment Provisions and Liberalization Schedule: Specialty Air Service***

Office of the Secretary
U.S. Department of Transportation
P-20/Room 10300
400 7th Street, S.W.
Washington, D.C. 20590
Tel: (202) 366-2892 Fax: (202) 366-7417

Office of Motor Carrier Standards
Federal Highway Administration
U.S. Department of Transportation
HCSI/Room 3107
400 7th Street, S.W.
Washington, D.C. 20590
Tel: (202) 366-1790 Fax: (202) 366-7908

Federal Railroad Administration
Office of Economic Analysis
Department of Transportation
RRP30/Room 8300
400 7th Street, S.W.
Washington, D.C. 20590
Tel: (202) 366-0354 Fax: (202) 366-7688

International Standards Coordinator for Hazardous
Materials Safety Research and Special Programs
Administration
U.S. Department of Transportation
DHM5 7th Street, S.W.
Washington, D.C. 20590
PUBLICATION LINE: (800) 752-6367
Tel: (202) 366-0656 Fax: (202) 366-5713

Industry and Economic Analysis
Federal Highway Administration
U.S. Department of Transportation
HPP11/Room 3324
400 7th Street, S.W.
Washington, D.C. 20590
Tel: (202) 366-9230 Fax: (202) 366-7696

NAFTA CHAPTER 13: TELECOMMUNICATIONS

13.1 SCOPE AND COVERAGE

- This chapter establishes provisions with respect to telecommunications, including access to and use of public telecommunications transport networks or services, including private networks; conditions for the provision of enhanced or value-added services; certain standards-related measures related to attachment of terminal or other equipment.

13.2 INFORMATION AND SOURCES

❑ ***For information on providing telecommunications services and equipment to Mexico and Canada***

Office of Telecommunications
U.S. Department of Commerce
Washington, D.C. 20230
Tel: (202) 482-4466
Fax: (202) 482-5834

National Telecommunications and Information
Administration,
U.S. Department of Commerce
Washington, D.C. 20230
Tel: (202) 482-1866

NAFTA CHAPTER 14:
FINANCIAL SERVICES

14.1 SCOPE AND COVERAGE

- This chapter applies to measures that apply to the financial institutions of a NAFTA Party, investments made in financial institutions within one NAFTA Party by nationals of another NAFTA Party and cross-border trade in financial services.

14.2 COMMITTEES AND WORKING GROUPS

❑ **14.21 FINANCIAL SERVICES COMMITTEE**
Chapter 14, Article 1412, Annex 1412(1)

TERMS OF REFERENCE:

- To supervise the implementation and further elaboration of Chapter 14, to inform the Commission of the results of annual meetings and to participate in dispute settlement in accordance with Article 1415. The Financial Services Committee has the authority to resolve disputes on its own.

LEADS:

CANADA

Frank Swedlove, Director
Financial Sector Division,
Department of Finance
20th Floor, East Tower
140 O'Connor
Ottawa, Ontario, K1A 0G5
Tel: (613) 992-4679,
Fax: (613) 943-8436

General Information:
Sylvia Rocheleau
Officer, Intergovernmental Relations
Financial Sector Division
L'Esplanade Laurier
20th Floor, East Tower
140 O'Connor St.
Ottawa, Ontario K1A 0G5
Tel: (613) 992-4475
Fax: (613) 943-8436

MEXICO

COMITE DE SERVICIOS FINANCIEOS

Responsable

Lic. Fernando Borja Mujica
Director General de Banca Multiple
Subsecretaria de Hacienda
Secretaria de Hacienda y Credito Publico, Insurgentes Sur N° 795, piso 3, Col. Napoles, 03810, Mexico, D.F.
Tels: 687 31 30
Fax: 687 36 27

Enlace

Dr. Fernando de Mateo V.
Director General de Negociaciones de Servicios y Coordinacion con Europa
Subsecretaria de Negociaciones Comerciales Internacionales
SECOFI, Alfonso Reyes N° 30, piso 18, Col. Condesa, 06140, Mexico, D.F.,
Tels: 729 91 40, ext. 6043
Fax: 729 93 81

UNITED STATES

Timothy Geidhner
Deputy Assistant Secretary for International Monetary and Financial Policy,
Treasury Department
Rm. 3221, Main Treasury Building
Washington, D.C., 20220
Tel: (202) 622-1252
Fax: (202) 622-0658

Assistant:
Bill Quin, Officer
Office of International Banking and Securities Markets
U.S. Treasury, Rm. 5321
Tel: (202) 622-1252
Fax: (202) 622-1254

14.3 INFORMATION SOURCES

❑ ***Contacts for NAFTA-Related Issues***

Shiela Riordon, Chief
Intergovernmental Relations Section
Financial Sector Division
L'Esplanade Laurier, 20th Floor
East Tower
140 O'Connor Street
Ottawa, Ontario K1A 0G5
Tel: (613) 992-5259 Fax: (613) 943-8436

Secretariat of Finance and Public Credit
Secretaria de Hacienda y Credito Publico
Direccion General Tecnica de Ingresos
Palacio Nacional
1er. Patio Mariano
Col. Centro
06066 Mexico, D.F.
Tel. (525) 518-5420 Fax: (525) 542-2821

❑ ***Chapter 19/Trade Remedies***

Terry Collins-Williams
Director, International Economic Division
L'Esplanade Laurier, 14th Floor
East Tower
140 O'Connor Street
Ottawa, Ontario K1A 0G5
Tel: (613) 996-8650 Fax: (613) 943-1177

Rudy Verspoor
Chief, Trade Remedies and General Economic Relations
L'Esplanade Laurier, 14th Floor
East Tower
140 O'Connor Street
Ottawa, Ontario K1A 0G5
Tel: (613) 996-0634 Fax: (613) 943-1177

International Finance Division
Department of Foreign Affairs and International Trade
Tel: (613) 995-7251 Fax: (613) 943-1100

Revenue Canada
NAFTA Information Desk
Revenue Canada - Customs, Excise and Taxation
6th Floor
191 Laurier Avenue West
Ottawa, Ontario K1A 0L5
Tel: 1-800-661-6121 Fax: (613) 954-4494

NAFTA Spanish Help Desk
Service Available in Spanish
Tel: (613) 941-0965

- ***Mexican Investment Board Faxline***

Attn.: Jenny DuPond
Mexican Investment Board
Paseo de la Reforma 915
Lomas de Chapultepec
11000, Mexico, D.F.
Tel: (525) 202-7804/328-9929
Fax: (525) 202-7925/328-9930

❑ ***The Mexican Foreign Trade Bank***

Support is extended for project planning and investment needs through final marketing, including transportation and storage

Periferico Sur #4333, Col. Jardines en la Montana
C.P. 14210, Mexico, D.F.
Tel: (525) 227 9008 Y 227 9009
1-800-835-7480
Fax: (525) 227-9070

NAFTA CHAPTER 15:
COMPETITION POLICY, MONOPOLIES AND STATE ENTERPRISES

15.1 SCOPE AND COVERAGE

- This chapter deals with competition policy and monopoly concerns. NAFTA Parties have committed themselves to the objectives of applying their domestic competition rules to prevent anticompetitive business practices and to use regulatory controls to assure that state enterprises or monopolies observe the commitments of their governments.

15.2 COMMITTEES AND WORKING GROUPS

❑ **15.21 WORKING GROUP ON TRADE AND COMPETITION POLICY**
Chapter 15, Article 1504

TERMS OF REFERENCE:

- To make recommendations on relevant issues concerning the relationship between competition laws and policies and trade in the free trade area.

LEADS:

CANADA

Rob Anderson
Acting Manager,
International Division,
Economic and International Affairs
Competition Bureau
21st Floor,
50 Victoria Street
Hull, Quebec K1A 0C9
Tel: (819) 953-4300
Fax: (819) 953-6400

Assistant:
Paul M. Feuer
International Division
Economic and International Affairs
Bureau of Competition Policy
21f, rue Victoria
Hull, P.Q. K1A 0C9
Tel: (819) 953-7759
Fax: (819) 953-6400

UNITED STATES

Charles Stark
Chief of Foreign Commerce Section
Anit-Trust Division
Department of Justice
Rm. 3264
10th and Constitution Ave. N.W.
Washington, D.C. 20530
Tel: (202) 514-2464
Fax: (202) 514-4508

Alternate Contact:

Caldwell Harrop
Tel: (202) 514-6127

MEXICO

GRUPO DE TRABAJO EN MATERIA DE COMERCIO Y COMPETENCIA

Responsable

Dr. Adriaan Ten Kate,
Director
General de Estudios Economicos
Comision Federal de Competencia
Monte Libano No. 225
Col. Lomas de Chapultepec
Delegacion Miguel Hidalgo, Mexico
Tel: (525) 283-6580
Fax: (525) 283-6599

Enlace

Lic. Greta Spota
Subdirector del area Internacional
Direccion General de Estudios Economicos, Comision Federal de Competencia

Col, Lomas de Chapultepec
Delegacion Miguel Hidalero
C.P. 11000 Mexico, D.F.
Tel: (525) 283-6596
Fax: (525) 283-6599

NAFTA CHAPTER 16:
TEMPORARY ENTRY

16.1 SCOPE AND COVERAGE

- This chapter establishes provisions to simplify the process for temporary, business-related admissions of citizens of the NAFTA Parties.

16.2 COMMITTEES AND WORKING GROUPS

❑ **16.21 TEMPORARY ENTRY WORKING GROUP**
Chapter 16, Article 1605

TERMS OF REFERENCE:

- To implement and administer Chapter 16; to develop measures to further facilitate temporary entry; to waive the labor certifications tests or procedures of similar effects for spouses of business persons who have been granted temporary entry for more than one year under Sections B, C or D of Annex 1603; and to propose modifications or additions to the Chapter.

LEADS:

CANADA

Dougall Aucoin
Citizenship and Immigration Canada
Journal Tower North 7th Fl.
300 Slater St.
Ottawa, Ontario
Tel: (613) 954-4214
Fax: (613) 941-9323

UNITED STATES

Jacquelyn Bednarz
Immigration and Naturalization Services
Tel: (202) 514-2982

MEXICO

GRUPO DE TRABAJO DE ENTRADA TEMPORAL

Responsable

Lic. Raul Solorzano
Instituto Nacional de Migracion
Subsecretaria de Poblacion y Servicios Migratorios
Secretaria de Gobernacion
Av. Chapultepec N° 284, piso 13, Col. Roma, 06700
Tel: (525) 626-7228
Fax: (525) 626-7299
(525) 626 72 99

Enlace

Dr. Fernando de Mateo V.
Director General de Negociaciones de Servicios y Coordinacion con Europa,
Subsecretaria de Negociaciones Comerciales Internacionales, SECOFI,
Alfonso Reyes N° 30, piso 18, Col. Condesa 06140, Mexico
Tels: 729 91 40, 729 91 41, ext. 6043
Fax: 729 93 81

16.3 LONG-TERM REVIEW PROCESS

TEMPORARY ENTRY WORKING GROUP
Article 1605

STATUS:

- This Working Group has met to discuss issues including: spousal coverage, professional category expansion, after-sales support, border-crossing fees, certification and licensing.

16.4 INFORMATION SOURCES

- ***Copy of guide for temporary entry of business persons under NAFTA***

  Citizenship and Immigration Canada
  Ottawa, Hull K1A 1L1

- ***For Canadian immigration information***

  Employment and Immigration Canada
  Tel: (613) 995-8131

- ***For information on NAFTA and business travel in the U.S.***

  Tel: (202) 783-3238 (U.S.)
  Tel: (202) 482-4464 (Mexico)
  Tel: (202) 482-3101 (Canada)

- ***For the telephone number of the nearest American Immigration and Naturalization Service Office***

  1-800-755-0777

- ***For visa information, general fact sheets on each NAFTA Party and its relations with the United States, publications, and tips for travelers***

  Office of Mexican Affairs,
  U.S. Dept. of State,
  2201 C Street, NW.
  Washington, D.C. 20520
  Tel: (202) 647-9292
  Fax: (202) 647-5752

  Office of Canadian Affairs
  U.S. Department of State
  Tel: (202) 647-2170
  Fax: (202) 647-4088

NAFTA CHAPTER 17:
INTELLECTUAL PROPERTY

17.1 SCOPE AND COVERAGE

- This chapter is directed at strengthening and harmonizing the domestic intellectual property laws of the NAFTA Parties.

17.2 INFORMATION SOURCES

❑ **CONTACT AND INQUIRY POINTS**
Article 1719(2) (contact point for information on intellectual property rights)

United States
Office of International Affairs
U.S. Customs Service
Department of the Treasury
1301 Constitution Ave., N.W.
Washington, D.C. 20229-0001
Tel: (202) 927-0400 Fax: (202) 927-2064

Mexico
Lic Jorge Amigo
Director General
Direccion General de
Desarrollo Tecnologico
Secretaria de Comercio y
Fomento Industrial
Azafran 18, 2o. piso
Mexico D.F. 08400
Tel: (525) 657-3751
(525) 650-7542
Fax: (525) 654-0771

Canada
Allan Hertz
Services, Investment and
Intellectual Property Division
Trade and Economic Policy
Branch
Department of Foreign
Affairs and Int'l Trade
L. B. Pearson Building
125 Sussex Drive
Ottawa, Ontario K1A 0G2
Tel: (613) 996-7175
Fax: (613) 944-0679

- ***For information on intellectual property rights in Canada***

Patents
Tel: (819) 997-1936

Trademarks
Tel: (819) 997-1420

Copyrights
Tel: (819) 997-1725

Industrial Designs
Tel: (819) 997-1725

- ***For an overview of property rights in Mexico***

Tel: (202) 482-4464

- ***For information on intellectual property rights and NAFTA***

U.S. Patent and Trademark
Office Box 4,
Washington, D.C. 20231
Tel: (703) 305-9300
Fax: (703) 305-8885

U.S. Copyright Office
Washington, D.C. 20559
Tel: (202) 707-8350
Fax: (202) 707-6859

NAFTA CHAPTER 18:
PUBLICATION, NOTIFICATION, AND ADMINISTRATION OF LAWS

18.1 SCOPE AND COVERAGE

- Chapter 18 sets out the framework for administering the NAFTA. Its aim is to ensure the effective administration, prompt and frequent sharing of information through notification and publication and the ability of all interested NAFTA Parties to comment on measures that might affect the operation of the Agreement.

18.2 INFORMATION SOURCES

❑ **CONTACT AND INQUIRY POINTS**
Article 1801 (contact point for administrative and institutional provisions)

United States
Office of North American Affairs
Office of the United States Trade Representative
600 17th Street, N.W.
Washington, D.C. 20506
Tel: (202) 395-4866 Fax: (202) 395-3911

Contact for practical day-to-day questions regarding NAFTA operation:

Julia Bender, Acting Director of NAFTA Coordination
Department of Commerce
NAFTA Business Development Office
Tel: (202) 482-0305

Mexico
Dr. Jaime Zabludovsky , Coordinador General
Subsecretaria de Negociaciones Comerciales Internacionales
Secretaria de Comercio y Fomento Industrial
Alfonso Reyes No.30 piso 16
Mexico, D.F. 06179
Tel: (525) 286-0822 Fax: (525) 286-3497

Canada
William Crosbie, Director
Multilateral Trade Inst. Div.
Trade & Econ. Policy Branch
Department of Foreign Affairs and International Trade
125 Sussex Drive, L.B. Pearson Building
Ottawa, Ontario K1A 0G2
Fax: (613) 944-0757

❑ ***General Information Contact:***

Department of Foreign Affairs
Henry Jarque
Multilateral Trade Institutions
125 Sussex Dr. , Ottawa, Ontario K1A 0G2
General Information: 1-800-267-8376 for referral

❑ ***Customs Issues:***
1-800-661-6121 for tariff and border administration issues

NAFTA CHAPTER 19:
REVIEW AND DISPUTE SETTLEMENT IN ANTIDUMPING AND COUNTERVAILING DUTY MATTERS

19.1 SCOPE AND COVERAGE

- Chapter 19 deals with the procedures for the review of antidumping and countervailing duty law determinations made by domestic judicial bodies as well as amendments of those laws.

19.2 COMMITTEES AND WORKING GROUPS

❑ **19.21 SPECIAL SECRETARIAT SECTION**
Chapter 19, Article 1908

TERMS OF REFERENCE:

- To facilitate the administrative operation of Chapter 20 and the work of panels and Committees convened pursuant to this Chapter.

❑ **19.22 EXTRAORDINARY CHALLENGE COMMITTEE**
Chapter 19, Article 1904(13), Annex 1904(13)

TERMS OF REFERENCE:

- To permit the NAFTA Parties to establish an Extraordinary Challenge Committee, composed of three members, within 15 days of a request pursuant to Article 1904(13). The Committee decisions shall be binding on the NAFTA Parties with respect to the particular matter.

❑ **19.23 SPECIAL COMMITTEE FOR SAFEGUARD OF PANEL REVIEW SYSTEM**
Chapter 19, Article 1905(2) Annex 1905(6)

TERMS OF REFERENCE:

- To examine complaints that a NAFTA Party's domestic law has prevented the establishment of a panel, prevented a panel from rendering a final decision or has failed to provide opportunity for review of a final determination.

19.3 LONG-TERM REVIEW PROCESS

CHAPTER 19, ARTICLE 1907

TERMS OF REFERENCE:

- To consult with officials of the competent investigating authorities on any problems that might arise with respect to the implementation or operation of the Chapter.

19.4 INFORMATION SOURCES

- ***For information on administrative procedures and investigations under Canada's antidumping and countervailing duty laws***

  The Director
  Policy and Administration
  Antidumping and Countervailing Division
  Revenue Canada Customs, Excise and Tax
  191 Laurier Avenue, W.
  Ottawa, Ontario K1A 0L5
  Tel: (613) 954-7254 Fax: (613) 941-2612

- ***For information on the status of ongoing U.S.antidumping or countervailing duty investigations on products from Mexico or Canada***

  Office of Investigations
  Import Administration
  U.S. Department of Commerce
  Washington, D.C. 20230
  Tel: (202) 482-5403 Fax: (202) 482- 1059

- ***For information on the status of current U.S. antidumping or countervailing duty cases on products from Mexico or Canada***

  Office of Antidumping Compliance
  Import Administration
  U.S. Department of Commerce
  Tel: (202) 482-2104 Fax: (202) 482-5105

Office of Countervailing Compliance
Import Administration
U.S. Department of Commerce
Tel: (202) 482-2786 Fax: (202) 482-4001

- ❑ ***For information on the status of antidumping or countervailing duty cases in Mexico or Canada against U.S. products***

Office of NAFTA
U.S. Department of Commerce
Tel: (202) 482-0305 Fax: (202) 482-5865

- ❑ ***For information regarding antidumping or countervailing duty cases currently subject to NAFTA dispute settlement proceedings***

United States
Secretary for the United States Section of the Secretariat (Article 2002(2c))
Mr. James R. Holbein
NAFTA Secretariat, United States Section
14th & Constitution N.W., Room 2061
Department of Commerce
Washington, D.C. 20230
Tel: (202) 482-5438 Fax: (202) 482-4148

Mexico
Lic. Rafael Figueroa Serrano
Coordinador General Subsecretaria de Negociaciones Comerciales Internacionales
Secretaria de Comercio y Fomento Industrial
Alfonso Reyes No. 30 piso 16
México D.F. 06179
Tel: (525) 286-0822 Fax: (525) 286-3497

Canada
Secretary for the Canadian Section of the Secretariat (Article 2002(2c))

Ms. Cathy Beehan
NAFTA Secretariat
Canadian Section
90 Sparks Street, Suite 705
Ottawa, Ontario K1P 5B4
Tel: (613) 992-9388 Fax: (613) 992-9392

NAFTA CHAPTER 20:
INSTITUTIONAL ARRANGEMENTS AND DISPUTE SETTLEMENT

20.1 SCOPE AND COVERAGE

- Chapter 20 establishes the administrative framework for the NAFTA, as well as the general dispute settlement procedures for issues that arise.

20.2 COMMITTEES AND WORKING GROUPS

❑ **20.21 FREE TRADE COMMISSION**
Chapter 20, Article 2001, Annex 2001(2)

TERMS OF REFERENCE:

- To supervise the implementation of the Agreement and oversee its further elaboration, resolve disputes on interpretation, and supervise the work of the Committees and Working Groups.

❏ 20.22 ADVISORY COMMITTEE ON PRIVATE COMMERCIAL DISPUTES

Chapter 20, Article 2022

TERMS OF REFERENCE:

- To report and provide recommendations to the Commission on issues concerning the availability, use and effectiveness of arbitration and other procedures for the resolution of private commercial disputes in the free trade area.

LEADS:

CANADA	MEXICO	UNITED STATES
Jonathan Fried, Director General, Trade Policy Bureau & NAFTA Coord. Dept. of Foreign Affairs & Int'l Trade 125 Sussex Drive Ottawa, Ontario, K1A 0G2 Tel: (613) 996-5677 Fax: (613) 996-2002 Assistant: Valerie Hughes Tel: (613) 943-2803 Fax: (613) 943-2804	Hugo Perezcano Tel: (525) 729-9134 Fax: (525) 729-9310	Contact: Jean Grier US Department of Commerce Tel: (202) 482-3215 Fax: (202) 482-4076

20.3 LONG-TERM REVIEW PROCESS

ADVISORY COMMITTEE ON PRIVATE COMMERCIAL DISPUTES
Chapter 20, Article 2022

STATUS:

- The Committee has decided that its work should focus on dispute settlement involving cases that are:
  1) Private (i.e., excluding cases in which a government is a NAFTA Party);
  2) International (those with a cross-border or transnational dimension); and
  3) Commercial (any relations of a commercial nature, contractual or not).

- The Committee has exchanged views on arbitration institutions and procedures in the three NAFTA Parties and has established Subcommittees to compile all available information on relevant laws and rules at the national and subnational level on existing and proposed centres for commercial arbitration, and to develop criteria for a future evaluation of their effectiveness;

- The Committee further:
  1) has examined the issue of whether there are sectors for which the increased use of arbitration and other forms of alternative dispute resolution would be appropriate;
  2) has considered means to promote the use of arbitration; and
  3) has agreed to compile information on the recognition and enforcement of arbitral awards.

- Two Canadian members on the Subcommittee on increased use of arbitration, David Haigh and Thomas Drucker, sent out a questionnaire to gather additional information on the use of nonjudicial dispute settlement in a range of industries and sectors in Canada.

20.4 INFORMATION SOURCES

❑ CONTACT AND INQUIRY POINTS

United States
Secretary for the United States Section of the Secretariat (Article 2002(2c))
Mr. James R. Holbein, NAFTA Secretariat
United States Section
14th & Constitution N.W., Room 2061
Department of Commerce
Washington, D.C. 20230
Tel: (202) 482-5438 Fax: (202) 482-4148

Mexico
Lic. Rafael Figueroa Serrano
Coordinador General Subsecretaria de Negociaciones Comerciales Internacionales
Secretaria de Comercio y Fomento Industrial
Alfonso Reyes No. 30 piso 16
México, D.F. 06179
Tel: (525) 286-0822 Fax: (525) 286-3497

Canada
Secretary for the Canadian Section of the Secretariat (Article 2002(2c))
Ms. Cathy Beehan
NAFTA Secretariat, Canadian Section
90 Sparks Street, Suite 705
Ottawa, Ontario K1P 5B4
Tel: (613) 992-9388 Fax: (613) 992-9392

PART III
NAFTA DISPUTE RESOLUTION PROVISIONS

Part III includes the various provisions relevant to dispute resolution under the NAFTA, including the separate Rules of Procedure for sections 1904 and 1905 and the Code of Conduct governing NAFTA panels. In particular, relevant sections under Chapters 1, 5, 8, 10, 11, 14, 15, 16, 18, 19, 20 and 21 of the NAFTA have been provided here and cross-referenced in the earlier parts. The Code of Conduct for dispute settlement sets out the criteria to be satisfied by NAFTA panelists under the different chapters.

NAFTA PROVISIONS

CHAPTER 1:
OBJECTIVES

Article 101: Establishment of the Free Trade Area

The Parties to this Agreement, consistent with Article XXIV of the *General Agreement on Tariffs and Trade*, hereby establish a free trade area.

Article 102: Objectives

1. The objectives of this Agreement, as elaborated more specifically through its principles and rules, including national treatment, most-favored-nation treatment and transparency, are to:

   a) eliminate barriers to trade in, and facilitate the cross-border movement of, goods and services between the territories of the Parties;

   b) promote conditions of fair competition in the free trade area;

c) increase substantially investment opportunities in the territories of the Parties;

d) provide adequate and effective protection and enforcement of intellectual property rights in each Party's territory;

e) create effective procedures for the implementation and application of this Agreement, for its joint administration and for the resolution of disputes; and

f) establish a framework for further trilateral, regional and multilateral cooperation to expand and enhance the benefits of this Agreement.

2. The Parties shall interpret and apply the provisions of this Agreement in the light of its objectives set out in paragraph 1 and in accordance with applicable rules of international law.

Article 103: Relation to Other Agreements

1. The Parties affirm their existing rights and obligations with respect to each other under the *General Agreement on Tariffs and Trade* and other agreements to which such Parties are party.

2. In the event of any inconsistency between this Agreement and such other agreements, this Agreement shall prevail to the extent of the inconsistency, except as otherwise provided in this Agreement.

Article 104: Relation to Environmental and Conservation Agreements

1. In the event of any inconsistency between this Agreement and the specific trade obligations set out in:

a) the *Convention on International Trade in Endangered Species of Wild Fauna and Flora*, done at Washington, March 3, 1973, as amended June 22, 1979,

b) the *Montreal Protocol on Substances that Deplete the Ozone Layer,* done at Montreal, September 16, 1987, as amended June 29, 1990,

c) the *Basel Convention on the Control of Transboundary Movements of Hazardous Wastes and Their Disposal*, done at Basel, March 22, 1989, on its entry into force for Canada, Mexico, and the United States, or

d) the agreements set out in Annex 104.1,

such obligations shall prevail to the extent of the inconsistency, provided that where a Party has a choice among equally effective and reasonably available means of complying with such obligations, the Party chooses the alternative that is the least inconsistent with the other provisions of this Agreement.

2. The Parties may agree in writing to modify Annex 104.1 to include any amendment to an agreement referred to in paragraph 1, and any other environmental or conservation agreement.

Article 105: Extent of Obligations

The Parties shall ensure that all necessary measures are taken in order to give effect to the provisions of this Agreement, including their observance, except as otherwise provided in this Agreement, by state and provincial governments.

Annex 104.1
Bilateral and Other Environmental Conservation Agreements

1. The *Agreement Between the Government of Canada and the Government of the United States of America Concerning the Transboundary Movement of Hazardous Waste*, signed at Ottawa, October 28, 1986.

2. The *Agreemnt Between the United States of America and the United Mexican States on Cooperation for the Protection and Improvement of the Environment in the Border Area*, sign at La Paz, Baja California Sur, August 14, 1983.

CHAPTER 5:
CUSTOMS PROCEDURES

Section D - Review and Appeal of Origin Determinations and Advance Rulings

Article 510: Review and Appeal

1. Each Party shall grant substantially the same rights of review and appeal of marking determinations of origin, country of origin determinations and advance rulings by its customs administration as it provides to importers in its territory to any person:

   a) who completes and signs a Certificate of Origin for a good that has been the subject of a determination of origin;

   b) whose good has been the subject of a country of origin marking determination pursuant to Article 311 (Country of Origin Marking); or

c) who has received an advance ruling pursuant to Article 509(1).

2. Further to Articles 1804 (Administrative Proceedings) and 1805 (Review and Appeal), each Party shall provide that the rights of review and appeal referred to in paragraph 1 shall include access to:

a) at least one level of administrative review independent of the official or office responsible for the determination under review; and

b) in accordance with its domestic law, judicial or quasi-judicial review of the determination or decision taken at the final level of administrative review.

CHAPTER 8: EMERGENCY ACTION

Article 801: Bilateral Actions

1. Subject to paragraphs 2 through 4 and Annex 801.1, and during the transition period only, if a good originating in the territory of a Party, as a result of the reduction or elimination of a duty provided for in this Agreement, is being imported into the territory of another Party in such increased quantities, in absolute terms, and under such conditions that the imports of the good from that Party alone constitute a substantial cause of serious injury, or threat thereof, to a domestic industry producing a like or directly competitive good, the Party into whose territory the good is being imported may, to the minimum extent necessary to remedy or prevent the injury:

a) suspend the further reduction of any rate of duty provided for under this Agreement on the good;

b) increase the rate of duty on the good to a level not to exceed the lesser of

i) the most-favored-nation (MFN) applied rate of duty in effect at the time the action is taken, and

ii) the MFN applied rate of duty in effect on the day immediately preceding the date of entry into force of this Agreement; or

c) in the case of a duty applied to a good on a seasonal basis, increase the rate of duty to a level not to exceed the MFN applied rate of duty that was in effect on the good for the corresponding season immediately preceding the date of entry into force of this Agreement.

2. The following conditions and limitations shall apply to a proceeding that may result in emergency action under paragraph 1:

a) a Party shall, without delay, deliver to any Party that may be affected written notice of, and a request for consultations regarding, the institution of a proceeding that could result in emergency action against a good originating in the territory of a Party;

b) any such action shall be initiated no later than one year after the date of institution of the proceeding;

c) no action may be maintained

i) for a period exceeding three years, except where the good against which the action is taken is provided for in the items in staging category C+ of the Schedule to Annex 302.2 of the Party taking the action and that Party determines that the affected industry has undertaken adjustment and requires an extension of the period of relief, in which case the period of relief may be extended for one year provided that the duty applied during the initial period of relief is substantially reduced at the beginning of the extension period, or

ii) beyond the expiration of the transition period, except with the consent of the Party against whose good the action is taken;

d) no action may be taken by a Party against any particular good originating in the territory of another Party more than once during the transition period; and

e) on the termination of the action, the rate of duty shall be the rate that, according to the Party's Schedule to Annex 302.2 for the staged elimination of the tariff, would have been in effect one year after the initiation of the action, and beginning January 1 of the year following the termination of the action, at the option of the Party that has taken the action

i) the rate of duty shall conform to the applicable rate set out in its Schedule to Annex 302.2, or

ii) the tariff shall be eliminated in equal annual stages ending on the date set out in its Schedule to Annex 302.2 for the elimination of the tariff.

3. A Party may take a bilateral emergency action after the expiration of the transition period to deal with cases of serious injury, or threat thereof, to a domestic industry arising from the operation of this Agreement only with the consent of the Party against whose good the action would be taken.

4. The Party taking an action under this Article shall provide to the Party against whose good the action is taken mutually agreed trade liberalizing compensation in the form of concessions

having substantially equivalent trade effects or equivalent to the value of the additional duties expected to result from the action. If the Parties concerned are unable to agree on compensation, the Party against whose good the action is taken may take tariff action having trade effects substantially equivalent to the action taken under this Article. The Party taking the tariff action shall apply the action only for the minimum period necessary to achieve the substantially equivalent effects.

5. This Article does not apply to emergency actions respecting goods covered by Annex 300-B (Textile and Apparel Goods).

Article 802: Global Actions

1. Each Party retains its rights and obligations under Article XIX of the GATT or any safeguard agreement pursuant thereto except those regarding compensation or retaliation and exclusion from an action to the extent that such rights or obligations are inconsistent with this Article. Any Party taking an emergency action under Article XIX or any such agreement shall exclude imports of a good from each other Party from the action unless:

a) imports from a Party, considered individually, account for a substantial share of total imports; and

b) imports from a Party, considered individually, or in exceptional circumstances imports from Parties considered collectively, contribute importantly to the serious injury, or threat thereof, caused by imports.

2. In determining whether:

a) imports from a Party, considered individually, account for a substantial share of total imports, those imports normally shall not be considered to account for a substantial share of total imports if that Party is not among the top five suppliers of the good subject to the proceeding, measured in terms of import share during the most recent three-year period; and

b) imports from a Party or Parties contribute importantly to the serious injury, or threat thereof, the competent investigating authority shall consider such factors as the change in the import share of each Party, and the level and change in the level of imports of each Party. In this regard, imports from a Party normally shall not be deemed to contribute importantly to serious injury, or the threat thereof, if the growth rate of imports from a Party during the period in which the injurious surge in imports occurred is appreciably lower than the growth rate of total imports from all sources over the same period.

3. A Party taking such action, from which a good from another Party or Parties is initially excluded pursuant to paragraph 1, shall have the right subsequently to include that good from the other Party or Parties in the action in the event that the competent investigating authority determines that a surge in imports of such good from the other Party or Parties undermines the effectiveness of the action.

4. A Party shall, without delay, deliver written notice to the other Parties of the institution of a proceeding that may result in emergency action under paragraph 1 or 3.

5. No Party may impose restrictions on a good in an action under paragraph 1 or 3:

a) without delivery of prior written notice to the Commission, and without adequate opportunity for consultation with the Party or Parties against whose good the action is proposed to be taken, as far in advance of taking the action as practicable; and

b) that would have the effect of reducing imports of such good from a Party below the trend of imports of the good from that Party over a recent representative base period with allowance for reasonable growth.

6. The Party taking an action pursuant to this Article shall provide to the Party or Parties against whose good the action is taken mutually agreed trade liberalizing compensation in the form of concessions having substantially equivalent trade effects or equivalent to the value of the additional duties expected to result from the action. If the Parties concerned are unable to agree on compensation, the Party against whose good the action is taken may take action having trade effects substantially equivalent to the action taken under Paragraph 1 or 3.

Article 803: Administration of Emergency Action Proceedings

1. Each Party shall ensure the consistent, impartial and reasonable administration of its laws, regulations, decisions and rulings governing all emergency action proceedings.

2. Each Party shall entrust determinations of serious injury, or threat thereof, in emergency action proceedings to a competent investigating authority, subject to review by judicial or administrative tribunals, to the extent provided by domestic law. Negative injury determinations shall not be subject to modification, except by such review. The competent investigating authority empowered under domestic law to conduct such proceedings should be provided with the necessary resources to enable it to fulfill its duties.

3. Each Party shall adopt or maintain equitable, timely, transparent and effective procedures for emergency action proceedings, in accordance with the requirements set out in Annex 803.3.

4. This Article does not apply to emergency actions taken under Annex 300-B (Textile and Apparel Goods).

Article 804: Dispute Settlement in Emergency Action Matters

No Party may request the establishment of an arbitral panel under Article 2008 (Request for an Arbitral Panel) regarding any proposed emergency action.

Article 805: Definitions

For purposes of this Chapter:

competent investigating authority means the "competent investigating authority" of a Party as defined in Annex 805;

contribute importantly means an important cause, but not necessarily the most important cause;

critical circumstances means circumstances where delay would cause damage that would be difficult to repair;

domestic industry means the producers as a whole of the like or directly competitive good operating in the territory of a Party;

emergency action does not include any emergency action pursuant to a proceeding instituted prior to January 1, 1994;

good originating in the territory of a Party means an originating good, except that in determining the Party in whose territory that good originates, the relevant rules of Annex 302.2 shall apply;

serious injury means a significant overall impairment of a domestic industry;

surge means a significant increase in imports over the trend for a recent representative base period;

threat of serious injury means serious injury that, on the basis of facts and not merely on allegation, conjecture or remote possibility, is clearly imminent; and

transition period means the 10-year period beginning on January 1, 1994, except where the good against which the action is taken is provided for in the items in staging category C+ of the Schedule to Annex 302.2 of the Party taking the action, in which case the transition period shall be the period of staged tariff elimination for that good.

Annex 801.1
Bilateral Actions

1. Notwithstanding Article 801, bilateral emergency actions between Canada and the United States on goods originating in the territory of either Party, other than goods covered by Annex 300-B (Textile and Apparel Goods), shall be governed in accordance with the terms of Article 1101 of the *Canada - United States Free Trade Agreement,* which is hereby incorporated into and made a part of this Agreement for such purpose.

2. For such purposes, "good originating in the territory of one Party" means "good originating in the territory of a Party" as defined in Article 805.

Annex 803.3
Administration of Emergency Action Proceedings

Institution of a Proceeding

1. An emergency action proceeding may be instituted by a petition or complaint by entities specified in domestic law. The entity filing the petition or complaint shall demonstrate that it is

representative of the domestic industry producing a good like or directly competitive with the imported good.

2. A Party may institute a proceeding on its own motion or request the competent investigating authority to conduct a proceeding.

Contents of a Petition or Complaint

3. Where the basis for an investigation is a petition or complaint filed by an entity representative of a domestic industry, the petitioning entity shall, in its petition or complaint, provide the following information to the extent that such information is publicly available from governmental or other sources, or best estimates and the basis therefor if such information is not available:

   a) product description - the name and description of the imported good concerned, the tariff subheading under which that good is classified, its current tariff treatment and the name and description of the like or directly competitive domestic good concerned;

   b) representativeness -

      i) the names and addresses of the entities filing the petition or complaint, and the locations of the establishments in which they produce the domestic good,

      ii) the percentage of domestic production of the like or directly competitive good that such entities account for and the basis for claiming that they are representative of an industry, and

      iii) the names and locations of all other domestic establishments in which the like or directly competitive good is produced;

c) import data - import data for each of the five most recent full years that form the basis of the claim that the good concerned is being imported in increased quantities, either in absolute terms or relative to domestic production as appropriate;

d) domestic production data - data on total domestic production of the like or directly competitive good for each of the five most recent full years;

e) data showing injury - quantitative and objective data indicating the nature and extent of injury to the concerned industry, such as data showing changes in the level of sales, prices, production, productivity, capacity utilization, market share, profits and losses, and employment;

f) cause of injury - an enumeration and description of the alleged causes of the injury, or threat thereof, and a summary of the basis for the assertion that increased imports, either actual or relative to domestic production, of the imported good are causing or threatening to cause serious injury, supported by pertinent data; and

g) criteria for inclusion - quantitative and objective data indicating the share of imports accounted for by imports from the territory of each other Party and the petitioner's views on the extent to which such imports are contributing importantly to the serious injury, or threat thereof, caused by imports of that good.

4. Petitions or complaints, except to the extent that they contain confidential business information, shall promptly be made available for public inspection on being filed.

Notice Requirement

5. On instituting an emergency action proceeding, the competent investigating authority shall publish notice of the institution of the proceeding in the official journal of the Party. The notice shall identify the petitioner or other requester, the imported good that is the subject of the proceeding and its tariff subheading, the nature and timing of the determination to be made, the time and place of the public hearing, dates of deadlines for filing briefs, statements and other documents, the place at which the petition and any other documents filed in the course of the proceeding may be inspected, and the name, address and telephone number of the office to be contacted for more information.

6. With respect to an emergency action proceeding instituted on the basis of a petition or complaint filed by an entity asserting that it is representative of the domestic industry, the competent investigating authority shall not publish the notice required by paragraph 5 without first assessing carefully that the petition or complaint meets the requirements of paragraph 3, including representativeness.

Public Hearing

7. In the course of each proceeding, the competent investigating authority shall:

   a) hold a public hearing, after providing reasonable notice, to allow all interested parties, and any association whose purpose is to represent the interests of consumers in the territory of the Party instituting the proceeding, to appear in person or by counsel, to present evidence and to be heard on the questions of serious injury, or threat thereof, and the appropriate remedy; and

b) provide an opportunity to all interested parties and any such association appearing at the hearing to cross-question interested parties making presentations at that hearing.

Confidential Information

8. The competent investigating authority shall adopt or maintain procedures for the treatment of confidential information, protected under domestic law, that is provided in the course of a proceeding, including a requirement that interested parties and consumer associations providing such information furnish nonconfidential written summaries thereof, or where they indicate that the information cannot be summarized, the reasons why a summary cannot be provided.

Evidence of Injury and Causation

9. In conducting its proceeding the competent investigating authority shall gather, to the best of its ability, all relevant information appropriate to the determination it must make. It shall evaluate all relevant factors of an objective and quantifiable nature having a bearing on the situation of that industry, including the rate and amount of the increase in imports of the good concerned, in absolute and relative terms as appropriate, the share of the domestic market taken by increased imports, and changes in the level of sales, production, productivity, capacity utilization, profits and losses, and employment. In making its determination, the competent investigating authority may also consider other economic factors, such as changes in prices and inventories, and the ability of firms in the industry to generate capital.

10. The competent investigating authority shall not make an affirmative injury determination unless its investigation demonstrates, on the basis of objective evidence, the existence of a clear causal link between increased imports of the good concerned and serious injury, or threat thereof. Where factors

other than increased imports are causing injury to the domestic industry at the same time, such injury shall not be attributed to increased imports.

Deliberation and Report

11. Except in critical circumstances and in global actions involving perishable agricultural goods, the competent investigating authority, before making an affirmative determination in an emergency action proceeding, shall allow sufficient time to gather and consider the relevant information, hold a public hearing and provide an opportunity for all interested parties and consumer associations to prepare and submit their views.

12. The competent investigating authority shall publish promptly a report, including a summary thereof in the official journal of the Party, setting out its findings and reasoned conclusions on all pertinent issues of law and fact. The report shall describe the imported good and its tariff item number, the standard applied and the finding made. The statement of reasons shall set out the basis for the determination, including a description of:

    a) the domestic industry seriously injured or threatened with serious injury;

    b) information supporting a finding that imports are increasing, the domestic industry is seriously injured or threatened with serious injury, and increasing imports are causing or threatening serious injury; and

    c) if provided for by domestic law, any finding or recommendation regarding the appropriate remedy and the basis therefor.

13. In its report, the competent investigating authority shall not disclose any confidential information provided pursuant to any

undertaking concerning confidential information that may have been made in the course of the proceedings.

Annex 805
Country-Specific Definitions

For purposes of this Chapter:

competent investigating authority means:

a) in the case of Canada, the Canadian International Trade Tribunal, or its successor;

b) in the case of Mexico, the designated authority within the Ministry of Trade and Industrial Development ("Secretaría de Comercio y Fomento Industrial"), or its successor; and

c) in the case of the United States, the U.S. International Trade Commission, or its successor.

CHAPTER 10:
GOVERNMENT PROCUREMENT

Section C - Bid Challenge

Article 1017: Bid Challenge

1. In order to promote fair, open and impartial procurement procedures, each Party shall adopt and maintain bid challenge procedures for procurement covered by this Chapter in accordance with the following:

   a) each Party shall allow suppliers to submit bid challenges concerning any aspect of the procurement process, which for the purposes of this Article begins after an entity has decided on its procurement requirement and continues through the contract award;

b) a Party may encourage a supplier to seek a resolution of any complaint with the entity concerned prior to initiating a bid challenge;

c) each Party shall ensure that its entities accord fair and timely consideration to any complaint regarding procurement covered by this Chapter;

d) whether or not a supplier has attempted to resolve its complaint with the entity, or following an unsuccessful attempt at such a resolution, no Party may prevent the supplier from initiating a bid challenge or seeking any other relief;

e) a Party may require a supplier to notify the entity on initiation of a bid challenge;

f) a Party may limit the period within which a supplier may initiate a bid challenge, but in no case shall the period be less than 10 working days from the time when the basis of the complaint became known or reasonably should have become known to the supplier;

g) each Party shall establish or designate a reviewing authority with no substantial interest in the outcome of procurements to receive bid challenge and make findings and recommendations concerning them;

h) on receipt of a bid challenge, the reviewing authority shall expeditiously investigate the challenge:

i) a Party may require its reviewing authority to limit its considerations to the challenge itself;

j) in investigating the challenge, the reviewing authority may delay the awarding of the proposed contract pending resolution of the challenge, except in cases of urgency or where the delay would be contrary to the public interest;

k) the reviewing authority shall issue a recommendation to resolve the challenge, which may include directing the entity to re-evaluate offers, terminate or re-compete the contract in question;

l) entities normally shall follow the recommendations of the reviewing authority;

m) each Party should authorize its reviewing authority, following the conclusion of a bid challenge procedure, to make additional recommendations in writing to an entity respecting any facet of the entity's procurement process that is identified as problematic during the investigation of the challenge, including recommendations for changes in the procurement procedures of the entity to bring them into conformity with this Chapter;

n) the reviewing authority shall provide its findings and recommendations respecting bid challenges in writing and in a timely manner, and shall make them available to the Parties and interested persons;

o) each Party shall specify in writing and shall make generally available all its bid challenge procedures; and

p) each Party shall ensure that each of its entities maintains complete documentation regarding each of its procurements, including a written record of all communications substantially affecting each procurement, for at least three years from the date the contract was awarded, to allow verification that the procurement process was carried out in accordance with this Chapter.

2. A Party may require that a bid challenge be initiated only after the notice of procurement has been published or, where a notice is not published, after tender documentation has been made available. Where a Party imposes such a requirement, the 10-working day period described in paragraph 1(f) shall begin no earlier than the date that the notice is published or the tender documentation is made available.

Section D - General Provisions

Article 1018: Exceptions

1. Nothing in this Chapter shall be construed to prevent a Party from taking any action or not disclosing any information which it considers necessary for the protection of its essential security interests relating to the procurement of arms, ammunition or war materials, or to procurement indispensable for national security or for national defense purposes.

2. Provided that such measures are not applied in a manner that would constitute a means of arbitrary or unjustifiable discrimination between Parties where the same conditions prevail or a disguised restriction on trade between the Parties, nothing in this Chapter shall be construed to prevent any Party from adopting or maintaining measures:

   a) necessary to protect public morals, order or safety;

   b) necessary to protect human, animal or plant life or health;

   c) necessary to protect intellectual property; or

   d) relating to goods or services of handicapped persons, of philanthropic institutions or of prison labor.

CHAPTER 11:
INVESTMENT

Section A - Investment

Article 1101: Scope and Coverage

1. This Chapter applies to measures adopted or maintained by a Party relating to:

   a) investors of another Party;

   b) investments of investors of another Party in the territory of the Party; and

   c) with respect to Articles 1106 and 1114, all investments in the territory of the Party.

2. A Party has the right to perform exclusively the economic activities set out in Annex III and to refuse to permit the establishment of investment in such activities.

3. This Chapter does not apply to measures adopted or maintained by a Party to the extent that they are covered by Chapter Fourteen (Financial Services).

4. Nothing in this Chapter shall be construed to prevent a Party from providing a service or performing a function such as law enforcement, correctional services, income security or insurance, social security or insurance, social welfare, public education, public training, health, and child care, in a manner that is not inconsistent with this Chapter.

Article 1102: National Treatment

1. Each Party shall accord to investors of another Party treatment no less favorable than it accords, in like circumstances, to its own investors with respect to the establishment, acquisition, expansion, management, conduct, operation, and sale or other disposition of investments.

2. Each Party shall accord to investments of investors of another Party treatment no less favorable than that it accords, in like circumstances, to investments of its own investors with respect to the establishment, acquisition, expansion, management, conduct, operation, and sale or other disposition of investments.

3. The treatment accorded by a Party under paragraphs 1 and 2 means, with respect to a state or province, treatment no less favorable than the most favorable treatment accorded, in the like circumstances, by that state or province to investors, and to investments of investors, of the Party of which it forms a part.

4. For greater certainty, no Party may:

   a) impose on an investor of another Party a requirement that a minimum level of equity in an enterprise in the territory of the Party be held by its nationals, other than nominal qualifying shares for directors or incorporators of corporations; or

   b) require an investor of another Party, by reasons of its nationality, to sell or otherwise dispose of an investment in the territory of the Party.

Article 1103: Most-Favored-Nation Treatment

1. Each Party shall accord to investors of another Party treatment no less favorable than it accords, in like circumstances, to investments of investors of any other Party or of a non-Party with respect to the establishment, acquisition, expansion, management, conduct, operation, and sale or other disposition of investments.

Article 1104: Standard of Treatment

Each Party shall accord to investors of another Party and to investments of investors of another Party the better of the treatment required by Articles 1102 and 1103.

Article 1105: Minimum Standards of Treatment

1. Each Party shall accord to investments of investors of another Party treatment in accordance with international law, including fair and equitable treatment and full protection and security.

2. Without prejudice to paragraph 1 and notwithstanding Article 1108(7)b), each Party shall accord to investors of another Party, and to investments of investors of another Party, nondiscriminatory treatment with respect to measures it adopts or maintains relating to losses suffered by investments in its territory owing to armed conflict or civil strife.

3. Paragraph 2 does not apply to existing measures relating to subsidies or grants that would be inconsistent with Article 1102 but for Article 1108(7)b).

Article 1106: Performance Requirements

1. No Party may impose or enforce any of the following requirements, or enforce any commitment or undertaking, in connection with the establishment, acquisition, expansion, management, conduct or operation of an investment of an investor of a Party or of a non-Party in its territory:

   a) to export a given level or percentage of goods or services;

   b) to achieve a given level or percentage of domestic content;

   c) to purchase, use or accord a preference to goods produced or services provided in its territory, or to purchase goods or services from persons in its territory;

   d) to relate in any way the volume or value of imports to the volume or value of exports or to the amount of foreign exchange inflows associated with such investment;

   e) to restrict sales of goods or services in its territory that such investment produces or provides by relating such sales in any way to the volume or value of its exports or foreign exchange earnings;

   f) to transfer technology, a production process or other proprietary knowledge to a person in its territory, except when the requirement is imposed or the commitment or undertaking is enforced by a court, administrative tribunal or competition authority to remedy an alleged violation of competition laws or to act in a manner not inconsistent with other provisions of this Agreement; or

   g) to act as the exclusive supplier of the goods it produces or services it provides to a specific region or world market.

2. A measure that requires an investment to use a technology to meet generally applicable health, safety or environment requirements shall not be construed to be inconsistent with paragraph 1(f). For greater certainty, Articles 1102 and 1103 apply to the measure.

3. No Party may condition the receipt or continued receipt of an advantage, in connection with an investment in its territory of an investor of a Party or of a non-Party, on compliance with any of the following requirements:

   a) to achieve a given level or percentage of domestic content;

   b) to purchase, use or accord a preference to goods produced in its territory, or to purchase goods from producers in its territory;

   c) to relate in any way the volume or value of imports to the volume or value of exports or to the amount of foreign exchange inflows associated with such investment; or

   d) to restrict sales of goods or services in its territory that such investment produces or provides by relating such sales in any way to the volume or value of its exports or foreign exchange earnings.

4. Nothing in paragraph 3 shall be construed to prevent a Party from conditioning the receipt or continued receipt of an advantage, in connection with an investment in its territory of an investor of a Party or of a non-Party, on compliance with a requirement to locate production, provide a service, train or employ workers, construct or expand particular facilities, or carry out research and development, in its territory.

5. Paragraphs 1 and 3 do not apply to any requirement other than the requirements set out in those paragraphs.

6. Provided that such measures are not applied in an arbitrary or unjustifiable manner, or do not constitute a disguised restriction on international trade or investment, nothing in paragraph 1(b) or (c) or 3(a) or (b) shall be construed to prevent any Party from adopting or maintaining measures, including environmental measures:

    a) necessary to secure compliance with laws and regulations that are not inconsistent with the provisions of this Agreement;

    b) necessary to protect human, animal or plant life or health; or

    c) necessary for the conservation of living or nonliving exhaustible natural resources.

Article 1107: Senior Management and Boards of Directors

1. No Party may require that an enterprise of that Party that is an investment of an investor of another Party appoint to senior management positions individuals of any particular nationality.

2. A Party may require that a majority of the board of directors, or any committee thereof, of an enterprise of that Party that is an investment of an investor of another Party, be of a particular nationality, or resident in the territory of the Party, provided that the requirement does not materially impair the ability of the investor to exercise control over its investment.

Article 1108: Reservations and Exceptions

1. Articles 1102, 1103, 1106 and 1107 do not apply to:

   a) any existing nonconforming measure that is maintained by

      i) a Party at the federal level, as set out in its Schedule to Annex I or III,

      ii) a state or province, for two years after the date of entry into force of this Agreement, and thereafter as set out by a Party in its Schedule to Annex I in accordance with paragraph 2, or

      iii) a local government;

   b) the continuation or prompt renewal of nonconforming measure referred to in subparagraph (a); or

   c) an amendment to any nonconforming measure referred to in subparagraph (a) to the extent that the amendment does not decrease the conformity of the measure, as it existed immediately before the amendment, with Articles 1102, 1103, 1106 and 1107.

2. Each Party may set out in its Schedule to Annex I, within two years of the date of entry into force of this Agreement, any existing nonconforming measure maintained by a state or province, not including a local government.

3. Articles 1102, 1103, 1106 and 1107 do not apply to any measure that a Party adopts or maintains with respect to sectors, subsectors or activities, as set out in its Schedule to Annex II.

4. No Party may, under any measure adopted after the date of entry into force of this Agreement and covered by its Schedule to Annex II, require an investor of another Party, by reason of its nationality, to sell or otherwise dispose of an investment existing at the time the measure becomes effective.

5. Articles 1102 and 1103 do not apply to any measure that is an exception to, or derogation from, the obligations under Article 1703 (Intellectual Property - National Treatment) as specifically provided for in that Article.

6. Article 1103 does not apply to treatment accorded by a Party pursuant to agreements, or with respect to sectors, set out in its Schedule to Annex IV.

7. Articles 1102, 1103 and 1107 do not apply to:

   a) procurement by a Party or a state enterprise; or

   b) subsidies or grants provided by a Party or a state enterprise, including government-supported loans, guarantees and insurance.

8. The provisions of:

   a) Article 1106(1)(a), (b) and (c), and 3(a) and (b) do not apply to qualification requirements for goods and services with respect to export promotion and foreign aid programs;

   b) Article 1106(1)(b), (c), (f) and (g), and 3(a) and (b) do not apply to procurement by a Party or a state enterprise; and

   c) Article 1106(3)(a) and (b) do not apply to requirements imposed by an importing Party relating to the content of goods necessary to qualify for preferential tariffs or preferential quotas.

Article 1109: Transfers

1. Each Party shall permit all transfers relating to an investment of an investor of another Party in the territory of the Party to be made freely and without delay. Such transfers include:

    a) profits, dividends, interest, capital gains, royalty payments, management fees, technical assistance and other fees, returns in kind and other amounts derived from the investment;

    b) proceeds from the sale of all or any part of the investment or from the partial or complete liquidation of the investment;

    c) payments made under a contract entered into by the investor, or its investment, including payments made pursuant to a loan agreement;

    d) payments made pursuant to Article 1110; and

    e) payments arising under Section B.

2. Each Party shall permit transfers to be made in a freely usable currency at the market rate of exchange prevailing on the date of transfer with respect to spot transactions in the currency to be transferred.

3. No Party may require its investors to transfer, or penalize its investors that fail to transfer, the income, earnings, profits or other amounts derived from, or attributable to, investments in the territory of another Party.

4. Notwithstanding paragraphs 1 and 2, a Party may prevent a transfer through the equitable, nondiscriminatory and good faith application of its laws relating to:

   a) bankruptcy, insolvency or the protection of the rights of creditors;

   b) issuing, trading or dealing in securities;

   c) criminal or penal offenses;

   d) reports or transfers of currency or other monetary instruments; or

   e) ensuring the satisfaction of judgments in adjudicatory proceedings.

5. Paragraph 3 shall not be construed to prevent a Party from imposing any measure through the equitable, nondiscriminatory and good faith application of its laws relating to the matters set out in subparagraphs (a) through (e)of paragraph 4.

6. Notwithstanding paragraph 1, a Party may restrict transfers of returns in kind in circumstances where it could otherwise restrict such transfers under this Agreement, including as set out in paragraph 4.

Article 1110: Expropriation and Compensation

1. No Party may directly or indirectly nationalize or expropriate an investment of an investor of another Party in its territory or take a measure tantamount to nationalization or expropriation of such an investment ("expropriation"), except:

   a) for public purpose;

   b) on a nondiscriminatory basis;

c) in accordance with due process of law and Article 1105(1); and

d) on payment of compensation in accordance with paragraphs 2 through 6.

2. Compensation shall be equivalent to the fair market value of the expropriated investment immediately before the expropriation took place ("date of expropriation"), and shall not reflect any change in value occurring because the intended expropriation had become known earlier. Valuation criteria shall include going concern value, asset value including declared tax value of tangible property, and other criteria, as appropriate, to determine fair market value.

3. Compensation shall be paid without delay and be fully realizable.

4. If payment is made in a G7 currency, compensation shall include interest at a commercially reasonable rate for that currency from the date of expropriation until the date of actual payment.

5. If a Party elects to pay in a currency other than a G7 currency, the amount paid on the date of payment, if converted into a G7 currency at the market rate of exchange prevailing on that date, shall be no less than if the amount of compensation owed on the date of expropriation had been converted into that G7 currency at the market rate of exchange prevailing on that date, and interest had accrued at a commercially reasonable rate for that G7 currency from the date of expropriation until the date of payment.

6. On payment, compensation shall be freely transferable as provided in Article 1109.

7. This Article does not apply to the issuance of compulsory licenses granted in relation to intellectual property rights, or to

the revocation, limitation or creation of intellectual property rights, to the extent that such issuance, revocation, limitation or creation is consistent with Chapter Seventeen (Intellectual Property).

8. For purposes of this Article and for greater certainty, a nondiscriminatory measure of general application shall not be considered a measure tantamount to an expropriation of a debt security or loan covered by this Chapter solely on the ground that the measure imposes costs on the debtor that cause it to default on the debt.

Article 1111: Special Formalities and Information Requirements

1. Nothing in Article 1102 shall be construed to prevent a Party from adopting or maintaining a measure that prescribes special formalities in connection with the establishment of investments by investors of another Party, such as a requirement that investors be residents of the Party or that investments be legally constituted under the laws or regulations of the Party, provided that such formalities do not materially impair the protection afforded by a Party to investors of another Party and investments of investors of another Party pursuant to this Chapter.

2. Notwithstanding Articles 1102 or 1103, a Party may require an investor of another Party or its investment in its territory, to provide routine information concerning that investment solely for informational or statistical purposes. The Party shall protect such business information that is confidential from any disclosure that would prejudice the competitive position of the investor or the investment. Nothing in this paragraph shall be construed to prevent a Party from otherwise obtaining or disclosing information in connection with the equitable and good faith application of its law.

Article 1112: Relation to Other Chapters

1. In the event of any inconsistency between this Chapter and another Chapter, the other Chapter shall prevail to the extent of the inconsistency.

2. A requirement by a Party that a service provider of another Party post a bond or other form of financial security as a condition of providing a service into its territory does not of itself make this Chapter applicable to the provision of that cross-border service. This Chapter applies to that Party's treatment of the posted bond or financial security.

Article 1113: Denial of Benefits

1. A Party may deny the benefits of this Chapter to an investor of another Party that is an enterprise of such Party and to investments of such investor if investors of a non-Party own or control the enterprise and the denying Party:

   a) does not maintain diplomatic relations with the non-Party; or

   b) adopts or maintains measures with respect to the non-Party that prohibit transactions with the enterprise or that would be violated or circumvented if the benefits of this Chapter were accorded to the enterprise or its investments.

2. Subject to prior notification and consultation in accordance with Article 1803 (Notification and Provision of Information) and 2006 (Consultations), a Party may deny the benefits of this Chapter to an investor of another Party that is an enterprise of such Party and to investments of such investors if investors of a non-Party own or control the enterprise and the enterprise has no substantial business activities in the territory of the Party under whose law it is constituted or organized.

Article 1114: Environmental Measures

1. Nothing in this Chapter shall be construed to prevent a Party from adopting, maintaining or enforcing any measure otherwise consistent with this Chapter that it consider appropriate to ensure that investment activity in its territory is undertaken in a manner sensitive to environmental concerns.

2. The Parties recognize that it is inappropriate to encourage investment by relaxing domestic health, safety or environmental measures. Accordingly, a Party should not waive or otherwise derogate from, or offer to waive or otherwise derogate from, such measures as an encouragement for the establishment, acquisition, expansion or retention in its territory of an investment of an investor. If a Party considers that another Party has offered such an encouragement, it may request consultations with the other Party and the two Parties shall consult with a view to avoiding any such encouragement.

Section B - Settlement of Disputes between a Party and Investor of Another Party

Article 1115: Purpose

Without prejudice to the rights and obligations of the Parties under Chapter Twenty (Institutional Arrangements and Dispute Settlement Procedures), this Section establishes a mechanism for the settlement of investment disputes that assures both equal treatment among investors of the Parties in accordance with the principle of international reciprocity and due process before an impartial tribunal.

Article 1116: Claim by an Investor of a Party on Its Own Behalf

1. An investor of a Party may submit to arbitration under this Section a claim that another Party has breached an obligation under:

a) Section A or Article 1503(2) (State Enterprises), or

b) Article 1502(3)(a) (Monopolies and State Enterprises) where the monopoly has acted in a manner inconsistent with the Party's obligations under Section A, and that the investor has incurred loss or damage by reason of, or arising out of, that breach.

2. An investor may not make a claim if more than three years have elapsed from the date on which the investor first acquired, or should have first acquired, knowledge of the alleged breach and knowledge that the investor has incurred loss or damage.

Article 1117: Claim by an Investor of a Party on Behalf of an Enterprise

1. An investor of a Party, on behalf of an enterprise of another Party that is a juridical person that the investor owns or controls directly or indirectly, may submit to arbitration under this Section a claim that the other Party has breached an obligation under

a) Section A or Article 1503(2) (State Enterprises), or

b) Article 1502(3)(a) (Monopolies and State Enterprises) where the monopoly has acted in a manner inconsistent with the Party's obligations under Section A,

and that the enterprise has incurred loss or damage by reason of, or arising out of, that breach.

2. An investor may not make a claim on behalf of an enterprise described in paragraph 1 if more than three years have elapsed from the date on which the enterprise first acquired, or should have first acquired, knowledge of the alleged breach and knowledge that the enterprise has incurred loss or damage.

3. Where an investor makes a claim under this Article and the investor or a noncontrolling investor in the enterprise makes a claim under Article 1116 arising out of the same events that gave rise to the claim under this Article, and two or more of the claims are submitted to arbitration under Article 1120, the claims should be heard together by a Tribunal established under Article 1126, unless the Tribunal finds that the interests of a disputing party would be prejudiced thereby.

4. An investment may not make a claim under this Section.

Article 1118: Settlement of a Claim through Consultation and Negotiation

The disputing parties should first attempt to settle a claim through consultation or negotiation.

Article 1119: Notice of Intent to Submit a Claim to Arbitration

The disputing investor shall deliver to the disputing Party written notice of its intention to submit a claim to arbitration at least 90 days before the claim is submitted, which notice shall specify:

a) the name and address of the disputing investor and, where a claim is made under Article 1117, the name and address of the enterprise;

b) the provisions of this Agreement alleged to have been breached and any other relevant provisions;

c) the issues and the factual basis for the claim; and

d) the relief sought and the approximate amount of damages claimed.

Article 1120: Submission of a Claim to Arbitration

1. Except as provided in Annex 1120.1, and provided that six months have elapsed since the events giving rise to a claim, a disputing investor may submit the claim to arbitration under:

   a) the ICSID Convention, provided that both the disputing Party and the Party of the investor are parties to the Convention;

   b) the Additional Facility Rules of ICSID, provided that either the disputing Party or the Party of the investor, but not both, is a party to the ICSID Convention; or

   c) the UNCITRAL Arbitration Rules.

2. The applicable arbitration rules shall govern the arbitration except to the extent modified by this Section.

Article 1121: Conditions Precedent to Submission of a Claim to Arbitration

1. A disputing investor may submit a claim under Article 1116 to arbitration only if:

   a) the investor consents to arbitration in accordance with the procedures set out in this Agreement; and

   b) the investor and, where the claim is for loss or damage to an interest in an enterprise of another Party that is a juridical person that the investor owns or controls directly or indirectly, the enterprise, waive their right to initiate or continue before any administrative tribunal or court under the law of any Party, or other dispute settlement procedure, any proceedings with respect to the measure of the disputing Party that is alleged to be a breach referred to in

Article 1116, except for proceedings for injunctive, declaratory or other extraordinary relief, not involving the payment of damages, before an administrative tribunal or court under the law of the disputing Party.

2. A disputing investor may submit a claim under Article 1117 to arbitration only if both the investor and the enterprise:

   a) consent to arbitration in accordance with the procedures set out in this Agreement; and

   b) waive their right to initiate or continue before any administrative tribunal or court under the law of any Party, or other dispute settlement procedures, any proceedings with respect to the measure of the disputing Party that is alleged to be a breach referred to in Article 1117, except for proceedings for injunctive, declaratory or other extraordinary relief, not involving the payment of damages, before an administrative tribunal or court under the law of the disputing Party.

3. A consent and waiver required by this Article shall be in writing, shall be delivered to the disputing Party and shall be included in the submission of a claim to arbitration.

4. Only where a disputing Party has deprived a disputing investor of control of an enterprise:

   a) a waiver from the enterprise under paragraph 1(b) or 2(b) shall not be required; and

   b) Annex 1120.1(b) shall not apply.

Article 1122: Consent to Arbitration

1. Each Party consents to the submission of a claim to arbitration in accordance with the procedures set out in this Agreement.

2. The consent given by paragraph 1 and the submission by a disputing investor of a claim to arbitration shall satisfy the requirement of:

   a) Chapter II of the ICSID Convention (Jurisdiction of the Centre) and the Additional Facility Rules for written consent of the parties;

   b) Article II of the New York Convention for an agreement in writing; and

   c) Article 1 of the Inter-American Convention for an agreement.

Article 1123: Number of Arbitrators and Method of Appointment

Except in respect of a tribunal established under Article 1126, and unless the disputing parties otherwise agree, the Tribunal shall comprise three arbitrators, one arbitrator appointed by each of the disputing parties and the third, who shall be the presiding arbitrator, appointed by agreement of the disputing parties.

Article 1124: Constitution of a Tribunal When a Party Fails to Appoint an Arbitrator or the Disputing Parties Are Unable to Agree on a Presiding Arbitrator

1. The Secretary-General shall serve as appointing authority for an arbitration under this Section.

2. If a Tribunal, other than a Tribunal established under Article 1126, has not been constituted within 90 days from the date that a claim is submitted to arbitration, the Secretary-General, on the request of either disputing party, shall appoint, in his discretion, the arbitrator or arbitrators not yet appointed, except that the

presiding arbitrator shall be appointed in accordance with paragraph 3.

3. The Secretary-General shall appoint the presiding arbitrator from the roster of presiding arbitrators referred to in paragraph 4, provided that the presiding arbitrator shall not be a national of the disputing Party or a national of the Party of the disputing investor. In the event that no such presiding arbitrator is available to serve, the Secretary-General shall appoint, from the ICSID Panel of Arbitrators, a presiding arbitrator who is not a national of any of the Parties.

4. On the date of entry into force of this Agreement, the Parties shall establish, and thereafter maintain, a roster of 45 presiding arbitrators meeting the qualifications of the Convention and rules referred to in Article 1120 and experienced in international law and investment matters. The roster members shall be appointed by consensus and without regard to nationality.

Article 1125: Agreement to Appointment of Arbitrators

For purposes of Article 39 of the ICSID Convention and Article 7 of Schedule C to the ICSID Additional Facility Rules, and without prejudice to an objection to an arbitrator based on Article 1124(3) or on a ground other than nationality:

a) the disputing Party agrees to the appointment of each individual member of a Tribunal established under the ICSID Convention or the ICSID Additional Facility Rules;

b) a disputing investor referred to in Article 1116 may submit a claim to arbitration, or continue a claim, under the ICSID Convention or the ICSID Additional Facility Rules, only on condition that the disputing investor agrees in writing to the appointment of each individual member of the Tribunal; and

c) a disputing investor referred to in Article 1117(1) may submit a claim to arbitration, or continue a claim, under the ICSID Convention or the ICSID Additional Facility Rules, only on condition that the disputing investor and the enterprise agree in writing to the appointment of each individual member of the Tribunal.

Article 1126: Consolidation

1. A Tribunal established under this Article shall be established under the UNCITRAL Arbitration Rules and shall conduct its proceedings in accordance with those Rules, except as modified by this Section.

2. Where a Tribunal established under this Article is satisfied that claims have been submitted to arbitration under Article 1120 that have a question of law or fact in common, the Tribunal may, in the interests of fair and efficient resolution of the claims, and after hearing the disputing parties, by order:

   a) assume jurisdiction over, and hear and determine together, all or part of the claims; or

   b) assume jurisdiction over, and hear and determine one or more of the claims, the determination of which it believes would assist in the resolution of the others.

3. A disputing party that seeks an order under paragraph 2 shall request the Secretary-General to establish a Tribunal and shall specify in the request:

   a) the name of the disputing Party or disputing investors against which the order is sought;

   b) the nature of the order sought; and

   c) the grounds on which the order is sought.

4. The disputing party shall deliver to the disputing Party or disputing investors against which the order is sought a copy of the request.

5. Within 60 days of receipt of the request, the Secretary-General shall establish a Tribunal comprising three arbitrators. The Secretary-General shall appoint the presiding arbitrator from the roster referred to in Article 1124(4). In the event that no such presiding arbitrator is available to serve, the Secretary-General shall appoint, from the ICSID Panel of Arbitrators, a presiding arbitrator who is not a national of any of the parties. The Secretary-General shall appoint the two other members from the roster referred to in Article 1124(4), and to the extent not available from that roster, from the ICSID Panel of Arbitrators, and to the extent not available from that Panel, in the discretion of the Secretary-General. One member shall be a national of the disputing Party and one member shall be a national of a Party of the disputing investors.

6. Where a Tribunal has been established under this Article, a disputing investor that has submitted a claim to arbitration under Article 1116 or 1117 and that has not been named in a request made under paragraph 3 may make a written request to the Tribunal that it be included in an order made under paragraph 2, and shall specify in the request:

   a) the name and address of the disputing investor;

   b) the nature of the order sought; and

   c) the grounds on which the order is sought.

7. A disputing investor referred to in paragraph 6 shall deliver a copy of its request to the disputing parties named in a request made under paragraph 3.

8. A Tribunal established under Article 1120 shall not have jurisdiction to decide a claim, or a part of a claim, over which a Tribunal established under this Article has assumed jurisdiction.

9. On application of a disputing party, a Tribunal established under this Article, pending its decision under paragraph 2, may order that the proceedings of a Tribunal established under Article 1120 be stayed, unless the latter Tribunal has already adjourned its proceedings.

10. A disputing Party shall deliver to the Secretariat, within 15 days of receipt by the disputing Party, a copy of:

    a) a request for arbitration made under paragraph (1) of Article 36 of the ICSID Convention

    b) a notice of arbitration made under Article 2 of Schedule C of the ICSID Additional Facility Rules; or

    c) a notice of arbitration given under the UNCITRAL Arbitration Rules.

11. A disputing Party shall deliver to the Secretariat a copy of a request made under paragraph 3:

    a) within 15 days of receipt of the request, in the case of a request made by a disputing investor;

    b) within 15 days of making the request, in the case of a request made by the disputing Party.

12. A disputing Party shall deliver to the Secretariat a copy of a request made under paragraph 6 within 15 days of receipt of the request.

13. The Secretariat shall maintain a public register of the documents referred to in paragraphs 10, 11 and 12.

Article 1127: Notice

A disputing Party shall deliver to the other Parties:

a) written notice of a claim that has been submitted to arbitration no later than 30 days after the date that the claim is submitted; and

b) copies of all pleadings filed in the arbitration.

Article 1128: Participation by a Party

On written notice to the disputing parties, a Party may make submissions to a Tribunal on a question of interpretation of this Agreement.

Article 1129: Documents

1. A Party shall be entitled to receive from the disputing Party, at the cost of the requesting Party a copy of:

   a) the evidence that has been tendered to the Tribunal; and

   b) the written argument of the disputing parties.

2. A Party receiving information pursuant to paragraph 1 shall treat the information as if it were a disputing Party.

Article 1130: Place of Arbitration

Unless the disputing parties agree otherwise, a Tribunal shall hold an arbitration in the territory of a Party that is a party to the New York Convention, selected in accordance with:

a) the ICSID Additional Facility Rules if the arbitration is under those Rules or the ICSID Convention; or

b) the UNCITRAL Arbitration Rules if the arbitration is under those Rules.

Article 1131: Governing Law

1. A Tribunal established under this Section shall decide the issues in dispute in accordance with this Agreement and applicable rules of international law.

2. An interpretation by the Commission of a provision of this Agreement shall be binding on a Tribunal established under this Section.

Article 1132: Interpretation of Annexes

1. Where a disputing Party asserts as a defense that the measure alleged to be a breach is within the scope of a reservation or exception set out in Annex I, Annex II, Annex III or Annex IV, on request of the disputing Party, the Tribunal shall request the interpretation of the Commission on the issue. The Commission, within 60 days of delivery of the request, shall submit in writing its interpretation to the Tribunal.

2. Further to Article 1131(2), a Commission interpretation submitted under paragraph 1 shall be binding on the Tribunal. If the Commission fails to submit an interpretation within 60 days, the Tribunal shall decide the issue.

Article 1133: Expert Reports

Without prejudice to the appointment of other kinds of experts where authorized by the applicable arbitration rules, a Tribunal, at the request of a disputing party or, unless the disputing parties disapprove, on its own initiative, may appoint one or more experts to report to it in writing on any factual issue concerning environmental, health, safety or other scientific matters raised by a disputing party in a proceeding, subject to such terms and conditions as the disputing parties may agree.

Article 1134: Interim Measures of Protection

A Tribunal may order an interim measure of protection to preserve the rights of a disputing party, or to ensure that the Tribunal's jurisdiction is made fully effective, including an order to preserve evidence in the possession or control of a disputing party or to protect the Tribunal's jurisdiction. A Tribunal may not order attachment or enjoin the application of the measure alleged to constitute a breach referred to in Article 1116 or 1117. For purposes of this paragraph, an order includes a recommendation.

Article 1135: Final Award

1. Where a Tribunal makes a final award against a Party, the Tribunal may award, separately or in combination, only:

   a) monetary damages and any applicable interest;

   b) restitution of property, in which case the award shall provide that the disputing Party may pay monetary damages and any applicable interest in lieu of restitution.

   A tribunal may also award costs in accordance with the applicable arbitration rules.

2. Subject to paragraph 1, where a claim is made under Article 1117(1):

   a) an award of restitution of property shall provide that restitution be made to the enterprise;

   b) an award of monetary damages and any applicable interest shall provide that the sum be paid to the enterprise; and

c) the award shall provide that it is made without prejudice to any right that any person may have in the relief under applicable domestic law.

3. A Tribunal may not order a Party to pay punitive damages.

Article 1136: Finality and Enforcement of an Award

1. An award made by a Tribunal shall have no binding force except between the disputing parties and in respect of the particular case.

2. Subject to paragraph 3 and the applicable review procedure for an interim award, a disputing party shall abide by and comply with an award without delay.

3. A disputing party may not seek enforcement of a final award until:

a) in the case of a final award made under the ICSID Convention

i) 120 days have elapsed from the date the award was rendered and no disputing party has requested revision or annulment of the award, or

ii) revision or annulment proceedings have been completed; and

b) in the case of a final award under the ICSID Additional Facility Rules or the UNCITRAL Arbitration Rules

i) three months have elapsed from the date the award was rendered and no disputing party has commenced a proceeding to revise, set aside or annul the award, or

ii) a court has dismissed or allowed an application to revise, set aside or annul the award and there is no further appeal.

4. Each Party shall provide for the enforcement of an award in its territory.

5. If a disputing Party fails to abide by or comply with a final award, the Commission, on delivery of a request by a Party whose investor was a party to the arbitration, shall establish a panel under Article 2008 (Request for an Arbitral Panel). The requesting Party may seek in such proceedings:

   a) a determination that the failure to abide by or comply with the final award is inconsistent with the obligations of this Agreement; and

   b) a recommendation that the Party abide by or comply with the final award.

6. A disputing investor may seek enforcement of an arbitration award under the ICSID Convention, the New York Convention or the Inter-American Convention regardless of whether proceedings have been taken under paragraph 5.

7. A claim that is submitted to arbitration under this Section shall be considered to arise out of a commercial relationship or transaction for purposes of Article I of the New York Convention and Article I of the Inter-American Convention.

Article 1137: General

Time when a Claim is Submitted to Arbitration

1. A claim is submitted to arbitration under this Section when:

   a) the request for arbitration under paragraph (1) of Article 36 of the ICSID Convention has been received by the Secretary-General;

   b) the notice of arbitration under Article 2 of Schedule C of the ICSID Additional Facility Rules has been received by the Secretary-General; or

   c) the notice of arbitration given under the UNCITRAL Arbitration Rules is received by the disputing Party.

Service of Documents

2. Delivery of notice and other documents on a Party shall be made to the place named for that Party in Annex 1137.2.

Receipts under Insurance or Guarantee Contracts

3. In an arbitration under this Section, a Party shall not assert, as a defense, counterclaim, right of setoff or otherwise, that the disputing investor has received or will receive, pursuant to an insurance or guarantee contract, indemnification or other compensation for all or part of its alleged damages.

Publication of an Award

4. Annex 1137.4 applies to the Parties specified in that Annex with respect to publication of an award.

Article 1138: Exclusions

1. Without prejudice to the applicability or nonapplicability of the dispute settlement provisions of this Section or of Chapter Twenty (Institutional Arrangements and Dispute Settlement Procedures) to other actions taken by a Party pursuant to Article 2102 (National Security), a decision by a Party to prohibit or restrict the acquisition of an investment in its territory by an investor of another Party, or its investment, pursuant to that Article shall not be subject to such provisions.

2. The dispute settlement provisions of this Section and of Chapter Twenty shall not apply to the matters referred to in Annex 1138.2.

Section C - Definitions

Article 1139: Definitions

For purposes of this Chapter:

disputing investor means an investor that makes a claim under Section B;

disputing parties means the disputing investor and the disputing Party;

disputing party means the disputing investor or the disputing Party;
disputing Party means a Party against which a claim is made under Section B;

enterprise means an "enterprise" as defined in Article 201 (Definitions of General Application), and a branch of an enterprise;

enterprise of a Party means an enterprise constituted or organized under the law of a Party, and a branch located in the territory of a Party and carrying out business activities there.

equity or debt securities includes voting and nonvoting shares, bonds. convertible debentures, stock options and warrants;

G7 Currency means the currency of Canada, France, Germany, Italy, Japan, the United Kingdom of Great Britain and Northern Ireland or the United States;

ICSID means the International Centre for Settlement of Investment Disputes;

ICSID Convention means the *Convention on the Settlement of Investment Disputes between States and Nationals of other States,* done at Washington, March 18, 1965;

Inter-American Convention means the *Inter-American Convention on International Commercial Arbitration,* done at Panama, January 30, 1975;

investment means:

a) an enterprise;

b) an equity security of an enterprise;

c) a debt security of an enterprise:

  i) where the enterprise is an affiliate of the investor, or

  ii) where the original maturity of the debt security is at least three years, but does not include a debt security, regardless of original maturity, of a state enterprise;

d) a loan to an enterprise:

   i) where the enterprise is an affiliate of the investor; or

   ii) where the original maturity of the loan is at least three years, but does not include a loan, regardless of original maturity, to a state enterprise;

e) an interest in an enterprise that entitles the owner to share in income or profits of the enterprise;

f) an interest in an enterprise that entitles the owner to share in the assets of that enterprise on dissolution, other than a debt security or a loan excluded from subparagraph c) or d);

g) real estate or other property, tangible or intangible, acquired in the expectation or used for the purpose of economic benefit or other business purposes; and

h) interests arising from the commitment of capital or other resources in the territory of a Party to economic activity in such territory, such as under

   i) contracts involving the presence of an investor's property in the territory of the Party, including turnkey or construction contracts, or concessions; or

   ii) contracts where remuneration depends substantially on the production, revenues or profits of an enterprise;

but investment does not mean,

i) claims to money that arise solely from

i) commercial contracts for the sale of goods or services by a national or enterprise in the territory of a Party to an enterprise in the territory of another Party, or

ii) the extension of credit in connection with a commercial transaction, such as trade financing, other than a loan covered by subparagraph (d); or

j) any other claims to money,

that do not involve the kinds of interests set out in subparagraphs (a) through (h);

investment of an investor of a Party means an investment owned or controlled directly or indirectly by an investor of such Party;

investor of a Party means a Party or state enterprise thereof, or a national or an enterprise of such Party, that seeks to make, is making or has made an investment;

investor of a non-Party means an investor other than an investor of a Party, that seeks to make, is making or has made an investment;

New York Convention means the *United Nations Convention on the Recognition and Enforcement of Foreign Arbitral Awards,* done at New York, June 10, 1958;

Secretary-General means the Secretary-General of ICSID;

transfers means transfers and international payments;

Tribunal means an arbitration tribunal established under Article 1120 or 1126; and

UNCITRAL Arbitration Rules means the arbitration rules of the United Nations Commission on International Trade Law, approved by the United Nations General Assembly on December 15, 1976.

Annex 1120.1
Submission of a Claim to Arbitration

Mexico

With respect to the submission of a claim to arbitration:

a) an investor of another Party may not allege that Mexico has breached an obligation under:

  i) Section A or Article 1503(2) (State Enterprises), or

  ii) Article 1502(3)(a) (Monopolies and State Enterprises) where the monopoly has acted in a manner inconsistent with the Party's obligations under Section A,

both in an arbitration under this Section and in proceedings before a Mexican court or administrative tribunal; and

b) where an enterprise of Mexico that is a juridical person that an investor of another Party owns or controls directly or indirectly alleges in proceedings before a Mexican court or administrative tribunal that Mexico has breached an obligation under:

  i) Section A or Article 1503(2) (State Enterprises), or

  ii) Article 1502(3)(a) (Monopolies and State Enterprises) where the monopoly has acted in a manner inconsistent with the Party's obligations under Section A, the investor may not allege the breach in an arbitration under this Section.

Annex 1137.2
Service of Documents on a Party Under Section B

Each Party shall set out in this Annex and publish in its official journal by January 1, 1994, the place for delivery of notice and other documents under this Section.

Annex 1137.4
Publication of an Award

Canada

Where Canada is the disputing Party, either Canada or a disputing investor that is a party to the arbitration may make an award public.

Mexico

Where Mexico is the disputing Party, the applicable arbitration rules apply to the publication of an award.

United States

Where the United States is the disputing Party, either the United States or a disputing investor that is a party to the arbitration may make an award public.

Annex 1138.2
Exclusions from Dispute Settlement

Canada

A decision by Canada following a review under the *Investment Canada* Act, with respect to whether or not to permit an acquisition that is subject to review, shall not be subject to the dispute settlement provisions of Section B or of Chapter Twenty (Institutional Arrangements and Dispute Settlement Procedures).

Mexico

A decision by the National Commission on Foreign Investment ("Comision Nacional de Inversiones Extranjeras") following a review pursuant to Annex I, page I-M-4, with respect to whether or not to permit an acquisition that is subject to review, shall not be subject to the dispute settlement provisions of Section B or of Chapter Twenty.

CHAPTER 14:
FINANCIAL SERVICES

Article 1410: Exceptions

1. Nothing in this Part shall be construed to prevent a Party from adopting or maintaining reasonable measures for prudential reasons, such as:

   a) the protection of investors, depositors, financial market participants, policy holders, policy-claimants, or persons to whom a fiduciary duty is owed by a financial institution or cross-border financial service provider;

   b) the maintenance of the safety, soundness, integrity or financial responsibility of financial institutions or cross-border financial service providers; and

c) ensuring the integrity and stability of a Party's financial system.

2. Nothing in this Part applies to nondiscriminatory measures of general application taken by any public entity in pursuit of monetary and related credit policies or exchange rate policies. This paragraph shall not affect a Party's obligations under Article 1106 (Performance Requirements) with respect to measures covered by Chapter Eleven (Investment) or Article 1109 (Transfers).

3. Article 1405 shall not apply to the granting by a Party to a financial institution of an exclusive right to provide a financial service referred to in Article 1401(3)(a).

4. Notwithstanding Article 1109(1), (2) and (3), as incorporated into this Chapter, and without limiting the applicability of Article 1109(4), as incorporated into this Chapter, a Party may prevent or limit transfers by a financial institution or cross-border financial services provider to, or for the benefit of, an affiliate of or person related to such institution or provider, through the equitable, nondiscriminatory and good faith application of measures relating to maintenance of the safety, soundness, integrity or financial responsibility of financial institutions or cross-border financial service providers. This paragraph does not prejudice any other provision of this Agreement that permits a Party to restrict transfers.

6. Each Party shall maintain or establish one or more inquiry points no later than 180 days after the date of entry into force of this Agreement, to respond in writing as soon as practicable, to all reasonable inquiries from interested persons regarding measures of general application covered by this Chapter.

Article 1412: Financial Services Committee

1. The Parties hereby establish the Financial Services Committee. The principal representative of each Party shall be an official of the Party's authority responsible for financial services set out in Annex 1412.1.

2. Subject to Article 2001(2)(d)(Free Trade Commission), the Committee shall:

   a) supervise the implementation of this Chapter and its further elaboration;

   b) consider issues regarding financial services that are referred to it by a Party; and

   c) participate in the dispute settlement procedures in accordance with Article 1415.

3. The Committee shall meet annually to assess the functioning of this Agreement as it applies to financial services. The Committee shall inform the Commission of the results of each annual meeting.

Article 1413: Consultations

1. A Party may request consultations with another Party regarding any matter arising under this Agreement that affects financial services. The other Party shall give sympathetic consideration to the request. The consulting Parties shall report the results of their consultations to the Committee at its annual meeting.

2. Consultations under this Article shall include officials of the authorities specified in Annex 1412.1.

3. A Party may request that regulatory authorities of another Party participate in consultations under this Article regarding that other

Party's measures of general application which may affect the operations of financial institutions or cross-border financial service providers in the requesting Party's territory.

4. Nothing in this Article shall be construed to require regulatory authorities participating in consultations under paragraph 3 to disclose information or take any action that would interfere with individual regulatory, supervisory, administrative or enforcement matters.

5. Where a Party requires information for supervisory purposes concerning a financial institution in another Party's territory or a cross-border financial service provider in another Party's territory, the Party may approach the competent regulatory authority in the other Party's territory to seek the information.

6. Annex 1413.6 shall apply to further consultations and arrangements.

Article 1414: Dispute Settlement

1. Section B of Chapter Twenty (Institutional Arrangements and Dispute Settlement Procedures) applies as modified by this Article to the settlement of disputes arising under this Chapter.

2. The Parties shall establish by January 1, 1994 and maintain a roster of up to 15 individuals who are willing and able to serve as financial services panelists. Financial services roster members shall be appointed by consensus for terms of three years, and may be reappointed.

3. Financial services roster members shall:

   a) have expertise or experience in financial services law or practice, which may include the regulation of financial institutions;

b) be chosen strictly on the basis of objectivity, reliability and sound judgment: and

c) meet the qualifications set out in Article 2009(2)(b) and (c) (Roster).

4. Where a Party claims that a dispute arises under this Chapter, Article 2011 (Panel Selection) shall apply, except that:

a) where the disputing Parties so agree, the panel shall be composed entirely of panelists meeting the qualifications in paragraph 3; and

b) in any other case,

i) each disputing Party may select panelists meeting the qualifications set out in paragraph 3 or in Article 2010(1) (Qualifications of Panelists), and

ii) if the Party complained against invokes Article 1410, the chair of the panel shall meet the qualifications set out in paragraph 3.

5. In any dispute where a panel finds a measure to be inconsistent with the obligations of this Agreement and the measure affects:

a) only the financial services sector, the complaining Party may suspend benefits only in the financial services sector:

b) the financial services sector and any other sector, the complaining Party may suspend benefits in the financial services sector that have an effect equivalent to the effect of the measure in the Party's financial services sector; or

c) only a sector other than the financial services sector, the complaining Party may not suspend benefits in the financial services sector.

Article 1415: Investment Disputes in Financial Services

1. Where an investor of another Party submits a claim under Article 1116 or 1117 to arbitration under Section B of Chapter Eleven (Investment - Settlement of Disputes between a Party and an Investor of Another Party) against a Party and the disputing Party invokes Article 1410, on request of the disputing Party, the Tribunal shall refer the matter in writing to the Committee for a decision. The Tribunal may not proceed pending receipt of a decision or report under this Article.

2. In a referral pursuant to paragraph 1, the Committee shall decide the issue of whether and to what extent Article 1410 is a valid defense to the claim of the investor. The Committee shall transmit a copy of its decision to the Tribunal and to the Commission. The decision shall be binding on the Tribunal.

3. Where the Committee has not decided the issue within 60 days of the receipt of the referral under paragraph 1, the disputing Party or the Party *of* the disputing investor may request the establishment of an arbitral panel under Article 2008 (Request for an Arbitral Panel). The panel shall be constituted in accordance with Article 1414. Further to Article 2017 (Final Report), the panel shall transmit its final report to the Committee and to the Tribunal. The report shall be binding on the Tribunal.

4. Where no request for the establishment of a panel pursuant to paragraph 3 has been made within 10 days of the expiration of the 60-day period referred to in paragraph 3, the Tribunal may proceed to decide the matter.

Article 1416: Definitions

For purposes of this Chapter:

cross-border financial service provider of a Party means a person of a Party that is engaged in the business of providing a financial service within the territory of the Party and that seeks to provide or provides financial services through the cross-border provision of such services;

cross-border provision of a financial service or cross border trade in financial services means the provision of a financial service:

a) from the territory of a Party into the territory of another Party,

b) in the territory of a Party by a person of that Party to a person of another Party, or

c) by a national of a Party in the territory of another Party,

but does not include the provision of a service in the territory of a Party by an investment in that territory;

financial institution means any financial intermediary or other enterprise that is authorized to do business and regulated or supervised as a financial institution under the law of the Party in whose territory it is located;

financial institution of another Party means a financial institution, including a branch, located in the territory of a Party that is controlled by persons of another Party;

financial service means a service of a financial nature, including insurance, and a service incidental or auxiliary to a service of a financial nature;

financial service provider of a Party means a person of a Party that is engaged in the business of providing a financial service within the territory of that Party;

investment means "investment" as defined in Article 1139 (Investment - Definitions), except that, with respect to loans and "debt securities" referred to in that Article:

a) a loan to or debt security issued by a financial institution is an investment only where it is treated as regulatory capital by the Party in whose territory the financial institution is located; and

b) a loan granted by or debt security owned by a financial institution, other than a loan to or debt security of a financial institution referred to in subparagraph (a), is not an investment;

for greater certainty:

c) a loan to, or debt security issued by, a Party or a state enterprise thereof is not an investment; and

d) a loan granted by or debt security owned by a cross-border financial service provider, other than a loan to or debt security issued by a financial institution, is an investment if such loan or debt security meets the criteria for investments set out in Article 1139;

investor of a Party means a Party or state enterprise thereof, or a person of that Party, that seeks to make, makes or has made an investment;

new financial service means a financial service not provided in the Party's territory that is provided within the territory of another Party, and includes any new form of delivery of a financial service or the sale of a financial product that is not sold in the Party's territory;

person of a Party means "person of a Party" as defined in Chapter Two (General Definitions) and, for greater certainty, does not include a branch of an enterprise of a non-Party;

public entity means a central bank or monetary authority of a Party, or any financial institution owned or controlled by a Party: and

self-regulatory organization means any nongovernmental body, including any securities or futures exchange or market, clearing agency, or other organization or association, that exercises its own or delegated regulatory or supervisory authority over financial service providers or financial institutions.

Annex 1412.1
Authorities Responsible for Financial Services

The authority of each Party responsible for financial services shall be:

a) for Canada, the Department of Finance of Canada;

b) for Mexico, the Secretaria de Hacienda y Crédito Publico; and

c) for the United States, the Department of the Treasury for banking and other financial services and the Department of Commerce for insurance services.

CHAPTER 15:
COMPETITION POLICY, MONOPOLIES AND STATE Enterprises

Article 1501: Competition Law

1. Each Party shall adopt or maintain measures to proscribe anti-competitive business conduct and take appropriate action with respect thereto, recognizing that such measures will enhance the fulfillment of the objectives of this Agreement. To this end the Parties shall consult from time to time about the effectiveness of measures undertaken by each Party.

2. Each Party recognizes the importance of cooperation and coordination among their authorities to further effective competition law enforcement in the free trade area. The Parties shall cooperate on issues of competition law enforcement policy, including mutual legal assistance, notification, consultation and exchange of information relating to the enforcement of competition laws and policies in the free trade area.

3. No Party may have recourse to dispute settlement under this Agreement for any matter arising under this Article.

Article 1502: Monopolies and State Enterprises

1. Nothing in this Agreement shall be construed to prevent a Party from designating a monopoly.

2. Where a Party intends to designate a monopoly and the designation may affect the interests of persons of another Party, the Party shall:

   a) wherever possible, provide prior written notification to the other Party of the designation; and

b) endeavor to introduce at the time of the designation such conditions on the operation of the monopoly as will minimize or eliminate any nullification or impairment of benefits in the sense of Annex 2004 (Nullification and Impairment).

3. Each Party shall ensure, through regulatory control, administrative supervision or the application of other measures, that any privately-owned monopoly that it designates and any government monopoly that it maintains or designates:

a) acts in a manner that is not inconsistent with the Party's obligations under this Agreement wherever such a monopoly exercises any regulatory, administrative or other governmental authority that the Party has delegated to it in connection with the monopoly good or service, such as the power to grant import or export licenses, approve commercial transactions or impose quotas, fees or other charges;

b) except to comply with any terms of its designation that are not inconsistent with subparagraph (c) or (d), acts solely in accordance with commercial considerations in its purchase or sale of the monopoly good or service in the relevant market, including with regard to price, quality, availability, marketability, transportation and other terms and conditions of purchase or sale;

c) provides nondiscriminatory treatment to investments of investors, to goods and to service providers of another Party in its purchase or sale of the monopoly good or service in the relevant market; and

d) does not use its monopoly position to engage, either directly or indirectly, including through its dealings with its parent, its subsidiary or other enterprise with common ownership, in anti-competitive practices in a nonmonopolized market in its territory that adversely affect an investment of an investor of another Party, including through the discriminatory provision of the monopoly good or service, cross-subsidization or predatory conduct.

4. Paragraph 3 does not apply to procurement by governmental agencies of goods or services for governmental purposes and not with a view to commercial resale or with a view to use in the production of goods or the provision of services for commercial sale.

5. For purposes of this Article "maintain" means designate prior to the date of entry into force of this Agreement and existing on January 1, 1994.

Article 1503: State Enterprises

1. Nothing in this Agreement shall be construed to prevent a Party from maintaining or establishing a state enterprise.

2. Each Party shall ensure, through regulatory control, administrative supervision or the application of other measures, that any state enterprise that it maintains or establishes acts in a manner that is not inconsistent with the Party's obligations under Chapters Eleven (Investment) and Fourteen Financial Services) wherever such enterprise exercises any regulatory, administrative or other governmental authority that the Party has delegated to it, such as the power to expropriate, grant licenses, approve commercial transactions or impose quotas, fees or other charges.

3. Each Party shall ensure that any state enterprise that it maintains or establishes accords nondiscriminatory treatment in the sale of its goods or services to investments in the Party's territory of investors of another Party.

Article 1504: Working Group on Trade and Competition

The Commission shall establish a Working Group on Trade and Competition, comprising representatives of each Party, to report, and to make recommendations on further work as appropriate, to the Commission within five years of the date of entry into force of this Agreement on relevant issues concerning the relationship between competition laws and policies and trade in the free trade area.

Article 1505: Definitions

For purposes of this Chapter:

designate means to establish, designate or authorize, or to expand the scope of a monopoly to cover an additional good or service, after the date of entry into force of this Agreement;

discriminatory provision includes treating:

a) a parent, a subsidiary or other enterprise with common ownership more favorably than an unaffiliated enterprise, or

b) one class of enterprises more favorably than another, in like circumstances;

government monopoly means a monopoly that is owned, or controlled through ownership interests, by the federal government of a Party or by another such monopoly;

in accordance with commercial considerations means consistent with normal business practices of privately-held enterprises in the relevant business or industry;

market means the geographic and commercial market for a good or service;

monopoly means an entity, including a consortium or government agency, that in any relevant market in the territory of a Party is designated as the sole provider or purchaser of a good or service, but does not include an entity that has been granted an exclusive intellectual property right solely by reason of such grant;

nondiscriminatory treatment means the better of national treatment and most-favored-nation treatment, as set out in the relevant provisions of this Agreement; and

state enterprise means, except as set out in Annex 1505, an enterprise owned, or controlled through ownership interests, by a Party.

Annex 1505
Country-Specific Definitions of State Enterprises

For purposes of Article 1503(3), "staet enterprise":

(a) with respect to Canada, means a Crown corporation within the meaning of the *Financial Administration Act* (Canada), a Crown corporation within the meaning of any comparable provincial law or equivalent entity that is incorporated under other applicable provincial law; and

(b) with respect to Mexico, does not include, the Compania Nacional de Subsistencias Populares (National Company for the Basic Commodities) and its existing affiliates, or any successor enterprise or its affiliates, for purposes of sales of maize, beans and powdered milk.

CHAPTER 16:
TEMPORARY ENTRY FOR BUSINESS PERSONS

Article 1606: Dispute Settlement

1. A Party may not initiate proceedings under Article 2007 (Commission - Good Offices, Conciliation and Mediation) regarding a refusal to grant temporary entry under this Chapter or a particular case arising under Article 1602(1) unless:

    a) the matter involves a pattern of practice; and

    b) the business person has exhausted the available administrative remedies regarding the particular matter.

2. The remedies referred to in paragraph (1)b) shall be deemed to be exhausted if a final determination in the matter has not been issued by the competent authority within one year of the institution of an administrative proceeding, and the failure to issue a determination is not attributable to delay caused by the business person.

CHAPTER 18:
PUBLICATION, NOTIFICATION AND ADMINISTRATION OF LAWS

Article 1801: Contact Points

Each Party shall designate a contact point to facilitate communications between the Parties on any matter covered by this Agreement. On the request of another Party, the contact point shall identify the office or official responsible for the matter and assist, as necessary, in facilitating communication with the requesting Party.

Article 1802: Publication

1. Each Party shall ensure that its laws, regulations, procedures and administrative rulings of general application respecting any matter covered by this Agreement are promptly published or otherwise made available in such a manner as to enable interested Persons and Parties to become acquainted with them.

2. To the extent possible, each Party shall:

   a) publish in advance any such measure that it proposes to adopt; and

   b) provide interested persons and Parties a reasonable opportunity to comment on such proposed measures.

Article 1803: Notification and Provision of Information

1. To the maximum extent possible, each Party shall notify any other Party with an interest in the matter of any proposed or actual measure that the Party considers might materially affect the operation of this Agreement or otherwise substantially affect that other Party's interests under this Agreement.

2. On request of another Party, a Party shall promptly provide information and respond to questions pertaining to any actual or proposed measure, whether or not that other Party has been previously notified of that measure.

3. Any notification or information provided under this Article shall be without prejudice as to whether the measure is consistent with this Agreement.

Article 1804: Administrative Proceedings

With a view to administering in a consistent, impartial and reasonable manner all measures of general application affecting matters covered by this Agreement, each Party shall ensure that in its administrative proceedings applying measures referred to in Article 1802 to particular persons, goods or services of another Party in specific cases that:

a) wherever possible, persons of another Party that are directly affected by a proceeding are provided reasonable notice, in accordance with domestic procedures, when a proceeding is initiated, including a description of the nature of the proceeding, a statement of the legal authority under which the proceeding is initiated and a general description of any issues in controversy;

b) such persons are afforded a reasonable opportunity to present facts and arguments in support of their positions prior to any final administrative action, when time, the nature of the proceeding and the public interest permit; and

c) its procedures are in accordance with domestic law.

Article 1805: Review and Appeal

1. Each Party shall establish or maintain judicial, quasi-judicial or administrative tribunals or procedures for the purpose of the prompt review and, where warranted, correction of final administrative actions regarding matters covered by this Agreement. Such tribunals shall be impartial and independent of the office or authority entrusted with administrative enforcement and shall not have any substantial interest in the outcome of the matter.

2. Each Party shall ensure that, in any such tribunals or procedures, the parties to the proceeding are provided with the right to:

   a) a reasonable opportunity to support or defend their respective positions; and

   b) a decision based on the evidence and submissions of record or, where required by domestic law, the record compiled by the administrative authority.

3. Each Party shall ensure, subject to appeal or further review as provided in its domestic law, that such decisions shall be implemented by, and shall govern the practice of. the offices or authorities with respect to the administrative action at issue.

Article 1806: Definitions

For purposes of this Chapter:

administrative ruling of general application means an administrative ruling or interpretation that applies to all persons and fact situations that fall generally within its ambit and that establishes a norm of conduct but does not include:

a) a determination or ruling made in an administrative or quasi-judicial proceeding that applies to a particular person, good or service of another Party in a specific case; or

b) a ruling that adjudicates with respect to a particular act or practice.

CHAPTER 19:
REVIEW AND DISPUTE SETTLEMENT IN ANTIDUMPING AND COUNTERVAILING DUTY MATTERS

Article 1901: General Provisions

1. Article 1904 applies only with respect to goods that the competent investigating authority of the importing Party, applying the importing Party's antidumping or countervailing duty law to the facts of a specific case, determines are goods of another Party.

2. For purposes of Articles 1903 and 1904, panels shall be established in accordance with the provisions of Annex 1901.2.

3. Except for Article 2203 (Entry into Force), no provision of any other Chapter of this Agreement shall be construed as imposing obligations on a Party with respect to the Party's antidumping law or countervailing duty law.

Article 1902: Retention of Domestic Antidumping Law and Countervailing Duty Law

1. Each Party reserves the right to apply its antidumping law and countervailing duty law to goods imported from the territory of any other Party. Antidumping law and countervailing duty law include, as appropriate for each Party, relevant statutes, legislative history, regulations, administrative practice and judicial precedents.

2. Each Party reserves the right to change or modify its antidumping law or countervailing duty law, provided that in the case of an amendment to a Party's antidumping or countervailing duty statute:

a) such amendment shall apply to goods from another Party only if the amending statute specifies that it applies to goods from that Party or from the Parties to this Agreement;

b) the amending Party notifies in writing the Parties to which the amendment applies of the amending statute as far in advance as possible of the date of enactment of such statute;

c) following notification, the amending Party, on request of any Party to which the amendment applies, consults with that Party prior to the enactment of the amending statute; and

d) such amendment, as applicable to that other Party, is not inconsistent with

i) the *General Agreement on Tariffs and Trade (GATT), the Agreement on Implementation of Article VI of the General Agreement on Tariffs and Trade* (the Antidumping Code) or the *Agreement on the Interpretation and Application of Articles VI, XVI and XIII of the General Agreement on Tariffs and Trade* (the Subsidies Code), or any successor agreement to which all the original signatories to this Agreement are party, or

ii) the object and purpose of this Agreement and this Chapter, which is to establish fair and predictable conditions for the progressive liberalization of trade between the Parties to this Agreement while maintaining effective and fair disciplines on unfair trade practices, such object and purpose to be ascertained from the provisions of this Agreement, its preamble and objectives, and the practices of the Parties.

Article 1903: Review of Statutory Amendments

1. A Party to which an amendment of another Party's antidumping or countervailing duty statute applies may request in writing that such amendment be referred to a binational panel for a declaratory opinion as to whether:

   a) the amendment does not conform to the provisions of Article 1902(2)(d)(i) or (ii); or

   b) such amendment has the function and effect of overturning a prior decision of a panel made pursuant to Article 1904 and does not conform to the provisions of Article 1902(2)(d)(i) or (ii).

   Such declaratory opinion shall have force or effect only as provided in this Article.

2. The panel shall conduct its review in accordance with the procedures of Annex 1903.2.

3. In the event that the panel recommends modifications to the amending statute to remedy a nonconformity that it has identified in its opinion:

   a) the two Parties shall immediately begin consultations and shall seek to achieve a mutually satisfactory solution to the matter within 90 days of the issuance of the panel's final declaratory opinion. Such solution may include seeking corrective legislation with respect to the statute of the amending Party:

   b) if corrective legislation is not enacted within nine months from the end of the 90-day consultation period referred to in subparagraph (a) and no other mutually satisfactory solution has been reached, the Party that requested the panel may

i) take comparable legislative or equivalent executive action, or

ii) terminate this Agreement with regard to the amending Party on 60 day written notice to that Party.

Article 1904: Review of Final Antidumping and Countervailing Duty Determinations

1. As provided in this Article, each Party shall replace judicial review of final antidumping and countervailing duty determinations with binational panel review.

2. An involved Party may request that a panel review, based on the administrative record, a final antidumping or countervailing duty determination of a competent investigating authority of an importing Party to determine whether such determination was in accordance with the antidumping or countervailing duty law of the importing Party. For this purpose, the antidumping or countervailing duty law consists of the relevant statutes, legislative history, regulations, administrative practice and judicial precedents to the extent that a court of the importing Party would rely on such materials in reviewing a final determination of the competent investigating authority. Solely for purposes of the panel review provided for in this Article, the antidumping and countervailing duty statutes of the Parties, as those statutes may be amended from time to time, are incorporated into and made a part of this Agreement.

3. The panel shall apply the standard of review set out in Annex 1911 and the general legal principles that a court of the importing Party otherwise would apply to a review of a determination of the competent investigating authority.

4. A request for a panel shall be made in writing to the other involved Party within 30 days following the date of publication of

the final determination in question in the official journal of the importing Party. In the case of final determinations that are not published in the official journal of the importing Party, the importing Party shall immediately notify the other involved Party of such final determination where it involves goods from the other involved Party, and the other involved Party may request a panel within 30 days of receipt of such notice. Where the competent investigating authority of the importing Party has imposed provisional measures in an investigation, the other involved Party may provide notice of its intention to request a panel under this Article, and the Parties shall begin to establish a panel at that time, Failure to request a panel within the time specified in this paragraph shall preclude review by a panel.

5. An involved Party on its own initiative may request review of a final determination by a panel and shall, on request of a person who would otherwise be entitled under the law of the importing Party to commence domestic procedures for judicial review of that final determination, request such review.

6. The panel shall conduct its review in accordance with the procedures established by the Parties pursuant to paragraph 14. Where both involved Parties request a panel to review a final determination, a single panel shall review that determination.

7. The competent investigating authority that issued the final determination in question shall have the right to appear and be represented by counsel before the panel. Each Party shall provide that other persons who, pursuant to the law of the importing Party, otherwise would have had the right to appear and be represented in a domestic judicial review proceeding concerning the determination of the competent investigating authority, shall have the right to appear and be represented by counsel before the panel.

8. The panel may uphold a final determination, or remand it for action not inconsistent with the panel's decision. Where the

panel remands a final determination, the panel shall establish as brief a time as is reasonable for compliance with the remand, taking into account the complexity of the factual and legal issues involved and the nature of the panel's decision. In no event shall the time permitted for compliance with a remand exceed an amount of time equal to the maximum amount of time (counted from the date of the filing of a petition, complaint or application) permitted by statute for the competent investigating authority in question to make a final determination in an investigation. If review of the action taken by the competent investigating authority on remand is needed, such review shall be before the same panel, which shall normally issue a final decision within 90 days of the date on which such remand action is submitted to it.

9. The decision of a panel under this Article shall be binding on the involved Parties with respect to the particular matter between the Parties that is before the panel.

10. This Agreement shall not affect:

    a) the judicial review procedures of any Party, or

    b) cases appealed under those procedures, with respect to determinations other than final determinations,

11. A final determination shall not be reviewed under any judicial review procedures of the importing Party if an involved Party requests a panel with respect to that determination within the time limits set out in this Article. No Party may provide in its domestic legislation for an appeal from a panel decision to its domestic courts.

12. This Article shall not apply where:

    a) neither involved Party seeks panel review of a final determination;

b) a revised final determination is issued as a direct result of judicial review of the original final determination by a court of the importing Party in cases where neither involved Party sought panel review of that original final determination; or

c) a final determination is issued as a direct result of judicial review that was commenced in a court of the importing Party before the date of entry into force of this Agreement.

13. Where, within a reasonable time after the panel decision is issued, an involved Party alleges that:

a) i) a member of the panel was guilty of gross misconduct, bias, or a serious conflict of interest, or otherwise materially violated the rules of conduct,

ii) the panel seriously departed from a fundamental rule of procedure; or

iii) the panel manifestly exceeded its powers, authority or jurisdiction set out in this Article. for example by failing to apply the appropriate standard of review, and

b) any of the actions set out in subparagraph (a) has materially affected the panel's decision and threatens the integrity of the binational panel review process,

that Party may avail itself of the extraordinary challenge procedure set out in Annex 1904.13.

14. To implement this Article, the Parties shall adopt rules of procedure by January 1, 1994. Such rules shall be based, where appropriate, on judicial rules of appellate procedure, and shall include rules concerning: the content and service of requests for panels; a requirement that the competent investigating authority transmit to the panel the administrative record of the proceeding; the protection of business proprietary, government classified,

and other privileged information (including sanctions against persons participating before panels for improper release of such information); participation by private persons; limitations on panel review to errors alleged by the Parties or private persons; filing and service; computation and extensions of time; the form and content of briefs and other papers; pre- and post-hearing conferences; motions; oral argument; requests for rehearing; and voluntary terminations of panel reviews. The rules shall be designed to result in final decisions within 315 days of the date on which a request for a panel is made, and shall allow:

a) 30 days for the filing of the complaint;

b) 30 days for designation or certification of the administrative record and its filing with the panel;

c) 60 days for the complainant to file its brief;

d) 60 days for the respondent to file its brief;

e) 15 days for the filing of reply briefs;

f) 15 to 30 days for the panel to convene and hear oral argument; and

g) 90 days for the panel to issue its written decision.

15. In order to achieve the objectives of this Article, the Parties shall amend their antidumping and countervailing duty statutes and regulations with respect to antidumping or countervailing duty proceedings involving goods of the other Parties, and other statutes and regulations to the extent that they apply to the operation of the antidumping and countervailing duty laws. In particular, without limiting the generality of the foregoing, each Party shall:

a) amend its statutes or regulations to ensure that existing procedures concerning the refund, with interest, of antidumping or countervailing duties operate to give effect to a final panel decision that a refund is due;

b) amend its statutes or regulations to ensure that its courts shall give full force and effect, with respect to any person within its jurisdiction, to all sanctions imposed pursuant to the laws of the other Parties to enforce provisions of any protective order or undertaking that such other Party has promulgated or accepted in order to permit access for purposes of panel review or of the extraordinary challenge procedure to confidential, personal, business property or other privileged information;

c) amend its statutes or regulations to ensure that

   i) domestic procedures for judicial review of a final determination may not be commenced until the time for requesting a panel under paragraph 4 has expired, and

   ii) as a prerequisite to commencing domestic judicial review procedures to review a final determination, a Party or other person intending to commence such procedures shall provide notice of such intent to the Parties concerned and to other persons entitled to commence such review procedures of the same final determination no later than 10 days prior to the latest date on which a panel may be requested; and

d) make the further amendments set out in its Schedule to Annex 1904.15.

Article 1905: Safeguarding the Panel Review System

1. Where a Party alleges that the application of another Party's domestic law:

   a) has prevented the establishment of a panel requested by the complaining Party;

   b) has prevented a panel requested by the complaining Party from rendering a final decision;

   c) has prevented the implementation of the decision of a panel requested by the complaining Party or denied it binding force and effect with respect to the particular matter that was before the panel; or

   d) has resulted in a failure to provide opportunity for review of a final determination by a panel or court of competent jurisdiction that is independent of the competent investigating authorities, that examines the basis for the competent investigating authority's determination and whether the competent investigating authority properly applied domestic antidumping and countervailing duty law in reaching the challenged determination, and that employs the relevant standard of review identified in Article 1911, the Party may request in writing consultations with the other Party regarding the allegations. The consultations shall begin within 15 days of the date of the request.

2. If the matter has not been resolved within 45 days of the request for consultations or such other period as the consulting Parties may agree, the complaining Party may request the establishment of a special committee.

3. Unless otherwise agreed by the disputing Parties, the special committee shall be established within 15 days of a request and perform its functions in a manner consistent with this Chapter.

4. The roster for special committees shall be that established under Annex 1904.13.

5. The special committee shall comprise three members selected in accordance with the procedures set out in Annex 1904.13.

6. The Parties shall establish rules of procedure in accordance with the principles set out in Annex 1905.6.

7. Where the special committee makes an affirmative finding with respect to one of the grounds specified in paragraph 1, the complaining Party and the Party complained against shall begin consultations within 10 days thereafter and shall seek to achieve a mutually satisfactory solution within 60 days of the issuance of the committee's report.

8. If, within the 60-day period, the Parties are unable to reach a mutually satisfactory solution to the matter, or the Party complained against has not demonstrated to the satisfaction of the special committee that it has corrected the problem or problems with respect to which the committee has made an affirmative finding, the complaining Party may suspend:

   a) the operation of Article 1904 with respect to the Party complained against; or

   b) the application to the Party complained against of such benefits under this Agreement as may be appropriate under the circumstances.

   If the complaining Party decides to take action under this paragraph, it shall do so within 30 days after the end of the 60-day consultation period.

9. In the event that a complaining Party suspends the operation of Article 1904 with respect to the Party complained against, the latter Party may reciprocally suspend the operation of Article

1904 within 30 days after the suspension of the operation of Article 1904 by the complaining Party. If either Party decides to suspend the operation of Article 1904, it shall provide written notice of such suspension to the other Party.

10. At the request of the Party complained against, the special committee shall reconvene to determine whether:

    a) the suspension of benefits by the complaining Party pursuant to paragraph 8b) is manifestly excessive; or

    b) the Party complained against has corrected the problem or problems with respect to which the committee has made an affirmative finding.

    The special committee shall within 45 days of the request, present a report to both Parties containing its determination, Where the special committee determines that the Party complained against has corrected the problem or problems, any suspension effected by the complaining Party or the Party complained against, or both, pursuant to paragraph 8 or 9 shall be terminated.

11. If the special committee makes an affirmative finding with respect to one of the grounds specified in paragraph 1, then effective as of the day following the date of issuance of the special committee's report:

    a) binational panel or extraordinary challenge committee review under Article 1904 shall be stayed

        i) in the case of review of any final determination of the complaining Party requested by the Party complained against, if such review was requested after the date on which consultations were requested pursuant to paragraph 1 and in no case more than 150 days prior to an affirmative finding by the special committee, or

ii) in the case of review of any final determination of the Party complained against requested by the complaining Party, on the request of the complaining Party; and

b) the time set out in Article 1904(4) or Annex 1904.13 for requesting panel or committee review shall not run unless and until resumed in accordance with paragraph 12.

12. If either Party suspends the operation of Article 1904 pursuant to paragraph 8(a), the panel or committee review stayed under paragraph 11(a) shall be terminated and the challenge to the final determination shall be irrevocably referred to the appropriate domestic court for decision, as provided below:

a) in the case of review of any final determination of the complaining Party requested by the Party complained against, on the request of either Party, or of a party to the panel review under Article 1904; or

b) in the case of review of any final determination of the Party complained against requested by the complaining Party, on the request of the complaining Party, or of a person of the complaining Party that is a party to the panel review under Article 1904.

If either Party suspends the operation of Article 1904 pursuant to paragraph 8(a), any running of time suspended under paragraph 11(b) shall resume.

If the suspension of the operation of Article 1904 does not become effective, panel or committee review stayed under paragraph 11(a), and any running of time suspended under paragraph 11 (b), shall resume.

13. If the complaining Party suspends the application to the Party complained against of such benefits under the Agreement as

may be appropriate under the circumstances pursuant to paragraph 8(b), panel or committee review stayed under paragraph 11(a), and any running of time suspended under paragraph 11(b), shall resume.

14. Each Party shall provide in its domestic legislation that, in the event of an affirmative finding by the special committee, the time for requesting judicial review of a final antidumping or countervailing duty determination shall not run unless and until the Parties concerned have negotiated a mutually satisfactory solution under paragraph 7, have suspended the operation of Article 1904 or the application of other benefits under paragraph 8.

Article 1906: Prospective Application

This Chapter shall apply only prospectively to:

a) final determinations of a competent investigating authority made after the date of entry into force of this Agreement; and

b) with respect to declaratory opinions under Article 1903, amendments to antidumping or countervailing duty statutes enacted after the date of entry into force of this Agreement.

Article 1907: Consultations

1. The Parties shall consult annually, or on the request of any Party, to consider any problems that may arise with respect to the implementation or operation of this Chapter and recommend solutions, where appropriate. The Parties shall each designate one or more officials, including officials of the competent investigating authorities, to be responsible for ensuring that consultations occur, when required, so that the provisions of this Chapter are carried out expeditiously.

2. The Parties further agree to consult on:

   a) the potential to develop more effective rules and disciplines concerning the use of government subsidies; and

   b) the potential for reliance on a substitute system of rules for dealing with unfair transborder pricing practices and government subsidization.

3. The competent investigating authorities of the Parties shall consult annually, or on the request of any Party, and may submit reports to the Commission, where appropriate. In the context of these consultations, the Parties agree that it is desirable in the administration of antidumping and countervailing duty laws to:

   a) publish notice of initiation of investigations in the importing Party's official journal, setting forth the name of the proceeding, the legal authority under which the proceeding is initiated, and a description of the goods at issue;

   b) provide notice of the times for submissions of information and for decisions that the competent investigating authorities are expressly required by statute or regulations to make;

   c) provide explicit written notice and instructions as to the information required from interested parties and reasonable time to respond to requests for information;

   d) accord reasonable access to information, noting that in this context

      i) "reasonable access" means access during the course of the investigation, to the extent practicable, so as to permit an opportunity to present facts and arguments as set out in sub-paragraph e) when it is not practicable to provide access to information during the investigation in such time as to permit an opportunity to present facts and arguments, reasonable access shall mean in time to permit the adversely affected party to make an informed decision as to whether to seek judicial or panel review, and

ii) "access to information" means access to representatives determined by the competent investigating authority to be qualified to have access to information received by that competent investigating authority, including access to confidential (business proprietary) information, but does not include information of such high degree of sensitivity that its release would lead to substantial and irreversible harm to the owner or which is required to be kept confidential in accordance with domestic legislation of a Party; any privileges arising under the domestic law of the importing Party relating to communications between the competent investigating authorities and a lawyer in the employ of, or providing advice to, those authorities may be maintained;

e) provide an opportunity tor interested parties to present facts and arguments to the extent time permits, including an opportunity to comment on the preliminary determination of dumping or of subsidization;

f) protect confidential (business proprietary) information received by the competent investigating authority to ensure that there is no disclosure except to representatives determined by the competent investigating authority to be qualified;

g) prepare administrative records, including recommendations of official advisory bodies that may be required to be kept, and any record of *ex parte* meetings that may be required to be kept;

h) provide disclosure of relevant information, including an explanation of the calculation or the methodology used to determine the margin of dumping or the amount of the subsidy, on which any preliminary or final determination of dumping or of subsidization is based, within a reasonable time after a request by interested parties;

i) provide a statement of reasons concerning the final determination of dumping or subsidization; and

j) provide a statement of reasons for final determinations concerning material injury to a domestic industry, threat of material injury to a domestic industry or material retardation of the establishment of such an industry.

Inclusion of an item in subparagraphs (a) through (j) is not intended to serve as guidance to a binational panel reviewing a final antidumping or countervailing duty determination pursuant to Article 1904 in determining whether such determination was in accordance with the antidumping or countervailing duty law of the importing Party.

Article 1908: Special Secretariat Provisions

1. The Parties shall establish a section within the Secretariat established pursuant to Article 2002 to facilitate the operation of this Chapter, including the work of panels or committees that may be convened pursuant to this Chapter.

2. The Secretaries of the Secretariat shall act jointly to provide administrative assistance to all panels or committees established pursuant to this Chapter. The Secretary for the Section of the Party in which a panel or committee proceeding is held shall prepare a record thereof and shall preserve an

authentic copy of the same in that Party's Section office. Such Secretary shall, on request, provide to the Secretary for the Section of any other Party a copy of such portion of the record as is requested, except that only public portions of the record shall be provided to the Secretary for the Section of any Party that is not an involved Party.

3. Each Secretary shall receive and file all requests, briefs and other papers properly presented to a panel or committee in any proceeding before it that is instituted pursuant to this Chapter and shall number in numerical order all requests for a panel or committee. The number given to a request shall be the file number for briefs and other papers relating to such request.

4. The Secretary for the Section of the Party in which a panel or committee proceeding is held shall forward to the Secretary for the Section of the other involved Party copies of all official letters, documents or other papers received or filed with that Party's Section office pertaining to any proceeding before a panel or committee, except for the administrative record, which shall be handled in accordance with paragraph 2. The Secretary for the Section of an involved Party shall provide on request to the Secretary for the Section of a Party that is not an involved Party in the proceeding a copy of such public documents as are requested.

Article 1909: Code of Conduct

The Parties shall, by the date of entry into force of this Agreement, exchange letters establishing a code of conduct for panelists and members of committees established pursuant to Articles 1903, 1904 and 1905.

Article 1910: Miscellaneous

On request of another Party, the competent investigating authority of a Party shall provide to the other Party copies of all public information submitted to it for purposes of an antidumping or countervailing duty investigation with respect to goods of that other Party.

Article 1911: Definitions

For purposes of this Chapter:

administrative record means, unless otherwise agreed by the Parties and the other persons appearing before a panel:

a) all documentary or other information presented to or obtained by the competent investigating authority in the course of the administrative proceeding, including any governmental memoranda pertaining to the case and including any record of *ex parte* meetings as may be required to be kept;

b) a copy of the final determination of the competent investigating authority, including reasons for the determination;

c) all transcripts or records of conferences or hearings before the competent investigating authority; and

d) all notices published in the official journal of the importing Party in connection with the administrative proceeding;

antidumping statute as referred to in Articles 1902 and 1903 means "antidumping statute" of a Party as defined in Annex 1911;

competent investigating authority means "competent investigating authority" of a Party as defined in Annex 1911;

countervailing duty statute as referred to in Articles 1902 and 1903 means "countervailing duty statute" of a Party as defined in Annex 1911;

domestic law for purposes of Article 1905(1) means a Party's constitution, statutes, regulations and judicial decisions to the extent they are relevant to the antidumping and countervailing duty laws;

final determination means final determination of a Party as defined in Annex 1911;

foreign interests includes exporters or producers of the Party whose goods are the subject of the proceeding or, in the case of a countervailing duty proceeding, the government of the Party whose goods are the subject of the proceeding;

general legal principles includes principles such as standing, due process, rules of statutory construction, mootness and exhaustion of administrative remedies;

goods of a Party means domestic products as these are understood in the *General Agreement on Tariff and Trade;*

importing Party means the Party that issued the final determination;

interested parties includes foreign interests;

involved Party means:

a) the importing Party; or

b) a Party whose goods are the subject of the final determination;

remand means a referral back for a determination not inconsistent with the panel or committee decision; and

standard of review means the "standard of review" for each Party as defined in Annex 1911.

Annex 1901.2
Establishment of Binational Panels

1. On the date of entry into force of this Agreement, the Parties shall establish and thereafter maintain a roster of individuals to serve as panelists in disputes under this Chapter. The roster shall include judges or former judges to the fullest extent practicable. The Parties shall consult in developing the roster, which shall include at least 75 candidates. Each Party shall select at least 25 candidates, and all candidates shall be citizens of Canada, Mexico or the United States. Candidates shall be of good character. high standing and repute, and shall be chosen strictly on the basis of objectivity, reliability, sound judgment and general familiarity with international trade law. Candidates shall not be affiliated with a Party, and in no event shall a candidate take instructions from a Party. The Parties shall maintain the roster, and may amend it, when necessary, after consultations.

2. A majority of the panelists on each panel shall be lawyers in good standing. Within 30 days of a request for a panel, each involved Party shall appoint two panelists, in consultation with the other involved Party. The involved Parties normally shall appoint panelists from the roster. If a panelist is not selected from the roster, the panelist shall be chosen in accordance with and be subject to the criteria of paragraph 1. Each involved Party shall have the right to exercise four peremptory challenges, to be exercised simultaneously and in confidence, disqualifying from appointment to the panel up to four candidates proposed by the other involved Party. Peremptory challenges and the selection of alternative panelists shall occur within 45 days of the request for the panel. If an involved Party fails to appoint its members to a panel within 30 days or if a panelist is struck and no alternative panelist is selected within 45 days, such panelist shall be selected by lot on the 31st or 46th

day, as the case may be, from that Party's candidates on the roster.

3. Within 55 days of the request for a panel, the involved Parties shall agree on the selection of a fifth panelist. If the involved Parties are unable to agree, they shall decide by lot which of them shall select, by the 61st day, the fifth panelist from the roster, excluding candidates eliminated by peremptory challenges.

4. On appointment of the fifth panelist, the panelists shall promptly appoint a chairman from among the lawyers on the panel by majority vote of the panelists. If there is no majority vote, the chairman shall be appointed by lot from among the lawyers on the panel.

5. Decisions of the panel shall be by majority vote and based on the votes of all members of the panel. The panel shall issue a written decision with reasons, together with any dissenting or concurring opinions of panelists.

6. Panelists shall be subject to the code of conduct established pursuant to Article 1909. If an involved Party believes that a panelist is in violation of the code of conduct, the involved Parties shall consult and if they agree, the panelist shall be removed and a new panelist shall be selected in accordance with the procedures of this Annex.

7. When a panel is convened pursuant to Article 1904 each panelist shall be required to sign:

   a) an application for a protective order for information supplied by the United States or its persons covering business proprietary and other privileged information;

b) an undertaking for information supplied by Canada or its persons covering confidential, personal, business proprietary and other privileged information; or

c) an undertaking for information supplied by Mexico or its persons covering confidential, business proprietary and other privileged information.

8. On a panelist's acceptance of the obligations and terms of an application for protective order or disclosure undertaking, the importing Party shall grant access to the information covered by such order or disclosure undertaking. Each Party shall establish appropriate sanctions for violations of protective orders or disclosure undertakings issued by or given to any Party. Each Party shall enforce such sanctions with respect to any person within its jurisdiction. Failure by a panelist to sign a protective order or disclosure undertaking shall result in disqualification of the panelist.

9. If a panelist becomes unable to fulfill panel duties or is disqualified, proceedings of the panel shall be suspended pending the selection of a substitute panelist in accordance with the procedures of this Annex.

10. Subject to the code of conduct established pursuant to Article 1909, and provided that it does not interfere with the performance of the duties of such panelist, a panelist may engage in other business during the term of the panel.

11. While acting as a panelist, a panelist may not appear as counsel before another panel.

12. With the exception of violations of protective orders or disclosure undertakings, signed pursuant to paragraph 7, panelists shall be immune from suit and legal process relating to acts performed by them in their official capacity.

Annex 1903.2
Panel Procedures Under Article 1903

1. The panel shall establish its own rules of procedure unless the Parties otherwise agree prior to the establishment of that panel. The procedures shall ensure a right to at least one hearing before the panel, as well as the opportunity to provide written submissions and rebuttal arguments. The proceedings of the panel shall be confidential, unless the two Parties otherwise agree. The panel shall base its decisions solely on the arguments and submissions of the two Parties.

2. Unless the Parties to the dispute otherwise agree, the panel shall, within 90 days after its chairman is appointed, present to the two Parties an initial written declaratory opinion containing findings of fact and its determination pursuant to Article 1903.

3. If the findings of the panel are affirmative, the panel may include in its report its recommendations as to the means by which the amending statute could be brought into conformity with the provisions of Article 1902(2)(d). In determining what, if any, recommendations are appropriate, the panel shall consider the extent to which the amending statute affects interests under this Agreement. Individual panelists may provide separate opinions on matters not unanimously agreed. The initial opinion of the panel shall become the final declaratory opinion, unless a Party to the dispute requests a reconsideration of the initial opinion pursuant to paragraph 4.

4. Within 14 days of the issuance of the initial declaratory opinion, a Party to the dispute disagreeing in whole or in part with the opinion may present a written statement of its objections and the reasons for those objections to the panel. In such event, the panel shall request the views of both Parties and shall reconsider its initial opinion. The panel shall conduct any further examination that it deems appropriate, and shall issue a final written opinion, together with dissenting or concurring views of

individual panelists, within 30 days of the request for reconsideration.

5. Unless the Parties to the dispute otherwise agree, the final declaratory opinion of the panel shall be made public, along with any separate opinions of individual panelists and any written views that either Party may wish to be published.

6. Unless the Parties to the dispute otherwise agree, meetings and hearings of the panel shall take place at the office of the amending Party's Section of the Secretariat.

Annex 1904.13
Extraordinary Challenge Procedure

1. The involved Parties shall establish an extraordinary challenge committee, composed of three members, within 15 days of a request pursuant to Article 1904(13). The members shall be selected from a 15-person roster comprised of judges or former judges of a federal judicial court of the United States or a judicial court of superior jurisdiction of Canada, or a federal judicial court of Mexico. Each Party shall name five persons to this roster. Each involved Party shall select one member from this roster and the involved Parties shall decide by lot which of them shall select the third member from the roster.

2. The Parties shall establish by the date of entry into force of the Agreement rules of procedure for committees. The rules shall provide for a decision of a committee within 90 days of its establishment.

3. Committee decisions shall be binding on the Parties with respect to the particular matter between the Parties that was before the panel. After examination of the legal and factual analysis underlying the findings and conclusions of the panel's decision in order to determine whether one of the grounds set out in Article 1904(13) has been established, and on finding that one

of those grounds has been established, the committee shall vacate the original panel decision or remand it to the original panel for action not inconsistent with the committee's decision; if the grounds are not established, it shall deny the challenge and, therefore, the original panel decision shall stand affirmed. If the original decision is vacated, a new panel shall be established pursuant to Annex 1901.2.

Annex 1904.15
Amendments to Domestic Laws

Schedule of Canada

Canada shall amend sections 56 and 58 of the *Special Import Measures Act,* as amended, to allow the United States with respect to goods of the United States or Mexico with respect to goods of Mexico or a United States or a Mexican manufacturer, producer or exporter, without regard to payment of duties, to make a written request for a redetermination; and section 59 to require the Deputy Minister to make a ruling on a request for a redetermination within one year of a request to a designated officer or other customs officer.

2. Canada shall amend section 18.3(1) of the *Federal Court Act,* as amended, to render that section inapplicable to the United States and to Mexico; and shall provide in its statutes or regulations that persons (including producers of goods subject to an investigation) have standing to ask Canada to request a panel review where such persons would be entitled to commence domestic procedures for judicial review if the final determination were reviewable by the Federal Court pursuant to section 18.1(4).

3. Canada shall amend the *Special Import Measures Act,* as amended, and any other relevant provisions of law, to provide that the following actions of the Deputy Minister shall be deemed

for the purposes of this Article to be final determinations subject to judicial review:

a) a determination by the Deputy Minister pursuant to section 41;

b) a re-determination by the Deputy Minister pursuant to section 59; and

c) a review by the Deputy Minister of an undertaking pursuant to section 53(1).

4. Canada shall amend Part II of the *Special Import Measures Act,* as amended, to provide for binational panel review respecting goods of Mexico and the United States.

5. Canada shall amend Part II of the *Special Import Measures Act,* as amended, to provide for definitions related to this Chapter, as may be required.

6. Canada shall amend Part II of the *Special Import Measures Act,* as amended, to permit the governments of Mexico and the United States to request binational panel review of final determinations respecting goods of Mexico and the United States.

7. Canada shall amend Part II of the *Special Import Measures Act,* as amended, to provide for the establishment of binational panels requested to review final determinations in respect of goods of Mexico and the United States.

8. Canada shall amend Part II of the *Special Import Measures Act,* as amended, to provide that binational panel review of a final determination shall be conducted in accordance with this Chapter.

9. Canada shall amend Part II of the *Special Import Measures Act, as* amended, to provide that an extraordinary challenge proceeding shall be requested and conducted in accordance with Article 1904 and Annex 1904.13.

10. Canada shall amend Part II of the *Special Import Measures* Act, as amended, to provide for a code of conduct, immunity for anything done or omitted to be done during the course of panel proceedings, the signing of and compliance with disclosure undertakings respecting confidential information, and remuneration for members of panels and committees established pursuant to this Chapter.

11. Canada shall make such amendments as are necessary to establish a Canadian Secretariat for this Agreement and generally to facilitate the operation of this Chapter and the work of the binational panels, extraordinary challenge committees and special committees convened under this Chapter.

Schedule of Mexico

Mexico shall amend its antidumping and countervailing duty statutes and regulations, and other statutes and regulations to the extent that they apply to the operation of the antidumping and countervailing duty laws, to provide the following:

a) elimination of the possibility of imposing duties within the five-day period after the acceptance of a petition;

b) substitution of the term *Initial Resolution* ("Resolución de Inicio") for the term *Provisional Resolution* ("Resolución Provisional") and the term *Provisional Resolution* ("Resolución Provisional") for the term *Resolution Reviewing the Provisional Resolution* ("Resolución que revisa a la Resolución Provisional");

c) full participation in the administrative process for interested parties, as well as the right to administrative appeal and judicial review of final determinations of investigations, reviews, product coverage or other final decisions affecting them;

d) elimination of the possibility of imposing provisional duties before the issuance of a preliminary determination;

e) the right to immediate access to review of final determinations by binational panels for interested parties, without the need to exhaust first the administrative appeal;

f) explicit and adequate timetables for determinations of the competent investigating authority and for the submission of questionnaires, evidence and comments by interested parties, as well as an opportunity for them to present facts and arguments in support of their positions prior to any final determination, to the extent time permits, including an opportunity to be adequately informed in a timely manner of and to comment on all aspects of preliminary determinations of dumping or subsidization;

g) written notice to interested parties of any of the actions or resolutions rendered by the competent investigating authority, including initiation of an administrative review as well as its conclusion;

h) disclosure meetings with interested parties by the competent investigating authority conducting its investigations and reviews, within seven calendar days after the date of publication in the *Diario Oficial de la Federación* ("Federal Official Journal") of preliminary and final determinations, to explain the margins of dumping and the amount of subsidies calculations and to provide the interested parties with copies of sample calculations and, if used, computer programs;

i) timely access by eligible counsel of interested parties during the course of the proceeding (including disclosure meetings) and on appeal, either before a national tribunal or a panel, to all information contained in the administrative record of the proceeding, including confidential information, excepting proprietary information of such a high degree of sensitivity that its release would lead to substantial and irreversible harm to the owner as well as government classified information, subject to an undertaking for confidentiality that strictly forbids use of the information for personal benefit and its disclosure to persons who are not authorized to receive such information; and for sanctions that are specific to violations of undertakings in proceedings before national tribunals or panels;

j) timely access by interested parties during the course of the proceeding, to all nonconfidential information contained in the administrative record and access to such information by interested parties or their representatives in any proceeding after 90 days following the issuance of the final determination;

k) a mechanism requiring that any person submitting documents to the competent investigating authority shall simultaneously serve on interested persons, including foreign interests, any submissions after the complaint;

l) preparation of summaries of *ex parte* meetings held between the competent investigating authority and any interested party and the inclusion in the administrative record of such summaries, which shall be made available to parties to the proceeding; if such summaries contain business proprietary information, the documents must be disclosed to a party's representative under an undertaking to ensure confidentiality;

m) maintenance by the competent investigating authority of an administrative record as defined in this Chapter and a requirement that the final determination be based solely on the administrative record;

n) informing interested parties in writing of all data and information the administering authority requires them to submit for the investigation, review, product coverage proceeding, or other antidumping or countervailing duty proceeding;

o) the right to an annual individual review on request by the interested parties through which they can obtain their own dumping margin or countervailing duty rate, or can change the margin or rate they received in the investigation or a previous review, reserving to the competent investigating authority the ability to initiate a review, at any time, on its own motion and requiring that the competent investigating authority issue a notice of initiation within a reasonable period of time after the request;

p) application of determinations issued as a result of judicial, administrative, or panel review to the extent they are relevant to interested parties in addition to the plaintiff, so that all interested parties will benefit;

q) issuance of binding decisions by the competent investigating authority if an interested party seeks clarification outside the context of an antidumping or countervailing duty investigation or review with respect to whether a particular product is covered by an antidumping or countervailing duty order;

r) a detailed statement of reasons and the legal basis for final determinations in a manner sufficient to permit interested parties to make an informed decision as to whether to seek judicial or panel review, including an explanation of methodological or policy issues raised in the calculation of dumping or subsidization;

s) written notice to interested parties and publication in the *Federal Official Journal* ("Diario Oficial de la Federación") of initiation of investigations setting forth the nature of the proceeding, the legal authority under which the proceeding is initiated, and a description of the product at issue;

t) documentation in writing of all advisory bodies' decisions or recommendations, including the basis for the decisions, and release of such written decisions to parties to the proceeding; all decisions or recommendations of any advisory body shall be placed in the administrative record and made available to parties to the proceeding; and

u) a standard of review to be applied by binational panels as set out in subparagraph (c) of the definition of "standard of review" in Annex 1911.

Schedule of the United States

1. The United States shall amend section 301 of the *Customs Courts Act of 1980,* as amended, and any other relevant provisions of law, to eliminate the authority to issue declaratory judgments in any civil action involving an antidumping or countervailing duty proceeding regarding a class or kind of Canadian or Mexican merchandise.

2. The United States shall amend section 405(a) of the *United States - Canada Free Trade Agreement Implementation Act of 1988, to* provide that the interagency group established under section 242 of the *Trade Expansion Act of 1962* shall prepare a list of individuals qualified to serve as members of binational panels, extraordinary challenge committees and special committees convened under this Chapter.

3. The United States shall amend section 405(b) of the *United States - Canada Free Trade Agreement Implementation Act of 1988, to* provide that panelists selected to serve on panels or committees convened pursuant to this Chapter, and individuals designated to assist such appointed individuals, shall not be considered employees of the United States.

4. The United States shall amend section 405(c) of the *United States - Canada Free Trade Agreement Implementation Act of 1988, to* provide that panelists selected to serve on panels or committees convened pursuant to this Chapter, and individuals designated to assist the individuals serving on such panels or committees, shall be immune from suit and legal process relating to acts performed by such individuals in their official capacity and within the scope of their functions as such panelists or committee members, except with respect to the violation of protective orders described in section 777f(d)(3) of the *Tariff Act of 1930,* as amended.

5. The United States shall amend section 405(d)of the *United States - Canada Free Trade Agreement Implementation Act of 1988*, to establish a United States Secretariat to facilitate the operation of this Chapter and the work of the binational panels, extraordinary challenge committees and special committees convened under this Chapter.

6. The United States shall amend section 407 of the *United States-Canada Free Trade Agreement Implementation Act of 1988*, to provide that an extraordinary challenge committee convened pursuant to Article 1904 and Annex 1904.13 shall have authority to obtain information in the event of an allegation that a member of a binational panel was guilty of gross misconduct, bias, or a serious conflict of interest, or otherwise materially violated the rules of conduct, and for the committee to summon the attendance of witnesses, order the taking of depositions and obtain the assistance of any district or territorial court of the United States in aid of the committee's investigation.

7. The United States shall amend section 408 of the *United States-Canada Free Trade Agreement Implementation Act of 1988,* to provide that, in the case of a final determination of a competent investigating authority of Mexico, as well as Canada, the filing with the United States Secretary of a request for binational panel review by a person described in Article 1904(5) shall be deemed, on receipt of the request by the Secretary, to be a request for binational panel review within the meaning of Article 1904(4).

8. The United States shall amend section 516A of the *Tariff Act of 1930*, as amended, to provide that judicial review of antidumping or countervailing duty cases regarding Mexican, as well as Canadian, merchandise shall not be commenced in the Court of International Trade if binational panel review is requested.

9. The United States shall amend section 516A(a) of the *Tariff Act of 1930*, as amended to provide that the time limits for commencing an action in the Court of International Trade with regard to antidumping or countervailing duty proceedings involving Mexican or Canadian merchandise shall not begin to run until the 31st day after the date of publication in the *Federal Register* of notice of the final determination or the antidumping duty order.

10. The United States shall amend section 516A(g) of the *Tariff Act of 1930,* as amended, to provide, in accordance with the terms of this Chapter, for binational panel review of antidumping and countervailing duty cases involving Mexican or Canadian merchandise. Such amendment shall provide that if binational panel review is requested such review will be exclusive.

11. The United States shall amend section 516A(g) of the *Tariff Act of 1930,* as amended, to provide that the competent investigating authority shall, within the period specified by any panel formed to review a final determination regarding Mexican

or Canadian merchandise, take action not inconsistent with the decision of the panel or committee.

12. The United States shall amend section 777 of the *Tariff Act of 1930*, as amended, to provide for the disclosure to authorized persons under protective order of proprietary information in the administrative record, if binational panel review of a final determination regarding Mexican or Canadian merchandise is requested.

13. The United States shall amend section 777 of the *Tariff Act of 1930,* as amended, to provide for the imposition of sanctions on any person who the competent investigating authority finds to have violated a protective order issued by the competent investigating authority of the United States or disclosure undertakings entered into with an authorized agency of Mexico or with a competent investigating authority of Canada to protect proprietary material during binational panel review.

Annex 1905.6
Special Committee Procedures

The Parties shall establish rules of procedure by the date of entry into force of this Agreement in accordance with the following principles;

a) the procedures shall assure a right to at least one hearing before the special committee as well as the opportunity to provide initial and rebuttal written submissions;

b) the procedures shall assure that the special committee shall prepare an initial report typically within 60 days of the appointment of the last member, and shall afford the Parties 14 days to comment on that report prior to issuing a final report 30 days after presentation of the initial report;

c) the special committee's hearings, deliberations, and initial report, and all written submissions to and communications with the special committee shall be confidential;

d) unless the Parties to the dispute otherwise agree, the decision of the special committee shall be published 10 days after it is transmitted to the disputing Parties, along with any separate opinions of individual members and any written views that either Party may wish to be published; and

e) unless the Parties to the dispute otherwise agree, meetings and hearings of the special committee shall take place at the office of the Section of the Secretariat of the Party complained against.

Annex 1911
Country-Specific Definitions

For purposes of this Chapter:

antidumping statute means:

a) in the case of Canada, the relevant provisions of the *Special Import Measures Act*, as amended, and any successor statutes;

b) in the case of the United States, the relevant provisions of Title VII of the *Tariff Act of 1930*, as amended, and any successor statutes;

c) in the case of Mexico, the relevant provisions of the *Foreign Trade Act Implementing Article 131 of the Constitution of the United Mexican States* ("Ley Reglamentaria del Artículo 131 de la Constitucion Politica de los Estados Unidos

Mexicanos en Matena de Comercio Exterior"), as amended, and any successor statutes; and

d) the provisions of any other statute that provides for judicial review of final determinations under subparagraph (a), (b) or (c), or indicates the standard of review to be applied to such determinations;

competent investigating authority means:

a) in the case of Canada,

   i) the Canadian International Trade Tribunal, or its successor, or

   ii) the Deputy Minister of National Revenue for Customs and Excise as defined in the *Special Import Measures Act,* as amended, or the Deputy Minister's successor;

b) in the case of the United States,

   i) the International Trade Administration of the United States Department of Commerce, or its successor, or

   ii) the United States International Trade Commission, or its successor; and

c) in the case of Mexico, the designated authority within the *Secretariat of Trade and Industrial Development* ("Secretaría de Comercio y Fomento Industrial"), or its successor;

countervailing duty statute means:

a) in the case of Canada, the relevant provisions of the *Special Import Measures Act,* as amended, and any successor statutes;

b) in the case of the United States, section 303 and the relevant provisions of Title VII of the *Tariff Act of 1930*, as amended, and any successor statutes;

c) in the case of Mexico, the relevant provisions of the *Foreign Trade Act Implementing Article 131 of the Constitution of the United Mexican States* ("Ley Reglamentaria del Articulo 131 de la Constitución Politica de los Estados Unidos Mexicanos en Materia de Comercio Exterior"), as amended, and any successor statutes; and

d) the provisions of any other status that provides for judicial review of final determinations under subparagraph (a), (b) or (c), or indicates the standard of review to be applied to such determinations;

final determination means:

a) in the case of Canada,

  i) an order or finding of the Canadian International Trade Tribunal under subsection 43(1) of the *Special Import Measures Act,*

  ii) an order by the Canadian International Trade Tribunal under subsection 76(4) of the *Special Import Measures Act,* as amended, continuing an order or finding made under subsection 43(1) of the Act with or without amendment,

  (iii) a determination by the Deputy Minister of National Revenue for Customs and Excise pursuant to section 41 of the *Special Import Measures Act,* as amended,

  (iv) a redetermination by the Deputy Minister pursuant to section 59 of the *Special Import Measures Act*, as amended,

(v) a decision by the Canadian International Trade Tribunal pursuant to subsection 76(3) of the *Special Import Measures Act,* as amended, not to initiate a review,

(vi) a reconsideration by the Canadian International Trade Tribunal pursuant to subsection 91(3) of the *Special Import Measures Act,* as amended, and

(vii) a review by the Deputy Minister of an undertaking pursuant to section 53(1) of the *Special Import Measures Act,* as amended;

b) in the case of the United States,

i) a final affirmative determination by the International Trade Administration of the U.S. Department of Commerce or by the U.S. International Trade Commission under section 705 or 735 of the *Tariff Act of 1930,* as amended, including any negative part of such a determination,

ii) a final negative determination by the International Trade Administration of the U.S. Department of Commerce or by the U.S. International Trade Commission under section 705 or 735 of the *Tariff Act of 1930,* as amended, including any affirmative part of such a determination,

(iii) a final determination, other than a determination in (iv), under section 751 of the *Tariff Act of 1930,* as amended,

(iv) a determination by the U.S. International Trade Commission under section 751f(b) of the *Tariff Act of 1930,* as amended, not to review a determination based on changed circumstances, and

(v) a final determination by the International Trade Administration of the U.S. Department of Commerce as to whether a particular type of merchandise is within the class or kind of merchandise described in an existing finding of dumping or antidumping or countervailing duty order; and

c) in the case of Mexico,

i) a final resolution regarding antidumping or countervailing duties investigations by the *Secretariat of Trade and Industrial Development* ("Secretaría de Comercio y Fomento Industrial"), pursuant to Article 13 of the *Foreign Trade Act Implementing Article 131 of the Constitution of the United Mexican States* ("Ley Reglamentaria del Articulo 131 de la Constitución Politica de los Estados Unidos Mexicanos en Materia de Comercio Exterior"), as amended,

ii) a final resolution regarding an annual administrative review of antidumping or countervailing duties by the *Secretariat of Trade and Industrial Development* ("Secretaría de Comercio y Fomento Industrial"), as described in paragraph (o) of its Schedule to Annex 1904.15, and

(iii) a final resolution by the *Secretariat of Trade and Industrial Development* ("Secretaría de Comercio y Fomento Industrial") as to whether a particular type of merchandise is within the class or kind of merchandise described in an existing antidumping or countervailing duty resolution; and

standard of review means the following standards, as may be amended from time to time by the relevant Party:

a) in the case of Canada, the grounds set out in subsection 18.1(4) of the *Federal Court Act,* as amended, with respect to all final determinations;

b) in the case of the United States,

   i) the standard set out in section 516A(b)(1)(B) of the *Tariff Act of 1930*, as amended, with the exception of a determination referred to in (ii), and

   ii) the standard set out in section 516Ab)(1)(a) of the *Tariff Act of 1930*, as amended, with respect to a determination by the U.S. International Trade Commission not to initiate a review pursuant to section 751(b) of the *Tariff Act of 1930,* as amended; and

c) in the case of Mexico, the standard set out in Article 238 of the *Federal Fiscal Code* ("Código Fiscal de la Federación"), or any successor statutes, based solely on the administrative record.

CHAPTER 20: INSTITUTIONAL ARRANGEMENTS AND DISPUTE SETTLEMENT PROCEDURES

Section A - Institutions

Article 2001: The Free Trade Commission

1. The Parties hereby establish the Free Trade Commission, comprising cabinet-level representatives of the Parties or their designees.

2. The Commission shall:

   a) supervise the implementation of this Agreement;

b) oversee its further elaboration;

c) resolve disputes that may arise regarding its interpretation or application;

d) supervise the work of all committees and working groups established under this Agreement, referred to in Annex 2001.2; and

e) consider any other matter that may affect the operation of this Agreement.

3. The Commission may:

a) establish, and delegate responsibilities to, ad hoc or standing committees working groups or expert groups;

b) seek the advice of nongovernmental persons or groups; and

c) take such other action in the exercise of its functions as the Parties may agree.

4. The Commission shall establish its rules and procedures. All decisions of the Commission shall be taken by consensus, except as the Commission may otherwise agree.

5. The Commission shall convene at least once a year in regular session. Regular sessions of the Commission shall be chaired successively by each Party.

Article 2002: The Secretariat

1. The Commission shall establish and oversee a Secretariat comprising national Sections.

2. Each Party shall:

a) establish a permanent office of its Section;

b) be responsible for

i) the operation and costs of its Section, and

ii) the remuneration and payment of expenses of panelists and members of committees and scientific review boards established under this Agreement, as set out in Annex 2002.2;

c) designate an individual to serve as Secretary for its Section, who shall be responsible for its administration and management; and

d) notify the Commission of the location of its Section's office.

3. The Secretariat shall:

a) provide assistance to the Commission;

b) provide administrative assistance to

i) panels and committees established under Chapter Nineteen (Review and Dispute Settlement in Antidumping and Countervailing Duty Matters), in accordance with the procedures established pursuant to Article 1908, and

ii) panels established under this Chapter, in accordance with procedures established pursuant to Article 2012; and

c) as the Commission may direct

i) support the work of other committees and groups established under this Agreement, and

ii) otherwise facilitate the operation of this Agreement.

Section B - Dispute Settlement

Article 2003: Cooperation

The Parties shall at all times endeavor to agree on the interpretation and application of this Agreement, and shall make every attempt through cooperation and consultations to arrive at a mutually satisfactory resolution of any matter that might affect its operation.

Article 2004: Recourse to Dispute Settlement Procedures

Except for the matters covered in Chapter Nineteen (Review and Dispute Settlement in Antidumping and Countervailing Duty Matters) and as otherwise provided in this Agreement, the dispute settlement provisions of this Chapter shall apply with respect to the avoidance or settlement of all disputes between the Parties regarding the interpretation or application of this Agreement or wherever a Party considers that an actual or proposed measure of another Party is or would be inconsistent with the obligations of this Agreement or cause nullification or impairment in the sense of Annex 2004.

Article 2005: GATT Dispute Settlement

1. Subject to paragraphs 2, 3 and 4, disputes regarding any matter arising under both this Agreement and the *General Agreement on Tariffs and Trade*, any agreement negotiated thereunder, or any successor agreement (GATT), may be settled in either forum at the discretion of the complaining Party.

2. Before a Party initiates a dispute settlement proceeding in the GATT against another Party on grounds that are substantially equivalent to those available to that Party under this Agreement, that Party shall notify any third Party of its intention. If a third Party wishes to have recourse to dispute settlement procedures under this Agreement regarding the matter, it shall inform promptly the notifying Party and those Parties shall consult with a view to agreement on a single forum. If those Parties cannot agree, the dispute normally shall be settled under this Agreement.

3. In any dispute referred to in paragraph 1 where the responding Party claims that its action is subject to Article 104 (Relation to Environmental and Conservation Agreements) and requests in writing that the matter be considered under this Agreement, the complaining Party may, in respect of that matter, thereafter have recourse to dispute settlement procedures solely under this Agreement.

4. In any dispute referred to in paragraph 1 that arises under Section B of Chapter Seven (Sanitary and Phytosanitary Measures) or Chapter Nine (Standards-Related Measures);

   a) concerning a measure adopted or maintained by a Party to protect its human, animal or plant life or health, or to protect its environment, and

   b) that raises factual issues concerning the environment, health, safety or conservation including directly related scientific matters,

   where the responding Party requests in writing that the matter be considered under this Agreement the complaining Party may, in respect of that matter, thereafter have recourse to dispute settlement procedures solely under this Agreement.

5. The responding Party shall deliver a copy of a request made pursuant to paragraph 3 or 4 to the other Parties and to its Section of the Secretariat. Where the complaining Party has initiated dispute settlement proceedings regarding any matter subject to paragraph 3 or 4, the responding Party shall deliver its request no later than 15 days thereafter. On receipt of such request, the complaining Party shall promptly withdraw from participation in those proceedings and may initiate dispute settlement procedures under Article 2007.

6. Once dispute settlement procedures have been initiated under Article 2007 or dispute settlement proceedings have been initiated under the GATT, the forum selected shall be used to the exclusion of the other, unless a Party makes a request pursuant to paragraph 3 or 4.

7. For purposes of this Article, dispute settlement proceedings under the GATT are deemed to be initiated by a Party's request for a panel, such as under Article XXIII:2 of the *General Agreement on Tariffs and Trade 1947*, or for a committee investigation, such as under Article 20.1 of the Customs Valuation Code.

Consultations

Article 2006: Consultations

1. Any Party may request in writing consultations with any other Party regarding any actual or proposed measure or any other matter that it considers might affect the operation of this Agreement.

2. The requesting Party shall deliver the request to the other Parties and to its Section of the Secretariat.

3. Unless the Commission otherwise provides in its rules and procedures established under Article 2001(4), a third Party that

considers it has a substantial interest in the matter shall be entitled to participate in the consultations on delivery of written notice to the other Parties and to its Section of the Secretariat.

4. Consultations on matters regarding perishable agricultural goods shall commence within 15 days of the date of delivery of the request.

5. The consulting Parties shall make every attempt to arrive at a mutually satisfactory resolution of any matter through consultations under this Article or other consultative provisions of this Agreement. To this end, the consulting Parties shall:

   a) provide sufficient information to enable a full examination of how the actual or proposed measure or other matter might affect the operation of this Agreement;

   b) treat any confidential or proprietary information exchanged in the course of consultations on the same basis as the Party providing the information; and

   c) seek to avoid any resolution that adversely affects the interests under this Agreement of any other Party.

Initiation of Procedures

Article 2007: Commission - Good Offices, Conciliation and Mediation

1. If the consulting Parties fail to resolve a matter pursuant to Article 2006 within;

   a) 30 days of delivery of a request for consultations,

   b) 45 days of delivery of such request if any other Party has subsequently requested or has participated in consultations regarding the same matter,

c) 15 days of delivery of a request for consultations in matters regarding perishable agricultural goods, or

d) such other period as they may agree,

any such Party may request in writing a meeting of the Commission.

2. A Party may also request in writing a meeting of the Commission where:

   a) it has initiated dispute settlement proceedings under the GATT regarding any matter subject to Article 2005(3) or (4), and has received a request pursuant to Article 2005(5) tor recourse to dispute settlement procedures under this Chapter; or

   b) consultations have been held pursuant to Article 513 (Working Group on Rules of Origin), Article 723 (Sanitary and Phytosanitary Measures–Technical Consultations) and Article 914 (Standards Related Measures Technical Consultations).

3. The requesting Party shall state in the request the measure or other matter complained of and indicate the provisions of this Agreement that it considers relevant, and shall deliver the request to the other Parties and to its Section of the Secretariat.

4. Unless it decides otherwise, the Commission shall convene within 10 days of delivery of the request and shall endeavor to resolve the dispute promptly.

5. The Commission may:

   a) call on such technical advisers or create such working groups or expert groups as it deems necessary,

b) have recourse to good offices, conciliation, mediation or such other dispute resolution procedures, or

c) make recommendations,

as may assist the consulting Parties to reach a mutually satisfactory resolution of the dispute.

6. Unless it decides otherwise, the Commission shall consolidate two or more proceedings before it pursuant to this Article regarding the same measure. The Commission may consolidate two or more proceedings regarding other matters before it pursuant to this Article that it determines are appropriate to be considered jointly.

Panel Proceedings

Article 2008: Request for an Arbitral Panel

1. If the Commission has convened pursuant to Article 2007(4), and the matter has not been resolved within:

   a) 30 days thereafter,

   b) 30 days after the Commission has convened in respect of the matter most recently referred to it, where proceedings have been consolidated pursuant to Article 2007(6), or

   c) such other period as the consulting Parties may agree, any consulting Party may request in writing the establishment of an arbitral panel. The requesting Party shall deliver the request to the other Parties and to its Section of the Secretariat.

2. On delivery of the request, the Commission shall establish an arbitral panel.

3. A third Party that considers it has a substantial interest in the matter shall be entitled to join as a complaining Party on delivery of written notice of its intention to participate to the disputing Parties and its Section of the Secretariat. The notice shall be delivered at the earliest possible time, and in any event no later than seven days after the date of delivery of a request by a Party for the establishment of a panel.

4. If a third Party does not join as a complaining Party in accordance with paragraph 3, it normally shall refrain thereafter from initiating or continuing:

   a) a dispute settlement procedure under this Agreement, or

   b) a dispute settlement proceeding in the GATT on grounds that are substantially equivalent to those available to that Party under this Agreement, regarding the same matter in the absence of a significant change in economic or commercial circumstances.

5. Unless otherwise agreed by the disputing Parties, the panel shall be established and perform its functions in a manner consistent with the provisions of this Chapter.

Article 2009: Roster

1. The Parties shall establish by January 1, 1994 and maintain a roster of up to 30 individuals who are willing and able to serve as panelists. The roster members shall be appointed by consensus for terms of three years, and may be reappointed.

2. Roster members shall:

   a) have expertise or experience in law, international trade, other matters covered by this Agreement or the resolution of disputes arising under international trade agreements and shall be chosen strictly on the basis of objectivity reliability and sound judgment;

b) be independent of, and not be affiliated with or take instructions trom, any Party; and

c) comply with a code of conduct to be established by the Commission.

Article 2010: Qualifications of Panelists

l. All panelists shall meet the qualifications set out in Article 2009(2).

2. Individuals may not serve as panelists for a dispute in which they have participated pursuant to Article 2007(5).

Article 2011: Panel Selection

1. Where there are two disputing Parties, the following procedures shall apply:

   a) The panel shall comprise five members.

   b) The disputing Parties shall endeavor to agree on the chair of the panel within 15 days of the delivery of the request for the establishment of the panel. If the disputing parties are unable to agree on the chair within this period, the disputing Party chosen by lot shall select within five days as chair an individual who is not a citizen of that Party.

   c) Within 15 days of selection of the chair, each disputing Party shall select two panelists who are citizens of the other disputing Party.

   d) If a disputing Party fails to select its panelists within such period, such panelists shall be selected by lot from among the roster members who are citizens of the other disputing Party.

2. Where there are more than two disputing Parties, the following procedures shall apply:

   a) The panel shall comprise five members.

   b) The disputing Parties shall endeavor to agree on the chair of the panel within 15 days of the delivery of the request for the establishment of the panel. If the disputing Parties are unable to agree on the chair within this period, the Party or Parties on the side of the dispute chosen by lot shall select within 10 days a chair who is not a citizen of such Party or Parties.

   c) Within 15 days of selection of the chair, the Party complained against shall select two panelists, one of whom is a citizen of a complaining Party, and the other of whom is a citizen of another complaining Party. The complaining Parties shall select two panelists who are citizens of the Party complained against.

   d) If any disputing Party fails to select a panelist within such period such panelist shall be selected by lot in accordance with the citizenship criteria of subparagraph (c).

3. Panelists shall normally be selected from the roster. Any disputing Party may exercise a peremptory challenge against any individual not on the roster who is proposed as a panelist by a disputing Party within 15 days after the individual has been proposed.

4. If a disputing Party believes that a panelist is in violation of the code of conduct, the disputing Parties shall consult and if they agree, the panelist shall be removed and a new Panelist shall be selected in accordance with this Article.

Article 2012: Rules of Procedure

1. The Commission shall establish by January I, 1994 Model Rules of Procedure, in accordance with the following principles:

   a) the procedures shall assure a right to at least one hearing before the panel as well as the opportunity to provide initial and rebuttal written submissions; and

   b) the panel's hearings, deliberations and initial report, and all written submissions to and communications with the panel shall be confidential.

2. Unless the disputing Parties otherwise agree, the panel shall conduct its proceedings in accordance with the Model Rules of Procedure.

3. Unless the disputing Parties otherwise agree within 20 days from the date of the delivery of the request for the establishment of the panel, the terms of reference shall be:

   > To examine, in the light of the relevant provisions of the Agreement, the matter referred to the Commission (as set out in the request for a Commission meeting) and to make findings, determinations and recommendations as provided in Article 2016(2).

4. If a complaining Party wishes to argue that a matter has nullified or impaired benefits, the terms of reference shall so indicate.

5. If a disputing Party wishes the panel to make findings as to the degree of adverse trade effects on any Party of any measure found not to conform with the obligations of the Agreement or to have caused nullification or impairment in the sense of Annex 2004, the terms of reference shall so indicate.

Article 2013: Third Party Participation

A Party that is not a disputing Party, on delivery of a written notice to the disputing Parties and to its Section of the Secretariat, shall be entitled to attend all hearings, to make written and oral submissions to the panel and to receive written submissions of the disputing Parties.

Article 2014: Role of Experts

On request of a disputing Party, or on its own initiative, the panel may seek information and technical advice from any person or body that it deems appropriate, provided that the disputing Parties so agree and subject to such terms and conditions as such Parties may agree.

Article 2015: Scientific Review Boards

1. On request of a disputing Party or, unless the disputing Parties disapprove, on its own initiative, the panel may request a written report of a scientific review board on any factual issue concerning environmental, health, safety or other scientific matters raised by a disputing Party in a proceeding, subject to such terms and conditions as such Parties may agree.

2. The board shall be selected by the panel from among highly qualified, independent experts in the scientific matters, after consultations with the disputing Parties and the scientific bodies set out in the Model Rules of Procedure established pursuant to Article 2012(1).

3. The participating Parties shall be provided:

    a) advance notice of, and an opportunity to provide comments to the panel on, the proposed factual issues to be referred to the board; and

b) a copy of the board's report and an opportunity to provide comments on the report to the panel.

4. The panel shall take the board's report and any comments by the Parties on the report into account in the preparation of its report.

Article 2016: Initial Report

1. Unless the disputing Parties otherwise agree, the panel shall base its report on the submissions and arguments of the Parties and on any information before it pursuant to Article 2014 or 2015.

2. Unless the disputing Parties otherwise agree, the panel shall, within 90 days after the last panelist is selected or such other period as the Model Rules of Procedure established pursuant to Article 2012(1) may provide, present to the disputing Parties an initial report containing:

   a) findings of fact, including any findings pursuant to a request under Article 2012(5);

   b) its determination as to whether the measure at issue is or would be inconsistent with the obligations of this Agreement or cause nullification or impairment in the sense of Annex 2004, or any other determination requested in the terms of reference; and

   c) its recommendations, if any, for resolution of the dispute.

3. Panelists may furnish separate opinions on matters not unanimously agreed.

4. A disputing Party may submit written comments to the panel on its initial report within 14 days of presentation of the report.

5. In such an event, and after considering such written comments, the panel, on its own initiative or on the request of any disputing Party, may:

   a) request the views of any participating Party;

   b) reconsider its report; and

   c) make any further examination that it considers appropriate.

Article 2017: Final Report

1. The panel shall present to the disputing Parties a final report, including any separate opinions on matters not unanimously agreed upon, within 30 days of presentation of the initial report, unless the disputing Parties otherwise agree.

2. No panel may, either in its initial report or its final report, disclose which panelists are associated with majority or minority opinions.

3. The disputing Parties shall transmit to the Commission the final report of the panel, including any report to a scientific review board established under Article 2015, as well as any written views that a disputing Party desires to be appended, on a confidential basis within a reasonable period of time after it is presented to them.

4. Unless the Commission decides otherwise, the final report of the panel shall be published 15 days after it is transmitted to the Commission.

Implementation of Panel Reports

Article 2018: Implementation of Final Report

1. On receipt of the final report of a panel, the disputing Parties shall agree on the resolution of the dispute, which normally shall

conform with the determinations and recommendations of the panel, and shall notify their Sections of the Secretariat of any agreed resolution of any dispute.

2. Wherever possible, the resolution shall be nonimplementation or removal of a measure not conforming with this Agreement or causing nullification or impairment in the sense of Annex 2004 or, failing such a resolution, compensation.

Article 2019: Nonimplementation - Suspension of Benefits

1. If in its final report a panel has determined that a measure is inconsistent with the obligations of this Agreement or causes nullification or impairment in the sense of Annex 2004 and the Party complained against has not reached agreement with any complaining Party on a mutually satisfactory resolution pursuant to Article 2018(1) within 30 days of receiving the final report, such complaining Party may suspend the application to the Party complained against of benefits of equivalent effect until such time as they have reached agreement on a resolution of the dispute.

2. In considering what benefits to suspend pursuant to paragraph 1:

   a) a complaining Party should first seek to suspend benefits in the same sector or sectors as that affected by the measure or other matter that the panel has found to be inconsistent with the obligations of this Agreement or to have caused nullification or impairment in the sense of Annex 2004; and

   b) a complaining Party that considers it is not practicable or effective to suspend benefits in the same sector or sectors may suspend benefits in other sectors.

3. On the written request of any disputing Party delivered to the other Parties and its Section of the Secretariat, the Commission shall establish a panel to determine whether the level of benefits suspended by a Party pursuant to paragraph 1 is manifestly excessive.

4. The panel proceedings shall be conducted in accordance with the Model Rules of Procedure. The panel shall present its determination within 60 days after the last panelist is selected or such other period as the disputing Parties may agree.

Section C - Domestic Proceedings and Private Commercial Dispute Settlement

Article 2020: Referrals of Matters from Judicial or Administrative Proceedings

1. If an issue of interpretation or application of this Agreement arises in any domestic judicial or administrative proceeding of a Party that any Party considers would merit its intervention, or if a court or administrative body solicits the views of a Party, that Party shall notify the other Parties and its Section of the Secretariat. The Commission shall endeavor to agree on an appropriate response as expeditiously as possible.

2. The Party in whose territory the court or administrative body is located shall submit any agreed interpretation of the Commission to the court or administrative body in accordance with the rules of that forum.

3. If the Commission is unable to agree, any Party may submit its own views to the court or administrative body in accordance with the rules of that forum.

Article 2021: Private Rights

No Party may provide for a right of action under its domestic law against any other Party on the ground that a measure of another Party is inconsistent with this Agreement.

Article 2022: Alternative Dispute Resolution

1. Each Party shall, to the maximum extent possible, encourage and facilitate the use of arbitration and other means of alternative dispute resolution for the settlement of international commercial disputes between private parties in the free trade area.

2. To this end, each Party shall provide appropriate procedures to ensure observance of agreements to arbitrate and for the recognition and enforcement of arbitral awards in such disputes.

3. A Party shall be deemed to be in compliance with paragraph 2 if it is a party to and is in compliance with the *1958 United Nations Convention on the Recognition and Enforcement of Foreign Arbitral Awards* or the *1975 Inter-American Convention on International Commercial Arbitration.*

4. The Commission shall establish an Advisory Committee on Private Commercial Disputes comprising persons with expertise or experience in the resolution of private international commercial disputes. The Committee shall report and provide recommendations to the Commission on general issues referred to it by the Commission respecting the availability, use and effectiveness of arbitration and other procedures for the resolution of such disputes in the free trade area.

Annex 2001.2
Committees and Working Groups

A. Committees:

I. Committee on Trade in Goods (Article 316)
2. Committee on Trade in Worn Clothing (Annex 300-B, Section 9.1)
3. Committee on Agricultural Trade (Article 706)
   - Advisory Committee on Private Commercial Disputes Regarding Agricultural Goods (Article 707)

4. Committee on Sanitary and Phytosanitary Measures (Article 722)
5. Committee on Standards–Related Measures (Article 913)
   - Land Transport Standards Sub-committee (Article 913(5))
   - Telecommunications Standards Sub-committee (Article 913(5))
   - Automotive Standards Council (Article 913(5))
   - Sub-committee on Labeling of Textile and Apparel Goods (Article 913(5))
6. Committee on Small Business (Article 1021)
7. Financial Services Committee (Article 1412)
8. Advisory Committee on Private Commercial Disputes (Article 2022(4))

B. Working Groups:

1. Working Group on Rules of Origin (Article 513)
   - Customs Subgroup (Article 513(6))
2. Working Group on Agricultural Subsidies (Article 705(6))
3. Bilateral Working Group (Mexico - United States) (Annex 703.2(A)(25))
4. Bilateral Working Group (Canada - Mexico) (Annex 703.2(B)(13))

5. Working Group on Trade and Competition (Article 1504)
6. Temporary Entry Working Group (Article 1605)

C. Other Committees and Working Groups Established under this Agreement

Annex 2002.2
Remuneration and Payment of Expenses

1. The Commission shall establish the amounts of remuneration and expenses that will be paid to the panelists, committee members and members of scientific review boards.

2. The remuneration of panelists or committee members and their assistants, members of scientific review boards, their travel and lodging expenses, and all general expenses of panels, committees or scientific review boards shall be borne equally by:

   a) in the case of panels or committees established under Chapter Nineteen (Review and Dispute Settlement in Antidumping and Countervailing Duty Matters), the involved Parties, as they are defined in Article 1911; or

   b) in the case of panels and scientific review boards established under this Chapter, the disputing Parties.

3. Each panelist or committee member shall keep a record and render a final account of the person's time and expenses, and the panel, committee or scientific review board shall keep a record and render a final account of all general expenses.

Annex 2004
Nullification and Impairment

1. If any Party considers that any benefit it could reasonably have expected to accrue to it under any provision of:

a) Part Two (Trade in Goods), except for those provisions of Annex 300-A (Automotive Sector) or Chapter Six (Energy) relating to investment.

b) Part Three (Technical Barriers to Trade),

c) Chapter Twelve (Cross-Border Trade in Services), or

d) Part Six (Intellectual Property),

is being nullified or impaired as a result of the application of any measure that is not inconsistent with this Agreement, the Party may have recourse to dispute settlement under this Chapter.

2. A Party may not invoke:

a) paragraph 1(a) or (b), to the extent that the benefit arises from any cross-border trade in services provision of Part Two, ot Three, or

b) paragraph 1 (c) or (d),

with respect to any measure subject to an exception under Article 2101 (General Exceptions).

CHAPTER 21:
EXCEPTIONS

Article 2102: National Security

1. Subject to Article 607 (Energy - National Security Measures) and 1018 (Government Procurement - Exceptions), nothing in this Agreement shall be construed:

a) to require any Party to furnish or allow access to any information the disclosure of which it determines to be contrary to its essential security interests;

b) to prevent any Party from taking any actions that it considers necessary for the protection of its essential security interests

   i) relating to the tariff in arms, ammunition and implements of war and to such traffic and transactions in other goods, materials, services and technology undertaken directly or indirectly for the purpose of supplying a military or other security establishment,

   ii) taken in time of war or other emergency in international relations, or

   (iii) relating to the implementation of national policies or international agreements respecting the nonproliferation of nuclear weapons or other nuclear explosive devices; or

c) to prevent any Party from taking action in pursuance of its obligations under the United Nations Charter for the maintenance of international peace and security.

RULES OF PROCEDURE FOR ARTICLE 1904 EXTRAORDINARY CHALLENGE COMMITTEES

DEPARTMENT OF EXTERNAL AFFAIRS

NORTH AMERICAN FREE TRADE AGREEMENT

RULES OF PROCEDURE FOR
ARTICLE 1904 EXTRAORDINARY CHALLENGE COMMITTEES

Preamble

The Parties,

Having regard to Chapter Nineteen of the North American Free Trade Agreement between Canada, the United Mexican States and the United States of America;

Acting pursuant to paragraph 2 of Annex 1904.13 to Chapter Nineteen of the Agreement;

Adopted the Rules of Procedure, which shall come into force on the same day as the Agreement enters into force and from that day shall govern all extraordinary challenge committee proceedings conducted pursuant to Article 1904 of the Agreement.

Short Title

1. These rules may be cited as the *NAFTA Extraordinary Challenge Committee Rules.*

Statement of General Intent

2. These rules are intended to give effect to the provisions of Chapter Nineteen of the Agreement with respect to extraordinary challenges conducted pursuant to Article 1904 of the Agreement and are designed to result in decisions within 90 days after the establishment of the committee. Where a procedural question arises that is not covered by these rules, a committee may adopt an appropriate procedure that is not inconsistent with the Agreement. In the event of any inconsistency between the provisions of these Rules and the Agreement, the Agreement shall prevail.

Interpretation

3. In these rules,

"Agreement" means the North American Free Trade Agreement; *(Accord) (Tratado)*

"Code of Conduct" means the code of conduct established by the Parties pursuant to Article 1909 of the Agreement; *(Code dc conduite) (Codigo de Conducta)*

"committee" means an extraordinary challenge committee *established pursuant to* Annex 1904.13 to Chapter Nineteen of *the Agreement; (comite) (comite)*

"counsel" means

a) with respect to *an* extraordinary challenge of a panel review of a final determination made in Canada, a person entitled to appear as counsel before the Federal Court of Canada,

b) with respect to an extraordinary challenge of a panel review of a final determination made in Mexico, a person entitled to appear as counsel before the Tribunal Fiscal de la Federacion, and

c) with respect to an extraordinary challenge of a panel review of a final determination made in the United States, a person entitled to appear as counsel before a federal court in the United States; *(avocat) (representante)*

"counsel of record" means a counsel referred to in subrule 12(1); *(avocat au dossier) (representante legal acreditado)*

"Deputy Minister" means the Deputy Minister of National Revenue for Customs and Excise, or the successor thereto, and includes any person authorized to perform a power, duty or function of the Deputy Minister under the *Special Import Measures Act,* as amended; *(sous-ministre) (Deputy Minister)*

"final determination" means, in the case of Canada, a definitive decision within the meaning of subsection 77.01(1) of the *Special Import Measures Act,* as amended; *(décision definitive) (resolucion definitiva)*

"investigating authority" means the competent investigating authority that issued the final determination that was the subject of the panel review to which an extraordinary challenge relates and includes, in respect of the issuance, amendment, modification or revocation of a Proprietary Information Access Order, any person authorized by the investigating authority; *(autorité chargée de l'enquete) (autoridad investigadora)*

"involved Secretariat" means the section of the Secretariat located in the country of an involved Party; *(Secretariat en cause) (Secretariado implicado)* "legal holiday" means

a) with respect to the Canadian Section of the Secretariat, every Saturday and Sunday, New Year's Day (January 1), Good Friday, Easter Monday, Victoria Day, Canada Day (July 1), Labor Day (first Monday in September), Thanksgiving Day (second Monday in October), Remembrance Day (November Il), Christmas Day (December 25), Boxing Day (December 26), any other day fixed as a statutory holiday by the Government of Canada or by the province in which the Section is located and any day on which the offices of the Canadian Section of the Secretariat are officially closed in whole or in part,

b) with respect to the Mexican Section of the Secretariat, every Saturday and Sunday, New Year's Day (January 1), Constitution Day (February S), Benito Juarez's Birthday (March 21), Labor Day (May 1), Battle of Puebla (May 5), Independence Day (September 16), Congressional Opening Day (November 1), Revolution Day (November 20), Transmission of the Federal Executive Branch (every six years on December 1), Christmas Day (December 25), any day designated as a statutory holiday by the Federal Laws 04 in the case of Ordinary Elections, by the Local Electoral Laws and any day on which the offices of the Mexican Section of the Secretariat are officially closed in whole or in part, and

c) with respect to the United States Section of the Secretariat, every Saturday and Sunday, New Year's Day (January 1), Martin Luther King's Birthday (third Monday in January), Presidents' Day (third Monday in February), Memorial Day (last Monday in May), Independence Day (July 4), Labor Day (first Monday in September), Columbus Day (second Monday in October), Veterans' Day (November 11),

Thanksgiving Day (fourth Thursday in November), Christmas Day (December 25), any other day designated as a holiday by the President or the Congress of the United States and any day on which the offices of the Government of the United States located in the District of Columbia or the offices of the United States Section of the Secretariat are officially closed in whole or in part; *(jour ferie) (dias inhabiles)*

"Mexico" means the United Mexican States; *(Mexique)*

"official publication" means

a) in the case of the Government of Canada, the *Canada Gazette,*

b) in the case of the Government of Mexico, the *Diario Oficial de la Federacion,* and

c) in the case of the Government of the United States, the *Federal Register, (journal officiel) (publicacion oficial)*

"panel" means a binational panel established pursuant to Annex 1901.2 to Chapter Nineteen of the Agreement, the decision of which is the subject of an extraordinary challenge; *(groupe spécial) (panel)*

"participant" means a Party who files a Request for an Extraordinary Challenge Committee or any of the following persons who files a Notice of Appearance pursuant to these rules:

a) the other involved Party,

b) a person who participated in the panel review that is the subject of the extraordinary challenge, and

c) a panelist against whom an allegation referred to in Article 1904.13a)I) of the Agreement is made; *(participant) (participante)*

"Party" means the Government of Canada, the Government of Mexico or the Government of the United States; *(Partie) (Parte)*

"person" means

a) an individual,

b) a Party,

c) an investigating authority,

d) a government of a province, state or other political subdivision of the country of a Party,

e) a department, agency or body of a Party or of a government referred to in paragraph (d), or

f) a partnership, corporation or association; *(personne) (persona)*

"personal information" means, with respect to an extraordinary challenge proceeding in which an allegation is made that a member of the panel was guilty of gross misconduct, bias or a serious conflict of interest or otherwise materially violated the rules of conduct, the information referred to in subrule 39(2) and rule 41; *(renseignements personnels) (informacion personal)* "pleading" means a Request for an Extraordinary Challenge Committee, a Notice of Appearance, a Change of Service Address, Notice of Change of Counsel of Record, a Notice of Motion, a brief or any other written submission filed by a participant; *(acte de procedure) (promocion)*

"privileged information" means

a) with respect to an extraordinary challenge of a panel review of a final determination made in Canada, information of the investigating authority that is subject to solicitor-client privilege under the laws of Canada, or that constitutes part of the deliberative process with respect to the final determination, with respect to which the privilege has not been waived,

b) with respect to an extraordinary challenge of a panel review of a final determination made in Mexico,

   i) information of the investigating authority that is subject to attorney-client privilege under the laws of Mexico, or

   ii) internal communications between officials of the Secretaria de Comercio y Fomento Industrial in charge of antidumping and countervailing duty investigations or communications between those officials and other government officials, where those communications constitute part of the deliberative process with respect to the final determination, and

c) with respect to an extraordinary challenge of a panel review of a final determination made in the United States, information of the investigating authority that is subject to the attorney-client, attorney work product or government deliberative process privilege under the laws of the United States and with respect to which the privilege has not been waived; *(renseignements protégés) (informacion privilegiada)*

"proof of service" means

a) with respect to an extraordinary challenge of a panel review of a final determination made in Canada or Mexico,

   i) an affidavit of service stating the name of the person who served the document, the date on which it was served, where it was served and the manner of service, or

   ii) a written acknowledgment of service by counsel for a participant stating the name of the person who served the document, the date on which it was served and the manner of service and, where the acknowledgment is signed by a person other than the counsel, the name of that person followed by a statement that the person is signing as agent for the counsel, and

b) with respect to an extraordinary challenge of a panel review of a final determination made in the United States, a certificate of service in the form of a statement of the date and manner of service and of the name of the person served, signed by the person who made service; *(preuve designifcation) (comprobante de envio)*

"proprietary information" means

a) with respect to an extraordinary challenge of a panel review of a final determination made in Canada, information referred to in subsection 84(3) of the *Special Import Measures* Act, as amended, or subsection 45(3) of the *Canadian International Trade Tribunal Act,* as amended, and with respect to which the person who designated or submitted the information has not withdrawn the person's claim as to the confidentiality of the information,

b) with respect to an extraordinary challenge of a panel review of a final determination made in Mexico, *informacion confidencial*, as defined under article 80 of the *Ley de Comercio Exterior* and its regulations, and

c) with respect to an extraordinary challenge of a panel review of a final determination made in the United States, business proprietary information under section 777(f) of the *Tariff Act of 1930,* as amended, and any regulations made under that Act; *(renseignements de nature exclusive) (informacion confidencial)*

"Proprietary Information Access Application" means

a) with respect to an extraordinary challenge of a panel review of a final determination made in Canada, a disclosure undertaking in the prescribed form, which form

   i) in respect of a final determination by the Deputy Minister, is available from the Deputy Minister, and

   ii) in respect of a final determination by the Tribunal, is available from the Tribunal,

b) with respect to an extraordinary challenge of a panel review of a final determination made in Mexico, a disclosure undertaking in the prescribed form, which form is available from the Secretaria de Comercio y Fomento Industrial, and

c) with respect to an extraordinary challenge of a panel review of a final determination made in the United States, a Protective Order Application

   i) in respect of a final determination by the International Trade Administration of the United States Department of Commerce, in a form prescribed by, and available from, the International Trade Administration of the United States Department of Commerce, and

   ii) in respect of a final determination by the United States International Trade Commission, in a form prescribed by, and available from, the United States International Trade Commission; *(demande relative de la communication de renseignements) (compromiso de confidencialidad)*

"Proprietary Information Access Order" means

a) in the case of Canada, a Disclosure Order issued by the Deputy Minister or the Tribunal pursuant to a Proprietary Information Access Application,

b) in the case of Mexico, a Disclosure Order issued by the Secretaria de Comercio y Fomento Industrial pursuant to a Proprietary Information Access Application, and

c) in the case of the United States, a Protective Order issued by the International Trade Administration of the United States Department of Commerce or the United States International Trade Commission pursuant to a Proprietary

Information Access Application *(ordonnance relative à la communication de renseignements) (autorizacion de acceso a la informacion confidencial)*

"responsible Secretariat" means, with respect to an extraordinary challenge of a panel review, the section of the Secretariat located in the country in which the final determination reviewed by the panel was made; *(Secretariat responsable) (Secretariado responsabie)*

"responsible Secretary" means the Secretary of the responsible Secretariat; *(secretaire responsable) (Secretario responsabie)*

"Secretariat" means the Secretariat established pursuant to Article 2002 of the Agreement; *(Secretariat) (Secretariado)*

"Secretary" means the Secretary of the United States Section of the Secretariat, the Secretary of the Mexican Section of the Secretariat or the Secretary of the Canadian Section of the Secretariat and includes any person authorized to act on behalf of that Secretary; *(secrétaire) (Secretario)*

"service address" means

a) with respect to a Party or panelist, the address filed with the Secretariat as the service address of the Party or panelist, including any facsimile number submitted with that address,

b) with respect to a participant other than a Party or panelist, the service address of the participant in the panel review, or

c) where a Change of Service Address has been filed by a Party, panelist or participant, the address set out as the new service address of the participant in that form, including any facsimile number submitted with that address: *(adresse aux fins de signification) (domicilio para oir y recibir notificaciones)*

"Tribunal" means the Canadian International Trade Tribunal or its successor and includes any person authorized to act on its behalf; *(Tribunal) (Tribunal)*

"United States" means the United States of America. *(États-Unis) (Estados Unidos)*

4. The definitions set forth in Article 1911 of the Agreement and Annex 1911 to Chapter 19 of the Agreement are hereby incorporated into these rules.

PART I
GENERAL

5. An extraordinary challenge proceeding commences on the day on which a Request for an Extraordinary Challenge Committee is filed with the Secretariat and terminates on the day on which a Notice of Completion of Extraordinary Challenge is effective.

6. The general legal principles of the country in which a final determination was made apply in an extraordinary challenge of the decision of a panel with respect to the final determination.

7. A committee may review any part of the record of the panel review relevant to the extraordinary challenge.

Internal Functioning of Committees

8.(1) For routine administrative matters governing its own internal functioning, a committee may adopt procedures not inconsistent with these rules or the Agreement.

(2) Subject to subrule *34b),* meetings of a committee may be conducted by means of a telephone conference call.

9. Only committee members may take part in the deliberations of a committee, which shall take place in private and remain secret. Staff of the involved Secretariats and assistants to committees members may be present by permission of the committee.

Computation of Time

10.(1) In computing any time period fixed in these rules or by an order or decision of a committee, the day from which the time period begins to run shall be excluded and, subject to subrules *(2)* and *(3),* the last day of the time period shall be included.

(2) Where the last day of a time period computed in accordance with subrule 1) falls on a legal holiday of the responsible Secretariat, that day and any other legal holidays of the responsible Secretariat immediately following that day shall be excluded from the computation.

(3) In computing any time period of five days or less fixed in these rules or by an order or decision of a committee, any legal holiday that falls within the time period shall be excluded from the computation.

11. A committee may extend any time period fixed in these rules if

    a) the extension is made in the interests of fairness and justice; and

    b) in fixing the extension, the committee takes into account the intent of the rules to secure just, speedy and inexpensive final resolutions of challenges to decisions of panels.

Counsel of Record

12.(1) Subject to subrule (2), the counsel of record for a participant in an extraordinary challenge proceeding shall be

    a) the counsel for the participant in the panel review; or

    b) in the case of a Party who was not a participant in the panel review or of a panelist, the counsel who signs any document filed on behalf of the Party or panelist in the extraordinary challenge proceeding.

(2) A participant may change its counsel of record by filing with the responsible Secretariat a Notice of Change of Counsel of Record signed by the new counsel, together with proof of service on the former counsel and other participants.

Costs

13. Each participant shall bear the costs of, and incidental to, its own participation in an extraordinary challenge proceeding.

Proprietary Information and Privileged Information

14.(1) Where proprietary information has been filed in a panel review that is the subject of an extraordinary challenge proceeding, every member of a committee, assistant to a committee member, court reporter, interpreter and translator shall provide the responsible Secretariat with a Proprietary Information Access Application.

(2) Upon receipt of a Proprietary Information Access Application, the responsible Secretary shall file with the appropriate investigating authority the Proprietary Information Access Application and any additional copies of those documents required by the investigating authority.

(3) The investigating authority shall issue the Proprietary Information Access Order and provide the responsible Secretariat with the original and any additional copies of those documents required by the responsible Secretariat.

(4) Upon receipt of a Proprietary Information Access Order, the responsible Secretary shall transmit the original Proprietary Information Access Order to the appropriate member of a committee, assistant to a committee member, court reporter, interpreter or translator.

15.(1) A member of a committee, assistant to a committee member, court reporter, interpreter or translator who amends or modifies a Proprietary Information Access Application shall provide a copy of the amendment or modification to the responsible Secretariat.

(2) Upon receipt of an amendment or modification to a Proprietary Information Access Application, the responsible Secretary shall file with the appropriate investigating authority that document

and any additional copies of that document required by the investigating authority.

(3) Upon receipt of an amendment or modification to a Proprietary Information Access Application, the investigating authority shall, as appropriate, amend, modify or revoke the Proprietary Information Access Order and provide the responsible Secretariat with the original of the amendment, modification or notice of revocation and any additional copies of the document required by the responsible Secretariat.

(4) Upon receipt of an amendment or modification to a Proprietary Information Access Order or a notice of revocation, the responsible Secretary shall transmit the amendment, modification or notice of revocation to the appropriate member of a committee, assistant to a committee member, court reporter, interpreter or translator.

16. The responsible Secretary shall serve Proprietary Information Access Orders granted to members of a committee, assistants to committee members, court reporters, interpreters or translators, and any amendments or modifications thereto or notices of revocation thereof, on all participants other than the investigating authority.

17. (1) A counsel of record, or a professional retained by, or under the control or direction of, a counsel of record, who has not been issued a Proprietary Information Access Order in the panel review or in these proceedings and who wishes disclosure of proprietary information in the file of an extraordinary challenge proceeding, shall file a Proprietary Information Access Application, as follows:

a) with the responsible Secretariat, four copies; and

b) with the investigating authority, one original and any additional copies that the investigating authority requires.

(2) A Proprietary Information Access Application referred to in subrule 1) shall be served on all participants.

(3) The investigating authority shall, within 10 days after a Proprietary Information Access Application is filed with it in accordance with subrule (1), serve on the person who filed the Proprietary Information Access Application

a) a Proprietary Information Access Order, or

b) a notification in writing setting out the reasons why a Proprietary Information Access Order is not issued.

18.(1) Where

a) an investigating authority refuses to issue a Proprietary Information Access Order to a counsel of record or to a professional retained by, or under the control or direction of, a counsel of record, or

b) an investigating authority issues a Proprietary Information Access Order with terms unacceptable to a counsel of record, the counsel of record may file with the responsible Secretariat a Notice of Motion requesting that the committee review the decision of the investigating authority.

(2) Where, after consideration of any response made by the investigating authority referred to in subrule (1), the committee decides that a Proprietary Information Access Order should be issued or that the terms of a Proprietary Information Access

Order should be amended or modified, the committee shall so notify counsel for the investigating authority.

(3) Where the final determination was made in the United States and the investigating authority fails to comply with the notification referred to in subrule (2). the committee may issue such orders as are just in the circumstances, including an order refusing to permit the investigating authority to make certain arguments in support of its case or striking certain arguments from its pleadings.

19.(1) Where a Proprietary Information Access Order is issued to a person in an extraordinary challenge proceeding, the person shall file with the responsible Secretariat a copy of the Proprietary Information Access Order.

(2) Where a Proprietary Information Access Order is revoked, amended or modified by an investigating authority, the investigating authority shall provide to the responsible Secretariat and to all participants a copy of the Notice of Revocation, amendment or modification.

20. In an extraordinary challenge proceeding that commences with a Request for an Extraordinary Challenge Committee pursuant to Article 1904.13a)I) of the Agreement, personal information shall be kept confidential

a) where a Notice of Motion is filed pursuant to subrule 41(1)c),

i) until the committee makes an order referred to in subrule 45(1)a), or

ii) where the committee makes an order referred to in subrule 45(1)b), indefinitely, unless otherwise ordered by the committee; and

b) in any other case, until the day after the expiration of the time period fixed, pursuant to rule 41, for filing a Notice of Motion referred to in subrule 41(1)c).

21. Where a person alleges that the terms of a Proprietary Information Access Application or Proprietary Information Access Order have been violated, the committee shall refer the allegations to the investigating authority for investigation and, where applicable, the imposition of sanctions in accordance with section 77.034 of the *Special Import Measures Act,* as amended, section 777f) of the *Tariff Act of 1930*, as amended, or article 93 of the Ley de *Comercio Exterior.*

Violation of Code of Conduct

22. Where a participant believes that a committee member or an assistant to a committee member is in violation of the Code of Conduct, the participant shall forthwith notify the responsible Secretary in writing of the alleged violation. The responsible Secretary shall promptly notify the other involved Secretary and the involved Parties of the allegations.

Pleadings and Simultaneous Translation of Extraordinary Challenge Proceedings in Canada

23. Rules 24 to 26 apply with respect to an extraordinary challenge of a panel review of a final determination made in Canada.

24. Either English or French may be used by any person, panelist or member of a committee in any document or oral proceeding.

25.(1) Subject to subrule (2), any order or decision including the reasons therefor, issued by a committee shall be made available simultaneously in both English and French where

a) in the opinion of the committee, the order or decision is in respect of a question of law of general public interest or importance; or

b) the proceedings leading to the issuance of the order or decision were conducted in whole or in part in both English and French.

(2) Where

a) an order or decision issued by a committee is not required by subrule 1) to be made available simultaneously in English and French, or

b) an order or decision is required by subrule 1i)a) to be made available simultaneously in both English and French but the committee is of the opinion that to make the order or decision available simultaneously in both English and French would occasion a delay prejudicial to the public interest or result in injustice or hardship to any participant, the order or decision, including the reasons therefor, shall be issued in the first instance in either English or French and thereafter at the earliest possible time in the other language, each version to be effective from the time the first version is effective.

(3) Nothing in subrule 1) or (2) shall be construed as prohibiting the oral delivery in either English or French of any order or decision or any reasons therefor.

(4) No order or decision is invalid by reason only that it was not made or issued in both English and French.

26.(1) Any oral proceeding conducted in both English and French shall be translated simultaneously.

(2) Where a participant requests simultaneous translation of an extraordinary challenge proceeding, the request shall be made as early as possible in the proceedings.

(3) Where a committee is of the opinion that there is a public interest in the extraordinary challenge proceedings, the committee may direct the responsible Secretary to arrange for simultaneous translation of the oral proceedings, if any.

PART II
WRITTEN PROCEEDINGS

27. Where these rules require that notice be given, it shall be given in writing.

Filing, Service and Communications

28.(1) No document is filed with the Secretariat until one original and five copies of the document are received by the responsible Secretariat during its normal business hours and within the time period fixed for filing.

(2) The responsible Secretariat shall accept, date and time stamp and place in the appropriate file every document submitted to the responsible Secretariat.

(3) Receipt, date and time stamping or placement in the file of a document by the responsible Secretariat does not constitute a waiver of any time period fixed for filing or an acknowledgment that the document has been filed in accordance with these rules.

29.(1) All documents filed by a participant, other than documents required by rule 58 to be served by the responsible Secretary and documents referred to in subrule 38(2), rule 39, subrule 40(2)a) and rule 41 shall be served by the participant on the counsel of record of each of the other participants or, where another participant is not represented by counsel, on the other participant.

(2) Subject to subrule 34a), a document may be served by

a) delivering a copy of the document to the service address of the participant;

b) sending a copy of the document to the service address of the participant by facsimile transmission or by expedited delivery courier or expedited mail service, such as express mail in the United States or Priority Post in Canada; or

c) personal service on the participant.

(3) A proof of service shall appear on, or be affixed to, all documents referred to in subrule (1).

(4) Where a document is served by expedited delivery courier or expedited mail service, the date of service set out in the affidavit of service or certificate of service shall be the day on which the document is consigned to the expedited delivery courier or expedited mail service.

30.(1) Where, under these rules, a document containing proprietary information, privileged information or personal information is required to be filed under seal with the Secretariat or is required to be served under seal, the document shall be filed or served in accordance with this rule and, where applicable, in accordance with rule 32.

(2) A document filed or served under seal shall be

a) bound separately from all other documents;

b) clearly marked

i) with respect to an extraordinary challenge of a panel review of a final determination made in Canada,

a) in the case of a document containing proprietary information, "Proprietary" "Confidential", "De nature exclusive" or Confidentiel, and

b) in the case of a document containing privileged information, "Privileged" or "Protégé", and

c) in the case of a document containing personal information, "Personal Information" or "Renseignements personnels",

ii) with respect to an extraordinary challenge of a panel review of a final determination made in Mexico,

a) in the case of a document containing proprietary information, "Confidencial ",

b) in the case of a document containing privileged information, "Privilegiada", and

c) in the case of a document containing personal information, "Informacion Personal", and

(iii) with respect to an extraordinary challenge of a panel review of a final determination made in the United States,

a) in the case of a document containing proprietary information, "Proprietary", and

b) in the case of a document containing privileged information, "Privileged", and

c) in the case of a document containing personal information, "Personal Information"; and

c) contained in an opaque inner wrapper and an opaque outer wrapper.

(3) An inner wrapper referred to in subrule (2)c) shall indicate

a) that proprietary information, privileged information or personal information is enclosed, as the case may be; and

b) the Secretariat file number of the extraordinary challenge proceeding.

31. Filing or service of proprietary information, privileged information or personal information with the Secretariat does not constitute a waiver of the designation of the information as proprietary information, privileged information or personal information.

32.(1) Where a participant files a pleading that contains proprietary information, the participant shall file two sets of the pleading in the following manner:

a) one set containing the proprietary information shall be filed under seal and

   i) with respect to an extraordinary challenge of a panel review of a final determination made in Canada, shall be labelled "Proprietary", "Confidential", "Confidentiel" or "De nature exclusive", with the top of each page that contains proprietary information marked with the word "Proprietary", "Confidential", "Confidentiel" or "De nature exclusive" and with the proprietary information enclosed in brackets,

   ii) with respect to an extraordinary challenge of a panel review of a final determination made in Mexico, shall be labelled "Confidencial", with the top of each page that contains proprietary information marked with the word "Confidencial" and with the proprietary information enclosed in brackets, and

   (iii) with respect to an extraordinary challenge of a panel review of a final determination made in the United States, shall be labelled "Proprietary", with the top of each page that contains proprietary information marked with the word "Proprietary" and with the proprietary information enclosed in brackets; and

b) no later than one day following the day on which the set of pleadings referred to in subrule a) is filed, another set not containing proprietary information shall be filed and

   i) with respect to an extraordinary challenge of a panel review of a final determination made in Canada, shall be labelled "Non-Proprietary", "Non-Confidential", "Non confidentiel" or "De nature non exclusive",

ii) with respect to an extraordinary challenge of a panel review of a final determination made in Mexico, shall be labelled "No-confidencial", and

(iii) with respect to an extraordinary challenge of a panel review of a final determination made in the United States, shall be labelled "Non-Proprietary",

with each page from which proprietary information has been deleted marked to indicate the location from which the proprietary information was deleted.

(2) Where a participant files a pleading that contains privileged information, the participant shall file two sets of the pleading in the following manner:

a) one set containing the privileged information shall be filed under seal and

i) with respect to an extraordinary challenge of a panel review of a final determination made in Canada, shall be labelled "Privileged" or "Protégé", with the top of each page that contains privileged information marked with the word "Privileged" or "Protége" and with the privileged information enclosed in brackets,

ii) with respect to an extraordinary challenge of a panel review of a final determination made in Mexico, shall be labelled "Privilegiada", with the top of each page that contains privileged information marked with the word "Privilegiada" and with the privileged information enclosed in brackets, and

(iii) with respect to an extraordinary challenge of a panel review of a final determination made in the United

States, shall be labelled "Privileged", with the top of each page that contains privileged information marked with the word "Privileged" and with the privileged information enclosed in brackets; and

b) no later than one day following the day on which the set of pleadings referred to in subrule a) is filed, another set not containing privileged information shall be filed and

i) with respect to an extraordinary challenge of a panel review of a final determination made in Canada. shall be labelled "Non-Privileged" or "Non protégé",

ii) with respect to an extraordinary challenge of a panel review of a final determination made in Mexico, shall be labelled "No-privilegiada", and

(iii) with respect to an extraordinary challenge of a panel review of a final determination made in the United States, shall be labelled "Non-Privileged"

with each page from which privileged information has been deleted marked to indicate the location from which the privileged information was deleted.

(3) Where a participant files a pleading that contains personal information, the pleading shall be filed under seal and

a) with respect to an extraordinary challenge of a panel review of a final determination made in Canada, shall be labelled "Personal Information" or "Renseignements personnels", with the top of each page that contains personal information marked with the words "Personal Information" or "Renseignements personnels" and with the personal information enclosed in brackets;

b) with respect to an extraordinary challenge of a panel review of a final determination made in Mexico, shall be labelled "Informacion Personal", with the top of each page that contains personal information marked with the words "Informacion personal" and with the personal information enclosed in brackets; and

c) with respect to an extraordinary challenge of a panel review of a final determination made in the United Slates, shall be labelled "Personal Information", with the top of each page that contains personal information marked with the words "Personal Information" and with the personal information enclosed in brackets.

33.(1) Subject to subrule *(2),* a document containing proprietary or privileged information shall be filed under seal in accordance with rule 30 and shall be served only on the Investigating authority and on those participants who have been granted access to the information under a Proprietary Information Access Order.

(2) Where all proprietary information contained in a document was submitted to the investigating authority by one participant, the document shall be served on that participant even if that participant has not been granted access to proprietary information under a Proprietary Information Access Order.

(3) A document containing personal information shall be filed under seal in accordance with rule 30 and shall be served only on persons or participants who have been granted access to the information under an order of the committee.

34. Where proprietary information, privileged information or personal information is disclosed to a person in an extraordinary challenge proceeding, the person shall not

a) file, serve or otherwise communicate the information by facsimile transmission; or

b) communicate the information by telephone.

35. Service on an investigating authority does not constitute service on a Party and service on a Party does not constitute service on an investigating authority.

Form and Content of Pleadings

36.(1) Every pleading filed in an extraordinary challenge proceeding shall contain the following information:

a) the title of, and any Secretariat file number assigned for, the extraordinary challenge proceeding;

b) a brief descriptive title of the pleading;

c) the name of the participant filing the pleading;

d) the name of counsel of record for the participant;

e) the service address, as defined in rule 3; and

f) the telephone number of the counsel of record of the participant or, where the participant is not represented by counsel, the telephone number of the participant

(2) Every pleading filed in an extraordinary challenge proceeding shall be on paper 8 ½ x 11 inches (216 millimetres by 279 millimetres) in size. The text of the pleading shall be printed, typewritten or reproduced legibly on one side only with a margin of approximately 1 ½ inches (40 millimetres) on the left-hand side with double spacing between each line of text, except for

quotations of more than 50 words, which shall be indented and single-spaced. Footnotes, titles, schedules, tables, graphs and columns of figures shall be presented in a readable form. Briefs and appendices shall be securely bound along the left-hand margin.

(3) Every pleading filed on behalf of a participant in an extraordinary challenge proceeding shall be signed by counsel for the participant or, where the participant is not represented by counsel, by the participant.

Requests for an Extraordinary Challenge Committee

37.(1) Where a Party, in its discretion, files with the responsible Secretary a Request for an Extraordinary Challenge Committee referred to in Article 1904.13a)ii) or (iii) of the Agreement, the Party shall file the Request (model form available from the Secretariat) within 30 days after the issuance, pursuant to rule 77 of the NAFTA Article 1904 Panel Rules, of the Notice of Final Panel Action in the panel review that is the subject of the Request.

(2) Where a Party, in its discretion, files with the responsible Secretary a Request for an Extraordinary Challenge Committee referred to in Article 1904.13a)I) of the Agreement, the Party shall file the Request (model form available from the Secretariat)

a) within 30 days after the issuance, pursuant to rule 77, of the *NAFTA Article 1904 Panel Rules,* of the Notice of Final Panel Action in the panel review that is the subject of the Request; or

b) subject to subrule (3), where the Party gained knowledge of the action of the panelist giving rise to the allegation more than 30 days after the panel issued a Notice of Final Panel Action, no more than 30 days after gaining knowledge of the action of the panelist.

(3) No Request for an Extraordinary Challenge Committee referred to in subrule (2) may be filed if two years or more have elapsed since the effective date of the Notice of Completion of Panel Review.

(4) Notwithstanding subrules (1) to (3), the running of the time periods referred to in this section

a) shall be suspended in the circumstances set out in Article 1905.11 of the Agreement; and

b) where suspended under subrule a), shall be resumed in the circumstances set out in Articles 1905.12 and 1905.13 of the Agreement

38.(1) Subject to subrule (2), every Request for an Extraordinary Challenge Committee shall be in writing and shall

a) include a concise statement of the allegations relied on, together with a concise statement of how the actions alleged have materially affected the panel's decision and the way in which the integrity of the panel review process is threatened;

b) contain the name of the Party in the panel review, name of counsel, service address and telephone number; and

c) where the panel decision was made in Canada, state whether the Party filing the Request for an Extraordinary Challenge Committee

i) intends to use English or French in pleadings and oral proceedings before the committee, and

ii) requests simultaneous translation of any oral proceedings.

(2) Where a Request for an Extraordinary Challenge Committee contains an allegation referred to in Article 1904.13a)I) of the Agreement, the identity of the panelist against whom such an allegation is made shall be revealed only in a confidential annex filed together with the Request and shall be disclosed only in accordance with rule 60.

39.(1) Every Request for an Extraordinary Challenge Committee (model form available from the Secretariat) shall be accompanied by

a) those items of the record of the panel review relevant to the allegations contained in the Request; and

b) an Index of the items referred to in subrule a).

(2) Where a Request contains an allegation referred to in Article 1904.13a)I) of the Agreement, the Request shall be accompanied by, in addition to the requirements of subrule (1),

a) any other material relevant to the allegations contained in the Request; and

b) if the Request is filed more than 30 days after the panel issued a Notice of Final Panel Action pursuant to rule 77 of the *NAFTA Article 1904 Panel Rules,* an affidavit certifying that the Party gained knowledge of the action of the panelist giving rise to the allegation no more than 30 days preceding the filing of the Request.

Notices of Appearance

40.(1) Within 10 days after the Request for an Extraordinary Challenge Committee is filed, a Party or participant in the panel review who proposes to participate in the extraordinary challenge proceeding shall file with the responsible Secretariat a Notice of Appearance (model form available from the Secretariat) containing the following information:

a) the name of the Party or participant, name of counsel, service address and telephone number;

b) a statement as to whether appearance is made

i) in support of the Request, or

ii) in opposition to the Request; and

c) where the extraordinary challenge is in respect of a panel review of a final determination made in Canada, a statement as to whether the person filing the Notice of Appearance

i) intends to use English or French in pleadings and oral proceedings before the committee, and

ii) requests simultaneous translation of any oral proceedings.

(2) Where a Party or participant referred to in subrule (1) proposes to rely on a document in the record of the panel review that is not specified in the Index filed with the Request for an Extraordinary Challenge Committee, the Party or participant shall file, with the Notice of Appearance,

a) the document; and

b) a statement identifying the document and requesting its inclusion in the extraordinary challenge record.

(3) On receipt of a document referred to in subrule (2), the responsible Secretary shall include the document in the extraordinary challenge record.

41.(1) Within 10 days after a Request for an Extraordinary Challenge Committee referred to in Article 1904.13a)l) of the Agreement is filed, a panelist against whom an allegation contained in the Request is made and who proposes to participate in the extraordinary challenge proceeding

a) shall file a Notice of Appearance;

b) may file, under seal, documents to be included in the extraordinary challenge record relevant to the panelist's defense against the allegation; and

c) may file an *ex parte* motion requesting that the extraordinary challenge proceeding be conducted *in camera.*

(2) Where a committee issues an order pursuant to subrule *45(1)a),* a panelist who filed documents described in subrule 45*i)b)* may, within five days after issuance of the order, withdraw any of those documents.

(3) Where a panelist withdraws documents pursuant to subrule (2), the committee shall not consider those documents.

Filing and Content of Briefs and Appendices

42.(1) The Party who has filed the Request for an Extraordinary Challenge Committee and every participant who has filed a Notice of Appearance under subrule *40(1)b)I)* shall file a brief, setting forth grounds and arguments in support of the Request, no later than 21 days after the Request for an Extraordinary Challenge Committee is filed.

(2) Every participant who has filed a Notice of Appearance under subrule *41 l)b)ii)* shall file a brief, setting forth grounds and arguments in opposition to the Request for an Extraordinary Challenge Committee, no later than 21 days after the expiration of the time period for filing of briefs referred to in subrule (1).

(3) The Party who has filed the Request for an Extraordinary Challenge Committee and every participant who has filed a Notice of Appearance under subrule 40(1)b)I) may file a brief, replying to the grounds and arguments set forth in the briefs filed pursuant to subrule (2), no later than 10 days after the expiration of the time period for filing of briefs referred to in subrule (2). Reply briefs shall be limited to rebuttal of matters raised in the briefs filed pursuant to subrule (2).

(4) Every brief filed under this rule shall be in the form required by rule 43.

(5) Appendices shall be filed with the briefs.

43.(1) Briefs shall contain information, in the following order, divided into five parts:

Part I:

a) A table of contents; and

b) A table of authorities cited:

The table of authorities shall contain references to all treaties, statutes and regulations cited, any cases primarily relied on in the briefs, set out alphabetically, and all other documents referred to except documents from the administrative record. The table of authorities shall refer to the page(s) of the brief where each authority is cited and mark, with an asterisk in the margin, those authorities primarily relied on.

Part II: A statement of the case:

This part shall contain a concise statement of the relevant facts with references to the panel record by page and, where applicable, by line.

Part III: A statement of the issues:

a) In the brief of the Party who files the Request for an Extraordinary Challenge Committee, this part shall contain a concise statement of the issues.

b) In the brief of any other participant, this part shall contain a concise statement of the position of the participant with respect to the issues.

Part IV: Argument:

This part shall consist of the argument, setting out concisely the points of law relating to the issues, with applicable citations to authorities and the panel record.

Part V: Relief:

This part shall consist of a concise statement precisely identifying the relief requested.

(2) Paragraphs in Parts I to V of a brief may be numbered consecutively.

(3) Authorities referred to in the briefs shall be included in an appendix, which shall be organized as follows: a table of contents, copies of all treaty and statutory references, references to regulations, cases primarily relied on in the briefs, set out alphabetically, all documents relied on from the panel record and all other materials relied on.

Motions

44.(1) Motions, other than motions referred to in subrule 41(1)c), may be considered at the discretion of the committee.

(2) A committee may dispose of a motion based upon the pleadings filed on the motion.

(3) A committee may hear oral argument in person or, subject to subrule 34b), direct that a motion be heard by means of a telephone conference call with the participants.

PART III
CONDUCT OF ORAL PROCEEDINGS

45.(1) The order of a committee on a motion referred to in subrule 41(1)c) shall set out

a) that the proceedings shall not be held *in camera*; or

b) that the proceedings shall be held *in camera* and

   i) that all the participants shall keep confidential all information received with respect to the extraordinary challenge proceeding and shall use the information solely for the purposes of the proceeding, and

   ii) which documents containing personal information the responsible Secretary shall serve under seal and on whom the documents shall be served.

(2) The responsible Secretary shall not serve any documents containing personal information until the time period for withdrawal of any documents pursuant to subrule 41(2) has expired.

46. A committee may decide the procedures to be followed in thc extraordinary challenge proceeding and may, for that purpose, hold a pre-hearing conference to determine such matters as the presentation of evidence and of oral argument.

47. The decision as to whether oral argument will be heard shall be in the discretion of the committee.

Oral Proceedings in Camera

48. During that part of oral proceedings in which proprietary information or privileged information is presented, a committee shall not permit any person other than the following persons to be present:

   a) the person presenting the proprietary information or privileged information;

b) a person who has been granted access to the proprietary information or privileged information under a Proprietary Information Access Order or an order of the panel or committee;

c) in the case of privileged information, a person as to whom the confidentiality of the privileged information has been waived; and

d) officials of, and counsel for, the investigating authority.

PART IV
RESPONSIBILITIES OF THE SECRETARY

49. The normal business hours of the Secretariat, during which the offices of the Secretariat shall be open to the public, shall be from 9:00 a.m. to 5:00 p.m. on each weekday other than

a) in the case of the Canadian Section of the Secretariat, legal holidays of that Section;

b) in the case of the Mexican Section of the Secretariat, legal holidays of that Section; and

c) in the case of the United States Section of the Secretariat, legal holidays of that Section.

50. On the completion of the selection of the members of a committee, the responsible Secretary shall notify the participants and the other involved Secretary of the names of the members of the committee.

51. The responsible Secretary shall provide administrative support for each extraordinary challenge proceeding and shall make the arrangements necessary for meetings and any oral

proceedings, including, if required, interpreters to provide simultaneous translation.

52. Each involved Secretary shall maintain a file for each extraordinary challenge, comprised of either the original or a copy of all documents filed, whether or not filed in accordance with these rules.

53. The responsible Secretary shall forward to the other involved Secretary a copy of all documents filed with the responsible Secretary and of all orders and decisions issued by a committee.

54. Where under these rules a notice or other document is required to be published, the responsible Secretary and the other involved Secretary shall each cause the document to be published in the official publication of the country in which that section of the Secretariat is located.

55.(1) Where a document containing proprietary information or privileged information is filed with the involved Secretariats, each involved Secretary shall ensure that

a) the document is stored, maintained, handled, and distributed in accordance with the terms of an applicable Proprietary Information Access Order;

b) the inner wrapper of the document is clearly marked to indicate that it contains proprietary information or privileged information; and

c) access to the document is limited to

i) in the case of proprietary information, officials of, and counsel for, the investigating authority, the person who submitted the proprietary information to the investigating authority and counsel of record for that person, and any persons who have been granted access to the information under a Proprietary Information Access Order, and

ii) in the case of privileged information relied upon in an extraordinary challenge of a decision of a panel with respect to a final determination made in the United States, committee members and their assistants and persons with respect to whom the panel ordered disclosure of the privileged information under rule 52 of the *NAFTA Article 1904 Panel Rules,* if those persons have filed with the responsible Secretariat a Proprietary Information Access Order with respect to the document.

(2) Where a document containing personal information is filed with the involved Secretariats, each involved Secretary shall ensure that

a) the document is stored, maintained, handled, and distributed in accordance with the terms of any applicable Proprietary Information Access Order;

b) the inner wrapper of the document is clearly marked to indicate that it contains personal information; and

c) access to the document is limited to persons granted access to the information pursuant to subrule 45(1)b).

56. No document filed in an extraordinary challenge proceeding shall be removed from the offices of the Secretariat except in the ordinary course of the business of the Secretariat or pursuant to the direction of a committee.

57.(1) Each involved Secretary shall permit access by any person to information in the file of an extraordinary challenge proceeding that is not proprietary information, privileged information or personal information.

(2) Each involved Secretary shall, in accordance with the terms of any applicable Proprietary Information Access Order or order of a panel or committee, permit access to proprietary information, privileged information or personal information in the file of an extraordinary challenge proceeding.

(3) Each involved Secretary shall, on request and on payment of the prescribed fee, provide copies of information in the file of an extraordinary challenge proceeding to any person who has been given access to that information.

58.(1) Where a Request for an Extraordinary Challenge Committee pursuant to Article 1904.13a)ii) or (iii) of the Agreement is filed with the responsible Secretariat, the responsible Secretary shall, upon receipt thereof,

a) forward a copy of the Request and Index to the other involved Secretary; and

b) serve a copy of the Request and Index on the other involved Party and on the participants in the panel review, together with a statement setting out the date on which the Request was filed and stating that all briefs of

i) the Party who has filed the Request and of every participant who files a Notice of Appearance in support of the Request shall be filed no later than 21 days after the date of filing of the Request,

ii) every participant who files a Notice of Appearance in opposition to the Request shall be filed no later than 21 days after the expiration of the time period, referred to in subrule I), for filing of briefs, and

(iii) the Party who has filed the Request and of every participant who files a brief under subrule I) in reply to the grounds and arguments set forth in the briefs filed pursuant to subrule ii) shall be filed no later than 10 days after the expiration of the time period, referred to in subrule ii), for filing of briefs.

(2) Where a Request for an Extraordinary Challenge Committee pursuant to Article 1904.13a)I) of the Agreement is filed, the responsible Secretary shall, upon receipt thereof,

a) forward a copy of the Request, Index and annex to the other involved Secretary; and

b) serve a copy of the Request, Index and annex on the other involved Party, on the panelist against whom the allegation contained in the Request is made and on the participants in the panel review, together with a statement setting out the date on which the Request was filed and stating that all briefs of

i) the Party who has filed the Request and of every participant who files a Notice of Appearance in support of the Request shall be filed no later than 21 days after the date of filing of the Request,

ii) every participant who files a Notice of Appearance in opposition to the Request shall be filed no later than 21 days after the expiration of the time period, referred to in subrule I), for filing of briefs, and

(iii) the Party who has filed the Request and of every participant who files a brief under subrule I) in reply to the grounds and arguments set forth in the briefs filed pursuant to subrule ii) shall be filed no later than 10 days after the expiration of the time period, referred to in subrule ii), for filing of briefs.

(3) The responsible Secretary shall serve orders and decisions of a committee and Notices of Completion of Extraordinary Challenge on the participants.

(4) Where the decision of a committee referred to in subrule (3) relates to a panel review of a final determination made in Canada, the decision shall be served by registered mail.

59. The responsible Secretary shall cause notice of a final decision of a committee issued pursuant to rule 63, and any order that the committee directs the Secretary to publish, to be published in the official publications of the involved Parties.

60. Where the time period fixed, pursuant to rule *41,* for filing an *ex parte* motion referred to in subrule 41(1)c) has expired, the responsible Secretary shall serve on all participants

a) where no motion is filed pursuant to that subrule, the documents referred to in rules 39 and 41;

b) where the committee issues an order referred to in subrule *45(1)a),* the documents referred to in rules 39 and 41 in accordance with any order of the committee; and

c) where the committee issues an order referred to in subrule *45(1)b),* the documents referred to in rules 39 and *41,* in accordance with subrule *45(1)b)ii)* and any order made by the committee.

PART V
ORDERS AND DECISIONS

61. All orders and decisions of a committee shall be made by a majority of the votes of all members of the committee.

62.(1) Where a Notice of Motion requesting dismissal of an extraordinary challenge proceeding is filed by a participant, the committee may issue an order dismissing the proceeding.

(2) Where the motion referred to in subrule 1) is consented to by all the participants and an affidavit to that effect is filed, or where all participants file Notices of Motion requesting dismissal, the extraordinary challenge proceeding is terminated.

63.(1) A final decision of a committee shall

a) affirm the decision of the panel;

b) vacate the decision of the panel; or

c) remand the decision of the panel to the panel for action not inconsistent with the final decision of the committee.

(2) Every final decision of a committee shall be issued in writing with reasons, together with any dissenting or concurring opinions of the members of the committee.

(3) Subrule (2) shall not be construed as prohibiting the oral delivery of the decision of a committee.

PART VI
COMPLETION OF EXTRAORDINARY CHALLENGES

64. Where all participants consent to the termination of the proceeding pursuant to rule 62, the responsible Secretary shall cause to be published in the official publications of the involved Parties a Notice of Completion of Extraordinary Challenge, effective on the day after the day on which the requirements of rule 62 have been met.

65. Where a committee issues its final decision, the responsible Secretary shall cause to be published in the official publications of the involved Parties a Notice of Completion of Extraordinary Challenge, effective on the day after the day on which

a) the committee affirms the decision of the panel;

b) the committee vacates the decision of the panel; or

c) where the committee remands the decision of the panel, the day the responsible Secretary gives notice to the committee that the panel has given notice that it has taken action not inconsistent with the committee's decision.

66. The members of the committee are discharged from their duties on the day on which a Notice of Completion of Extraordinary Challenge is effective.

Stays and Suspensions

67.(1) A Party may make a request, pursuant to Article 1905.11 a)ii) of the Agreement, that an ongoing extraordinary challenge proceeding be stayed by filing the request with the responsible Secretariat.

(2) A Party who files a request under subrule (1) shall forthwith give written notice of the request to the other involved Party and to the other involved Secretariat.

(3) On receipt of a request under subrule (1), the responsible Secretary shall

a) immediately give written notice of the stay of the extraordinary challenge proceedings to all participants in the extraordinary challenge proceedings; and

b) publish a notice of the stay of the extraordinary challenge proceedings in the official publications of the involved Parties.

68. On receipt of a report containing an affirmative finding with respect to a ground specified in Article 1905.1 of the Agreement, the responsible Secretary for extraordinary challenge proceedings referred to in Article 1905.11a)I) of the Agreement shall

a) immediately give notice in writing to all participants in those proceedings; and

b) publish a notice of the affirmative finding in the official publications of the involved Parties.

69.(1) A Party who intends to suspend the operation of Article 1904 of the Agreement pursuant to Article 1905.8 or 1905.9 of the Agreement shall endeavor to give written notice of that intention to the other involved Party and to the involved Secretaries at least five days prior to the suspension.

(2) On receipt of a notice under subrule (1), the involved Secretaries shall publish a notice of the suspension in the official publications of the involved Parties.

RULES OF PROCEDURE FOR ARTICLE 1905 SPECIAL COMMITTEES

DEPARTMENT OF EXTERNAL AFFAIRS

NORTH AMERICAN FREE TRADE AGREEMENT

RULES OF PROCEDURE FOR
ARTICLE 1905 SPECIAL COMMITTEES

The Parties,

Having regard to chapter Nineteen of the North American Free Trade Agreement between Canada, the United Mexican States and the United States of America;

Acting pursuant to Article 1905.6 of the Agreement;

Adopt the following Rules of Procedure, which shall come into force on the same day as the Agreement enters into force and from that day shall govern all special committee proceedings conducted pursuant to Article 1905 of the Agreement.

Short Title

1. The rules may be cited as the *Article 1905 Special Committee Rules*.

Statement of General Intent

2. These rules apply to special committee proceedings conducted pursuant to Article 1905 of the Agreement, unless the involved Parties otherwise agree. Where a procedural questions arises that is not covered by these rules, a special committee may adopt an appropriate procedure that is not inconsistent with the Agreement. In the event of any inconsistency between the provisions of these rules and the Agreement, the Agreement shall prevail.

Interpretation

3. In these rules,

"Agreement" means the North American Free Trade Agreement (*Accord) (Tratado)*

"Complaining Party" means a Party who requests, pursuant to Article 1905.2 of the Agreement, that a special committee be established; (*Partie plaignante*) (*Parte reclamante*)

"involved Secretariat" means the responsible Secretariat or the section of the Secretariat located in the country of the other involved Party; (*Secretariat en cause*) (*Secretariado implicado*)

"legal holiday" means

a) with respect to the Canadian Section of the Secretariat, every Saturday and Sunday, New Year's Day (January 1), Good Friday, Easter Monday, Victoria Day, Canada Day (July 1), Labor Day (first Monday in September), Thanksgiving Day (second Monday in October), Remembrance Day (November 11), Christmas Day (December 25), Boxing Day (December 26), any other day fixed as a statutory holiday by the Government of Canada or by the province in which the section is located and any day on which the offices of the Canadian Section of the Secretariat are officially closed in whole or in part,

b) with respect to the Mexican Section of the Secretariat, every Saturday and Sunday, New Year's Day (January 1), Constitution Day (February 5), Benito Juarez's Birthday (March 21), Labor Day (May 1), Battle of Puebla (May 5), Independence Day (September 16), Congressional Opening Day (November 1), Revolution Day (November 20), Transmission of the Federal Executive Branch (every sixth year on December 1), Christmas Day (December 25), any day designated as a statutory holiday by the Federal Laws or, in the case of Ordinary Elections, by the Local Electoral Laws and any day on which the offices of the Mexican Section of the Secretariat are officially closed in whole or in part, and

c) with respect to the United States Section of the Secretariat, every Saturday and Sunday, New Year's Day (January 1), Martin Luther King's Birthday (third Monday in January), Memorial Day (last Monday in May), Independence Day (July 4), Labor Day (first Monday in September), Columbus Day (second May in October), Veteran's Day (November 11), Thanksgiving Day (fourth Thursday in November), Christmas Day (December 25), any day designated as a holiday by the President or the Congress of the United States and any day on which the offices of the Government of the United States located in the District of Columbia or the offices of the United States Section of the Secretariat are officially closed in whole in part; (*jour ferie*) (*dias inhabiles*)

"Mexico" means the United Mexican States; (*Mexique*) (*Mexico*)

"official publication" means

a) in the case of the Government of Canada, the Canada Gazette,

b) in the case of the Government of Mexico, the *Diario Oficial de la Federacion*, and

c) in the case of the Government of the United States, the *Federal Register*; (*journal officiel*) (*publicacion oficial*)

"Party" means the Government of Canada, the Government of Mexico or the Government of the United States; (*Partie*) (*Parte*)

"Responding Party" means the Party against whom an allegation is made under Article 1905.1 of the Agreement; (*Partie visee par la plainte*) (*Parte demandada*)

"responsible Secretariat" means the section of the Secretariat of the Responding Party; (*Secretariat responsable*) (*Secretariado responsable*)

"responsible Secretary" means the Secretary of the responsible Secretariat; (*secretaire responsable*) (*Secretario responsable*)

"Secretariat" means the Secretariat established pursuant to Article 2002 of the Agreement; (*Secretario responsable*)

"Secretary" means the Secretary of the United States Section of the Secretariat, the Secretary of the Mexican Section of the Secretariat, or the Secretary of the Canadian Section of the Secretariat and includes any person authorized to act on behalf of that Secretary; (*secretaire) (Secretario)* "special committee" means a special committee established pursuant to Article 1905 of the Agreement; (*comite special*) (*comite especial*)

"United States" means the United States of America. (*Etats-Unis*) (*Estados Unidos*)

Operation of the Special Committee

4.(1) Subject to subrule (2), unless the involved Parties otherwise agree, special committee meetings shall take place at the offices of the responsible Secretariat or at such alternative location as the committee members may agree.

(2) A special committee may conduct meetings or exchange information by any means, including by means of a telephone conference call or facsimile or computer transmission.

5. The members of a special committee shall select from among themselves a chairperson, who shall preside over all meetings and hearings of the special committee.

6. The chairperson of the special committee shall fix the date and time of its meetings in consultation with other special committee members and the responsible Secretary.

7. All reports, findings, determinations and decisions of a special committee shall be made or issued by a majority vote of all members of the special committee.

8. A special committee proceeding commences on the day on which a request for a special committee is filed with the responsible Secretariat and terminates on the day on which a

notice of completion of the special committee proceeding is issued pursuant to rule 36.

9.(1) A special committee may adopt internal procedures of its own, not inconsistent with these rules, for routine administrative matters.

(2) A special committee may delegate to its chairperson the authority to make decisions regarding internal procedures or routine administrative matters.

10. The terms of reference of a special committee shall be limited to

a) making a finding as to whether any allegations set out in Article 1905.1 of the Agreement made by the Complaining Party regarding the application of the Responding Party's domestic law are substantiated;

b) determining whether a suspension of benefits by the Complaining Party pursuant to Article 1905.8b) of the Agreement is manifestly excessive; and

c) determining whether the Responding Party has corrected a problem with respect to which the special committee has made an affirmative finding.

Service of Documents

11. A document to be filed by an involved Party with the responsible Secretariat shall

a) be served on the other involved Party by express courier, overnight mail or by any other means agreed upon by the involved Parties; and

b) when filed, be accompanied by a proof of service certifying that the document has been served on the other involved Party, indicating the manner, date and time of service.

Written Submissions

12. All written submissions and responses filed with a responsible Secretariat shall be accompanied by four copies thereof.

13.(1) A request for the establishment of a special committee under Article 1905.2 of the Agreement shall be made by filing the request with the responsible Secretariat.

(2) On the filing of a request under subrule (1), the responsible Secretary and the other involved Secretary shall cause a notice of the filing of the request to be published in the official publications of the countries in which their sections of the Secretariat are located.

14. The written initial submission of a Complaining Party shall be filed with the responsible Secretariat no later than 10 days after the date on which the last member of the special committee is appointed.

15. A written response by the Responding Party shall be filed with the responsible Secretariat no later than 20 days after the filing of the initial submission of the Complaining Party.

16. A special committee may allow each involved Party the opportunity to make an equal number of further written submissions, within such time as may be fixed by the special committee, having regard to the time limits fixed by Annex 1905.6 to Chapter Nineteen of the Agreement.

17. The responsible Secretary shall forward to the other involved Secretary a copy of all documents filed with the responsible Secretariat and of all reports, findings, determinations and decisions issued by the special committee.

Hearings

18.(1) At least one hearing shall be held before the special committee presents its initial report.

(2) The date and time of hearings shall be fixed by the special committee in consultation with the involved Parties and the responsible Secretary.

(3) A verbatim transcript shall be taken of all hearings.

19. Unless the involved Parties otherwise agree, special committee hearings shall take place at the offices of the responsible Secretariat.

20.(1) All special committee members must be present during hearings.

(2) No later than five days before the date of a hearing, each involved Party shall deliver to the responsible Secretariat and to the other involved Party a list of the names of the persons who will present oral arguments at the hearing on behalf of that Party and of other representatives or advisers of the Party who will be attending the hearing.

21. Oral proceedings shall be conducted in the following order, ensuring that each involved Party is given equal time:

a) the argument of the Complaining Party;

b) the argument of the Responding Party;

c) a reply of the Complaining Party; and

d) a counter-reply of the Responding Party.

22. At the request of an involved Party or at the initiative of the special committee, with the agreement of both involved Parties and subject to such terms and conditions as both involved Parties may agree upon, the special committee may call upon any person to provide information concerning the matter in dispute.

Language of Proceedings

23. Written and oral proceedings may be in either English, French or Spanish, or in any combination thereof.

24. Unless the involved Parties otherwise agree, the reports, findings, determinations and decisions of a special committee shall be issued in an official language of the Responding Party and, if necessary, shall be promptly translated into an official language of the other involved Party.

Special Committee Deliberations

25.(1) The deliberations of a special committee shall take place in private and remain confidential.

(2) Only special committee members may take part in the deliberations of a special committee.

(3) Staff of the involved Secretariats, assistants to the special committee members and any necessary support staff may be

present during deliberations of a special committee by permission of the special committee.

Reports

26. In accordance with paragraph *b)* of Annex 1905.6 to Chapter Nineteen of the Agreement, a special committee shall prepare and present to the involved Parties an initial report, wherever practicable, within 60 days after the appointment of the last member of the special committee.

27. The involved Parties may comment in writing or, at the request of the special committee, orally, on an initial report of a special committee within 14 days after the initial report is presented.

28. An initial report of a special committee shall be kept confidential.

29.(1) A special committee shall issue a final report, together with any separate opinions rendered by individual committee members, within 30 days after the presentation of its initial report.

(2) Any separate opinions rendered by individual special committee members shall be anonymous.

(3) On the issuance of a final report under subrule (1), the responsible Secretary shall immediately forward copies of the report to the involved Parties.

(4) Unless the involved Parties otherwise agree,

a) within 10 days after the final report is forwarded to the involved Parties, the involved Secretaries shall cause a notice that a final report has been issued by a special committee to be published in the official publications of the involved Parties, indicating that copies of the report and of any separate opinions by individual members or written views of either involved Party are available to the public at the offices of the responsible Secretariat; and

b) the responsible Secretariat shall make available to the public copies of the final report of a special committee, together with any separate opinions by individual members and any written views that either involved Party may wish to be published.

Reconvening of Special Committee

30. Where a special committee has made an affirmative finding with respect to grounds specified in Article 1905.1 of the Agreement, a Responding Party may request that the special committee be reconvened by filing a request with the responsible Secretariat

a) where the Responding Party is requesting that the special committee determine whether the Responding Party has corrected a problem with respect to which the special committee has made an affirmative finding, at any time after the affirmative finding was made; or

b) where the Responding Party is requesting that the special committee determine whether a suspension of benefits by the Complaining Party under Article 1905.8 of the Agreement is manifestly excessive, at any time after the suspension was made.

31.(1) Where a request referred to in subrule *30a) is* filed before the fortieth day of the 60-day consultation period referred to in Article 1905.8 of the Agreement, the special committee shall endeavor to present a report containing its determination to the involved Parties before the sixtieth day of that period, and may for that purpose make such orders as to filing of written submissions and responses and the holding of a hearing as the special committee considers necessary under the circumstances.

(2) Rules *32 to 34* apply with respect to requests referred to in subrule *30a)* that are filed on or after the fortieth day of the 60-day consultation period referred to in Article 1905.8 and to requests referred to in subrule 30b).

32.(1) At the time of filing a request pursuant to rule *30,* the Responding Party shall file a written submission in support of the request.

(2) A Complaining Party shall file a written response to a submission referred to in subrule (1) within 20 days after that submission is filed.

33.(1) At the time of filing a request pursuant to rule 30 or a written response pursuant to subrule 32(2), an involved Party may request an opportunity to present oral argument in support of its request or response.

(2) Where an involved Party requests an opportunity to present oral argument pursuant to subrule (1), the special committee may hold a hearing, at which both involved Parties shall be granted an equal opportunity to present oral argument.

34. The special committee shall, within 45 days of the filing of a request pursuant to rule 30, present to the involved Parties a written report containing its determination pursuant to Article 1905.10 of the Agreement.

35. Subrules 29(2) to (4) apply, with such modifications as are necessary, to reports referred to in subrule 31(1) and rule 34.

Completion of Special Committee Proceedings

36.(1) On completion of a special committee proceeding, as determined by the special committee in consultation with the involved Parties, the special committee shall request the responsible Secretary to issue a notice of completion of the proceeding.

(2) A notice referred to in subrule (1) is effective the day after it is issued.

(3) The responsible Secretary shall cause a notice issued under subrule (1) to be published in the official publications of the involved Parties.

37. The members of a special committee are discharged from their duties on the day on which a notice of completion of the special committee proceeding is effective.

Confidentiality

38. All written submissions to, and communications with, a special committee and all documents filed with the involved Secretariats shall be kept confidential.

39.(1) All hearings of a special committee, and all transcripts thereof, shall be kept confidential.

(2) It is the responsibility of each involved Party to ensure that the persons attending oral proceedings of a special committee on its behalf maintain the confidentiality of the proceedings.

Ex Parte Contacts

40.(1) No special committee or member of a special committee shall meet or contact one involved Party in the absence of the other involved Party.

(2) No special committee member shall discuss a matter before the special committee with the involved Parties in the absence of other special committee members.

Extension and Computation of Time

41. A time period fixed by these rules may be extended with the consent of both involved Parties or by a decision of a special committee.

42.(1) In computing any time period fixed in or under these rules, the day or date from which the time period begins to run shall be excluded and, subject to subrule (2), the last day of the time period shall be included.

(2) Where the last day of a time period computed in accordance with subrule 1) falls on a legal holiday of the responsible Secretariat, that day and any other legal holidays of the responsible Secretariat immediately following that day shall be excluded from the computation.

(3) In computing any time period of five days or less fixed in these rules or by a decision of a special committee, any legal holiday that falls within the time period shall be excluded from the computation.

Responsibilities of the Responsible Secretary

43. The responsible Secretary shall provide administrative support for each special committee proceeding and shall make the arrangements necessary for the hearings and meetings of the special committee, including the provision of court reporters.

44. The responsible Secretary shall maintain a file for each special committee proceeding, comprised of the original or a copy of all documents filed, whether or not filed in accordance with these rules, in the special committee proceeding.

Death or Incapacity

45. Where a special committee member is disqualified, dies or otherwise becomes unable to fulfil special committee duties,

a) special committee proceedings and computations of time shall be suspended, pending the appointment of a substitute member, and

b) where the disability, disqualification or death occurs after oral argument has begun, the chairperson may order that the matter be reheard, on such terms as are appropriate, after selection of a substitute member.

Translation and Interpretation

46.(1) Subject to rule 47, each involved Party shall,

a) within a reasonable period of time after the appointment of the last special committee member, advise the responsible Secretary in writing of the language in which its written submissions will be made and in which it wishes to receive the written submissions of the other involved Party; and

b) within a reasonable period of time before the date of a hearing, advise the responsible Secretary in writing of the language in which it will present oral arguments at the hearing and in which it wishes to hear oral arguments.

(2) On receipt of advice pursuant to subrule (1), the responsible Secretary shall promptly notify the other involved Secretary, the other involved Party and the special committee.

47.(1) In lieu of the procedure set out in rule 46, a Party may advise its Secretary of

a) the language in which its written submissions will be made in all special committee proceedings and in which it wishes to receive written submissions of any other Party involved in a special committee proceeding; and

b) the language in which it will present oral arguments, and in which it wishes to hear oral arguments, at all special committee hearings.

(2) On receipt of advice pursuant to subrule (1), a Secretary shall promptly notify the other Secretaries and Parties accordingly.

48. Where the responsible Secretary is advised that written submissions or oral arguments in a special committee proceeding will be in more than one language or on the basis of a request of a special committee member, the responsible Secretary shall arrange for the translation of the written submissions or for the provision of interpreters to provide simultaneous translation at the hearing, as the case may be.

49. Any time period applicable to a special committee proceeding shall be suspended for the period necessary to complete the translation of any written submission.

50.(1) The costs incurred in the preparation of a translation of a written submission shall be borne by the Party filing the submission.

(2) Costs for interpretation of oral arguments and for the translation of the special committee's reports shall be shared equally by the involved Parties

CODE OF CONDUCT FOR DISPUTE SETTLEMENT PROCEDURES UNDER CHAPTERS 19 AND 20 OF THE NORTH AMERICAN FREE TRADE AGREEMENT

DEPARTMENT OF EXTERNAL AFFAIRS

NORTH AMERICAN FREE TRADE AGREEMENT

CODE OF CONDUCT FOR DISPUTE SETTLEMENT PROCEDURES UNDER CHAPTERS 19 AND 20 OF THE NORTH AMERICAN FREE TRADE AGREEMENT

PREAMBLE

Whereas the Parties place prime importance on the integrity and impartiality of proceedings conducted pursuant to Chapters 19 and 20 of the North American Free Trade Agreement between the Government of Canada, the Government of the United Mexican States and the Government of the United States of America, this Code of Conduct is hereby established to ensure that these principles are respected.

INTERPRETATION

A. In this Code of Conduct,

"Agreement" means the North American Free Trade Agreement: *(Accord) (Trarado)*

"assistant" means a person who, under the terms of appointment of a member, conducts research or provides support for the member; *(adjoint) (asisrentc)*
"candidate" means

a) an individual whose name appears on a roster or list established under Article 1414, Annex 1901.2 or 1904.13 or Article 2009,

b) an individual who is under consideration for appointment as a member of a panel pursuant to Annex 1901.2 or Article 1903, 1904 or 2011, or

c) an individual who is under consideration for appointment as a member of a committee pursuant to Annex 1904.13 or Article 1905; *(candidat) (candidato)*

"member" means

a) a member of a panel constituted pursuant to Annex 1901.2 or Article 1414, 1903, 1904, 2008 or 2011,

b) a member of an extraordinary challenge committee constituted pursuant to Annex 1904.13, or

c) a member of a special committee constituted pursuant to Article 1905; *(membre) (miembro)*

"participant" has the meaning assigned in the *Rules of Procedure for Article 1904 Binational Panel Reviews; (participant) (participante)*

"Party" means a Party to the Agreement; *(Partie) (Panel)*

"proceeding", unless otherwise specified, means

a) a panel review under Article 1903 or 1904,

b) an extraordinary challenge proceeding under Annex 1904.13,

c) a special committee proceeding under Article 1905,

d) a panel proceeding under Chapter 20, or

e) a proceeding in a dispute arising under Chapter 11 or 14 to which Chapter 20 applies: (*procedure*) (*procedimiento*)

"Secretariat" means the Secretariat established pursuant to Article 2002: (*Secretariat*) (*Secretariado*) and

"staff" means in respect of a member, means persons under the direction and control of the member, other than assistants. (*personnel*) (*personal*)

B. Any reference made in this Code of Conduct to an Article, Annex or Chapter is a reference to the appropriate Article, Annex or Chapter of the Agreement.

I. RESPONSIBILITIES TO THE PROCESS

Every candidate, member and former member shall avoid impropriety and the appearance of impropriety and shall observe high standards of conduct so that the integrity and impartial of the dispute settlement process is preserved.

II. DISCLOSURE OBLIGATIONS

[Introductory Note:

The governing principle of this Code of Conduct is that a candidate or member must disclose the existence of any interest, relationship or matter that is likely to affect the candidate's or member's independence or impartiality or that might reasonably create an appearance of impropriety or an apprehension of bias is created where a reasonable person, with knowledge of all the relevant circumstances that a reasonable inquiry would disclose, would conclude that a candidate's or member's ability to carry out the duties with integrity, impartiality and competence is impaired.

These disclosure obligations, however, should not be interpreted so that the burden of detailed disclosure makes it impractical for persons in the legal or business community to serve as members, thereby depriving the Parties and participants of the services of those who might be best qualified to serve as members. Thus, candidates and members should not be called upon to disclose interests, relationships or matters whose bearing on their role in the proceeding would be trivial.

Throughout the proceeding, candidates and members have a continuing obligations to disclose interests, relationships and matters that may bear on the integrity or impartiality of the dispute settlement process.

This Code of Conduct does not determine whether or under what circumstances the Parties will disqualify a candidate or member from being appointed to, or serving as a member of, a panel or committee on the basis of disclosures made.]

A. A candidate shall disclose any interest, relationship or matter that is likely to affect the candidate's independence or impartiality or that might reasonably create an appearance of impropriety or an apprehension of bias in the proceeding. To this end, a candidate shall make all reasonable efforts to become aware of any such interests, relationships and matters.

The candidate shall disclose such interests, relationships and matters by completing an Initial Disclosure Statement provided by the Secretariat and sending it to the Secretariat.

Without limiting the generality of the foregoing, candidates shall disclose the following interests, relationships and matters:

1) any financial or personal interest of the candidate

    a) in the proceeding or in its outcome, and

    b) in an administrative proceeding, a domestic court proceeding or another panel or committee proceeding that involves issues that may be decided in the proceeding for which the candidate is under consideration;

(2) any financial interest of the candidate's employer, partner, business associate or family member

    a) in the proceeding or in its outcome, and

    b) in an administrative proceeding, a domestic court proceeding or another panel or committee proceeding that involves issues that may be decided in the proceeding for which the candidate is under consideration:

(3) any past or existing financial, business, professional. family or social relationship with any interested parties in the proceeding, or their counsel, or any such relationship involving a candidate's employer. partner, business associate or family member: and

(4) public advocacy or legal or other representation concerning an issue in dispute in the proceeding or involving the same goods.

B. A member in an Article 1904 proceeding shall, after receiving the complaint, disclose any interests, advocacy or representation referred to in paragraph *A(1)b)* or *(2)b)* or subsection (4) by completing a Supplementary Disclosure Statement provided by the Secretariat and sending it to the Secretariat for consideration by the appropriate Parties.

C. Once appointed, a member shall continue to make all reasonable efforts to become aware of any interests, relationships or matters referred to in section A and shall disclose them. The obligation to disclose is a continuing duty which requires a member to disclose any such interests, relationships and matters that may arise during any stage of the proceeding.

The member shall disclose such interests, relationships and matters by communicating them in writing to the Secretariat for consideration by the appropriate Parties.

III. THE PERFORMANCE OF DUTIES BY CANDIDATES AND MEMBERS

A. A candidate who accepts an appointment as a member shall be available to perform, and shall perform a member's duties thoroughly and expeditiously throughout the course of the proceeding.

B. A member shall ensure that the Secretariat can, at all reasonable times, contact the member in order to conduct panel or committee business.

C. A member shall carry out all duties fairly and diligently.

D. A member shall comply with the provisions of Chapter 19 or *20* and the applicable rules.

E. A member shall not deny other members the opportunity to participate in all aspects of the proceeding.

F. A member shall consider only those issues raised in the proceeding and necessary to a decision and shall not delegate the duty to decide to any other person, except as provided in the applicable rules.

G. A member shall take all reasonable steps to ensure that the member's assistant and staff comply with Parts I, II and VI of this Code of Conduct.

H. A member shall not engage in ex *parte* contacts concerning the proceeding.

I. A candidate or member shall not communicate matters concerning actual or potential violations of this Code of Conduct unless the communication is to the Secretariat or is necessary to ascertain whether that candidate or member has violated or may violate the Code.

IV. INDEPENDENCE AND IMPARTIALITY OF MEMBERS

A. A member shall be independent and impartial. A member shall act in a fair manner and shall avoid creating an appearance of impropriety or an apprehension of bias.

B. A member shall not be influenced by self-interest, outside pressure, political considerations, public clamour, loyalty to a Party or fear of criticism.

C. A member shall not, directly or indirectly, incur any obligation or accept any benefit that would in any way interfere, or appear to interfere, with the proper performance of the member's duties.

D. A member shall not use the member's position on the panel or committee to advance any personal or private interests. A member shall avoid actions that may create the impression that others are in a special position to influence the member. A member shall make every effort to prevent or discourage others from representing themselves as being in such a position.

E. A member shall not allow past or existing financial, business, professional, family or social relationships or responsibilities to influence the member's conduct or judgment.

F. A member shall avoid entering into any relationship, or acquiring any financial or personal interest, that is likely to affect the member's impartiality or that might reasonably create an appearance of impropriety or an apprehension of bias.

DUTIES IN CERTAIN SITUATIONS

A. For a period of one year after the completion of an Article 1904 proceeding, a former member shall not personally advise or represent any participant in the proceeding with regard to antidumping or countervailing duty matters.

B. In the case of an Article 1904 proceeding, a member or a former member shall not represent a participant in an administrative proceeding, a domestic court proceeding or another Article 1904 proceeding involving the same goods.

C. A former member shall avoid actions that may create the appearance that the member was biased in carrying out the member's duties or would benefit from the decision of the panel or committee.

VI. MAINTENANCE OF CONFIDENTIALITY

A. A member or former member shall not at any time disclose or use any non-public information concerning the proceeding or acquired during the proceeding except for the purposes of the proceeding and shall not, in any case, disclose or use any such information to gain personal advantage or advantage for others or to affect adversely the interest of another.

B. A member shall not disclose a declaratory opinion under Article 1903 or a panel or extraordinary challenge committee order or decision under Article 1904 prior to its issuance by the panel or committee.

C. A member shall not disclose a special committee report or decision under Article 1905 prior to its public release by the Secretariat. A member or former member shall not at any time disclose which members are associated with majority or minority opinions in an Article 1905 proceeding.

D. A member shall not disclose a panel report issued under Chapter 20 prior to its publication by the Commission. A member or former member shall not at any time disclose which members are associated with majority or minority opinions In a proceeding under Chapter 20.

E. A member or former member shall not at any time disclose the deliberations of a panel or committee, or any member's view, except as required by law.

VII. RESPONSIBILITIES OF ASSISTANTS AND STAFF

Parts I (Responsibilities to the Process), II (Disclosure Obligations) and VI (Maintenance of Confidentiality) of this Code of Conduct apply also to assistants and staff.

INDEX

Additional Facility Rules, 45, 46, 240, 242–244, 247, 250, 252
Administrative Structure, 8, 31, 36
Advisory Committee on Private Commercial Disputes, 9, 10, 30, 31, 129, 198, 199, 335, 336
Alternative Dispute Resolution, 30, 199, 335
Antidumping Laws, 55, 84, 277
Automated Data Exchange Subgroup, 11, 148

Bid Challenge Procedure, 220, 222
Bilateral Action, 25, 26, 207, 214
Bilateral Working Group, 10, 133, 336
Border Facilities Subgroup, 11, 147

Chair, 16, 17, 49, 54, 77, 78, 85, 263, 327, 328
Chapter 11, 1, 2, 6, 41-45, 48, 49, 163, 224, 405
Chapter 14, 6, 11, 41-43, 175, 259
Chapter 19, iii, 1, 2, 6, 55-59, 63, 68, 71, 79, 80, 86, 177, 191, 192, 277, 351, 409
  Assessing Duties, 74
  binational panel review of a final determination, 303
  consultation, 83
  Countervailing Duties, 55
  Dumping , 55
  enforcement, 76
  Extraordinary challenge procedures, 80
  making domestic final determinations, 72
  Material Injury, 55, 61, 293
  obligations owed, 56
  Panel Decisions, 78
  Panel reviews permitted for, 58
  Preliminary Determinations, 60
  Procedures for Making Declaratory Opinions, 85
  Request for a Panel, 76
  Review of Statutory Amendments, 84
  roster, 77
  Rules of procedure, 80
  safeguard the functioning of, 83
  standard of review, 75
  Time Limitations, 80
  types of final determinations, 72
  Undertakings, 73

Chapter 20, 1, 2, 5-8, 12, 13, 19, 20, 24, 28-30, 34, 43, 48, 49, 53, 77, 79, 80, 134, 191, 197, 317, 405, 411, 412
administrative structure, 8
applies to, 5
Committees and Working Groups, 8
consultations, 12
does not apply to, 6
Free Trade Commission, 8
GATT, 14
Implementation and Enforcement, 18
may apply to, 6
Model Rules of Procedure, 12, 329
Scope and Coverage , 5, 201
Secretariat, 8
Stages of Proceedings, 12
Transparency and Due Process Requirements, 12
who can initiate, 7
Working Group, 10
Chapter 20 Alternative, 28
Choice of Forum, 19
Committee on Agricultural Trade, 9, 125, 127, 129, 133-135, 336
Committee on Sanitary and Phytosanitary Measures, 9, 130, 336
Committee on Small Business, 10, 336
Committee on Standards-Related Measures, 9, 132, 133, 143, 152
Committee on Trade in Goods, 9, 105, 336
Committee on Trade in Worn Clothing, 9, 106, 336
Committees and Working Groups, viii, 8–11, 93, 94, 105, 113, 125, 141, 143, 157, 165, 175, 181, 183, 191, 197, 318, 336, 337
Competition Law, 6, 29, 181, 227, 268, 271
Complaints by Private Parties, 38
Consultations, vii, 2, 11–14, 20, 25, 28, 32, 36–38, 44, 83, 85, 86, 130, 141, 143, 149, 158, 208, 211, 236, 237, 239, 261, 262, 268, 279, 286–291, 297, 320, 322–324, 330, 391, 394, 397–399
Countervailing Duties, 55, 56, 66, 69, 70, 84, 285, 316
Customs Procedures, 2, 21, 23, 113, 115, 121, 206
appeal of the redetermination, 23
request for redetermination, 21
Customs Subgroup, 10, 114, 115, 117, 336

Dangerous Goods Subgroup, 11
Due Process Requirements, 8, 12
Dumping, 11, 55, 56-63, 67, 68, 70–74, 292, 293, 305, 307, 308, 316

Emergency Action, 2, 6, 10, 23–28, 141, 207–214, 217, 219
Bilateral Action, 25
Chapter 20 Alternative, 28
Global Action, 25
Provisions, 24
Environmental Cooperation, 31, 98
administrative structure, 31
Complaints by Private Parties, 35
Joint Public Advisory Committee, 32
special forum selection, 34
Evaluation Committee of Experts, 37
Exclusions, 42, 210, 253, 259, 322
Extraordinary Challenge Committee, 82, 192, 288, 301, 304, 308, 309, 340–342, 346, 351, 357, 369–375, 381, 382, 404, 411
Extraordinary Challenge Procedures, 80

Final Determination, 2, 29, 56–59, 62, 66, 67, 69, 70, 72–80, 85, 192, 273, 280–283, 285, 286, 288–290, 293, 295, 296, 302, 303, 305–307, 310, 311, 313–317, 341, 342, 346–351, 357, 358, 362, 364–367, 380, 383
Financial Services Committee, 10, 11, 51, 175, 261, 336
Free Trade Commission, 2, 8, 9, 12-15, 28, 51, 116, 141, 197, 261, 317

GATT, 14–16, 19, 20, 25, 26, 34, 84, 85, 100, 107, 117, 141, 159, 210, 278, 320–322, 324, 326
Global Action, 25–27, 210, 219
Government Procurement, 2, 6, 10, 28, 123, 157–160, 220, 338

ICSID Convention, 45, 46, 49, 52, 163, 240, 242–244, 246, 247, 250–254
Implementation and Enforcement, 18, 33, 39, 52
Initiate a claim, 7, 44, 57
Initiate a review, 307, 315, 317
Investor–State Arbitration Procedures, 43
  Additional Facility Rules, 45
  applies to, 41
  Arbitral Tribunal Formation, 49
  Chapter 11, 42, 43
  Chapter 14, 42, 43
  Conditions Precedent to , 48
  Consolidation of Claims, 50
  damages, 52
  does not apply to, 48
  ICSID Convention, 49
  New York Convention, 50
  Procedures, 88, 49
  prudential reason, 43, 51
  Scope and Coverage, 41
  suspending benefits, 53
  UNCITRAL Arbitration Rules, 47
  who can initiate a claim, 44

Joint Public Advisory Committee, 32

Labour Cooperation, 36
  Administrative Structure, 36
  Commission for Labor Cooperation, 36
  National Administrative Offices, 36
  Special Council Session, 38

Maritime Subgroup, 11, 148
Material Injury, 55, 57–59, 61–63, 65–67, 71–74, 293
Ministerial Council, 36, 37
Model Rules of Procedure, 12, 15, 329, 330, 331, 334

National Administrative Office, 36

Operations Subgroup, 11, 147

Panel Selection, 16, 49, 263, 327
Preliminary Determination, 60–71, 292, 305
Private Commercial Disputes, 6, 9, 10, 30, 31, 129, 198, 199, 334, 335
  Advisory Committee on Private Commercial Disputes, 30
  Advisory Committee on Private Commercial Disputes Regarding Agricultural Goods, 31
  Alternate Dispute Resolution, 30
Private Parties, 1, 30, 31, 35, 58, 71, 72, 335
Procedural Matters, 25, 32, 37, 50

Rail Subgroup, 11, 146
Redetermination of Origin, 23
Reports, 15, 17, 28, 33, 36, 39, 52, 135, 152, 233, 248, 291, 332, 391, 394–396, 399, 403
Review of Statutory Amendments, 84, 279

Roster, 16, 17, 33, 39, 43, 49, 77, 82, 83, 243, 245, 262, 263, 287, 297, 298, 301, 326, 328, 404

Science and Technology Subgroup, 11, 148
Scope and Coverage, 5, 41, 56, 105, 113, 123, 125, 141, 143, 157, 163, 165, 173, 175, 181, 183, 187, 189, 191, 197, 224
SECOFI, 8, 24, 57, 68–71, 74, 100, 101, 106–108, 142, 144, 145, 149, 152, 155, 158, 176, 186
Secretariat, 8, 9, 13, 15, 32, 35–37, 39, 45, 56, 68–70, 72, 79, 95, 98, 100, 101, 103, 108, 177, 191, 194, 195, 200, 246, 293, 301, 304, 309, 312, 313, 316, 318, 319, 322–326, 330, 333, 334, 342–344, 350–357, 360, 361, 363, 368, 369, 371, 372, 378–381, 385, 386, 388–395, 397, 399, 400, 405, 407–409, 411, 414
Special Committee, 83, 84, 192, 286–288, 290, 304, 308, 309, 311, 312, 387, 388, 391–405, 411
Standard of Review, 75, 76, 280, 283, 286, 297, 308, 313, 314, 316

Telecommunications Standards Subcommittee, 336
Temporary Entry, 6, 10, 29, 95, 147, 183-185, 273, 337
Temporary Entry Working Group, 10, 183, 184, 337
Third Party, 51, 321, 322, 326, 330
Time Limitations, 13, 15, 44, 80
Traffic Control Devices Subgroup, 11, 146
Transportation Consultative Group, 11, 147
Tribunals, 12, 48, 212, 275, 306

UNCITRAL Arbitration Rules, 47, 50, 240, 244, 248, 250, 252, 257

Undertakings, 71–73, 220, 227, 285, 299, 303, 304, 306, 311, 315, 348

XVehicle Weight & Dimension Subgroup, 11, 146
Vehicle/Driver Compliance Subgroup, 11, 146

Working Group on Agricultural Subsidies, 10, 127, 336
Working Group on Dumping and Antidumping Duties, 11
Working Group on Emergency Action, 10, 141
Working Group on Government Procurement, 10
Working Group on Rules of Origin, 10, 113, 115, 116, 324, 336
Working Group on Services and Investment, 10, 165
Working Group on Trade and Competition, 10, 181, 271, 336